D1648560

DISRUPTING D.C.

Disrupting D.C.
The Rise of Uber and the Fall of the City

Katie J. Wells, Kafui Attoh,
and Declan Cullen

PRINCETON UNIVERSITY PRESS

PRINCETON AND OXFORD

Published by Princeton University Press
41 William Street, Princeton, New Jersey 08540
99 Banbury Road, Oxford OX2 6JX

press.princeton.edu

All Rights Reserved

Library of Congress Cataloging-in-Publication Data

Names: Wells, Katie J., author. | Attoh, Kafui Ablode,
    1983– author. | Cullen, Declan, author.
Title: Disrupting D.C. : the rise of Uber and the fall of the city /
    Katie J. Wells, Kafui Attoh, and Declan Cullen.
Description: Princeton : Princeton University Press, [2023] |
    Includes bibliographical references and index.
Identifiers: LCCN 2022053161 (print) | LCCN 2022053162 (ebook) | ISBN
    9780691249759 (hardback ; alk. paper) | ISBN 9780691249773 (ebook)
Subjects: LCSH: Uber (Firm) | Ridesharing—Political aspects—Washington
    (D.C.) | Urban transportation—Political aspects—Washington (D.C.) |
    Urbanization—Washington (D.C.) | Urban policy—Washington (D.C.)
Classification: LCC HE5620.R53 W45 2023 (print) | LCC HE5620.
    R53 (ebook) | DDC 388.4/13212—dc23/eng/20221109
LC record available at https://lccn.loc.gov/2022053161
LC ebook record available at https://lccn.loc.gov/2022053162

British Library Cataloging-in-Publication Data is available

Editorial: Meagan Levinson and Erik Beranek
Production Editorial: Natalie Baan
Production: Erin Suydam
Publicity: Kate Hensley and Kathryn Stevens
Copyeditor: Will DeRooy

This book has been composed in Adobe Text and Gotham

Printed on acid-free paper. ∞

Printed in Canada

10 9 8 7 6 5 4 3 2 1

CONTENTS

PREFACE

In December 2011, Washington, D.C., became the sixth munici-
pality in the United States to receive its introduction to Uber's
famed car service—a service allowing customers to both hail and
pay for a luxury sedan using their smartphones. As had been the
case in San Francisco, Seattle, Boston, and New York City, Uber's
expansion into the nation's capital was not without controversy.
Indeed, within a month, local regulators targeted Uber in a highly
publicized sting for operating without a livery license. Six months
later, the company faced additional resistance from D.C. Council
members concerned about the company's impact on the local taxi
industry. Over the course of a year, D.C. became not only the first
city in the country where Uber faced resistance from municipal
legislators but also the first city where such resistance was overcome and anti-Uber legislation defeated. This history was not lost
on Uber.

According to Uber CEO Travis Kalanick in 2013, it was in D.C.
that the company first created a "playbook" for how to deal with
intransigent regulators and to win in the realm of local politics.[1]
In 2016, a D.C.-based lobbyist for Uber only reiterated this point
to us. Washington, D.C., he argued, had not only "adopted our
[i.e., Uber's] view of the world"; it had become "one of the best
models for us."[2] On the one hand, this book is about the growth and
development of Uber in D.C. and the nature of the "playbook"
and blueprint developed there. It examines how Uber has changed
the city, as well as how the city has informed Uber's global expansion. On the other hand, this book explores how Uber's successes

in D.C. and elsewhere reflect and shape what we expect from cities and from urban politics more generally.

The arguments developed in this book derive from over a hundred interviews with people living and working in D.C.—from Uber and taxi drivers to elected officials, urban planners, and local journalists—whose lives have intersected with Uber's operation in the city. Taken together, their experiences offer a complex picture of Uber's role in the city. They serve to confirm many of the extant criticisms of Uber and the rapacious style of neoliberal capitalism that it represents. They reveal the Silicon Valley buzzword "disruption" as a euphemism for lowering labor standards, bypassing local regulations, and opening up new areas of life to competition in the market. The stories in the following chapters confirm criticisms of Uber on economic grounds, too. Despite more than a decade in operation, Uber has yet to prove consistently profitable. To quote the writer Cory Doctorow, a company like Uber is best described as a "bezzle"—a word coined by economist John Kenneth Galbraith.[3] The bezzle, Galbraith explains, is the inventory of embezzled money that amasses before the victims of the scheme finally realize that they have been had.[4] As a quintessential bezzle, Uber has reshaped cities, restructured entire industries, and redefined whole areas of urban life.

Still, the accounts in the following pages suggest that Uber is more than a bezzle or a symbol of neoliberal excess. To the Uber drivers with whom we spoke in D.C., it was a way to make money in the wake of the 2008 recession; it was a job that was stressful but meaningful. For many, it served as a safety net. For city legislators and policymakers, it was a way to address holes in transportation infrastructure and to respond to complaints from constituents that the taxi industry was racist and sclerotic. It was also central to the effort to market D.C. as a hub for innovation and to appeal to the tech industry.

Those who lauded Uber or who championed its impact on their lives are neither simply victims nor dupes. Not only were Uber's benefits obvious; they were commonsense. For us, these findings stood athwart any effort, however gratifying, to simply denounce Uber or its role in cities. As a result, this book strives to offer an analysis of the political, economic, and social conditions that gave rise to Uber, that made it popular, and that made it a common-sense solution to various urban problems. We hope to draw attention to those conditions and to center them in a critique of the gig economy that refuses to conflate the symptoms with the disease.

In the time since we first drafted this book, the conditions central to Uber's success have only become more apparent. In the summer of 2022 and in the face of record inflation, the *Washington Post* reported that executives at Uber, Lyft, and DoorDash cited the economic strain facing workers across the economy as cause for investor confidence.[5] Uber CEO Dara Khosrowshahi claimed there had been an explosion of new driver sign-ups from workers desperate for extra money given the rising cost of living. A full-scale recession, an executive at ride-hailing competitor Lyft admitted, might be even better, from a purely economic standpoint. As perverse as this may seem, these admissions were a reminder that the ride-hailing industry's growth has never been a sign of urban economic strength or urban innovation and has always been a sign of urban weakness, desperation, and low expectations.

Kafui Attoh, Katie J. Wells, and Declan Cullen
Poughkeepsie, NY—Washington, D.C.
November 2022

Low Expectations

FIGURE 0.1. Protest in Dupont Circle, July 19, 2016. Reproduced from Borderstan.com with permission by ARL Now.

Metro's a loser! We took an Uber!
—ANTI-METRO PROTESTORS IN WASHINGTON, D.C.[1]

And so once you go into politics, it's not like Pinterest where people are putting up pins. You're changing the way cities work, and so that's fundamentally a third rail.
—TRAVIS KALANICK, UBER CEO[2]

The D.C. fight confirmed everything we needed to know:
Just like Uber was seriously disrupting the status quo in
the taxi industry itself, we could disrupt the status quo
of governing too. Calling entrenched interests out on
corruption and pay-to-play politics wasn't new. Using
your own app to mobilize your customers to swamp their
elected officials with complaints was. This would be the
thesis behind dozens of campaigns we've run for startups
ever since.

—BRADLEY TUSK, UBER CONSULTANT[3]

In late July 2016, Dupont Circle in Washington, D.C., hosted one
of the more curious protests of recent times. Under the headline
"Mystery Group of Young People Protests for Metro Privatization," journalist Raye Weigel described the event as resembling
an "after-party" for a "fraternity rush."[4] Part of Weigel's assessment was the preponderance of young men in polo shirts, cargo
shorts, and boat shoes. Another part of it, however, was the tone
of the hastily scrawled messages on the posters they carried. Along
with signs reading "Do you even Metro, bro?" and "Privatize the
DC Metro, #Si se puede" there were some that were even more
colorful—"Thomas the Govt. Train, you're fired" and "The Metro
is more lit than my mixtape" (a pointed reference to the rash
of track fires that had recently shuttered large sections of the
Metro system). As Weigel reported, there were chants as well.
In a video released by *Borderstan* (an online news aggregator for
the Dupont Circle, U Street, and Columbia Heights neighborhoods), protestors can be heard chanting: "Metro's a loser! We
took an Uber!"[5]

With all the makings of a practical joke, the protest fizzled as
quickly as it had started. Nevertheless, it served as yet another
reminder of a Metro system that for many in D.C. seemed broken
beyond repair. When the D.C. Metro was constructed in the 1970s,
explains historian Zachary Schrag in *The Great Society Subway*, it
represented a "monument to confidence in the public realm."[6] Like

the Apollo missions or the creation of the National Endowment for the Arts, the capital's new transportation system embodied the ideals of the Great Society: a belief in the "power of government to do good" and a commonsense commitment to promoting public investments "suited to the grandeur and dignity of the world's richest nation."[7] Quoting Lyndon B. Johnson, Schrag adds, Metro was an attempt to build "a place where the city of man serves not only the needs of the body and the demands of commerce but the desire for beauty and the hunger for community."[8]

As the protest at Dupont Circle seemed to suggest, by 2016 Metro no longer represented the "power of government to do good" or "the hunger for community." The system was literally on fire. In January 2015, an electrical fire in a tunnel near L'Enfant Station had left a mother of two dead from smoke inhalation. In August of the same year, a derailment had paralyzed large chunks of the system for hours. On the eve of the papal visit in early October, local commuters experienced yet more delays following a fire at a Metro power plant. In April 2016, the launch of the semi-ironic "IsMetroOnFire.com"—a website giving visitors real-time updates on which transit lines were currently engulfed in flames—illustrated the depth of the crisis.[9]

Few in D.C. may have taken the demand to privatize Metro seriously, coming as it did from a group of "meme-crazed millennials."[10] Yet they did touch on some emerging realities. The Metro system *was* unreliable and ostensibly dangerous. And so, for many in D.C., car services like Uber and Lyft—often cheaper and more convenient than taxis—were a welcome alternative. "Metro's a loser! We took an Uber!" was not simply a chant but a description of how people traveled to work. By 2016, both Uber and Lyft had become household names (see appendix D). And while Metro's failures would raise the profiles of these ride-hailing companies considerably, their growth and success were attributable to other factors. As will become clear in the following pages, some of those factors were technological and economic; others were political and ideological.

Uber did more than offer an alternative to D.C.'s existing transportation regime. It offered an alternative view of the public realm itself. Unlike Johnson's Great Society, in Uber's world the public realm was defined less by confidence and ambition than by apathy and a deep cynicism. Rather than an expression of heightened expectations or a self-assured belief in the power of government to meet people's material and social needs, the rise of Uber expresses a set of lowered expectations.

This argument contradicts much of what was promised by the on-demand or gig economy (alternatively called the app-based economy, online platform economy, or sharing economy). At least part of the growth and success of companies like Uber and Lyft (and Airbnb, TaskRabbit, Grubhub, and countless others) can be attributed to the expansion of broadband Internet, the ubiquity of smartphones, and new programming tools and Internet services.[11] Such technological innovations have opened up entirely new areas of economic activity while giving unprecedented power to corporations and diligent entrepreneurs eager to disrupt industries long believed to be immune to innovation.[12] The growth of these enterprises has relied on the extension of new information and communication technologies into ever more areas of people's social and economic lives. In addition, these enterprises have benefited from structural shifts in the broader economy. As writer and digital economy scholar Nick Srnicek argues, it is no coincidence that so many gig-economy companies trace their origins to the 2008 economic crisis.[13] In a postrecession environment defined by both low interest rates and low rates of return on a "wide range of financial assets," investors were incentivized to find returns wherever possible.[14] This strategy involved taking on additional risk by "investing in unprofitable and unproven tech companies."[15] For tech companies associated with the gig economy, the economic conditions following the recession were favorable not only for raising venture capital but also for finding a workforce among the recently laid off and those otherwise facing a sudden loss of income.

The history of Uber offers a far more complex portrait of the gig economy. Rather than a simple story of financial capitalism, technological innovation, or a "diligent, intelligent and frugal elite" (to borrow from Marx's quip on the "idyllic" origins of modern capitalism), the story of Uber is a story about the use and exertion of political force.[16] It is a story in which Uber, in some instances, broke the law and then bent urban politics to its design, forcefully lobbying legislators to change the law it had just broken. This use of political power is what Uber CEO Travis Kalanick has called "principled confrontation" and what others have described more evocatively as "corporate civil disobedience."[17] And "disobedience," in fact, was how Uber entered Washington, D.C.

As mentioned in the preface, in 2011 D.C. became the sixth city in the United States introduced to Uber's nascent sedan service.[18] As it had in San Francisco, Seattle, Boston, New York City, and Chicago, Uber entered D.C. with neither the approval nor the blessing of local regulators. In a matter of weeks, in a highly publicized sting by the D.C. Taxicab Commission, an Uber vehicle was impounded and its driver ticketed.[19] Although Uber had faced similar resistance from regulators in San Francisco and New York City, D.C. was the first city where pushback came from municipal legislators. It was also the first city where such political resistance was overcome.

How did this take place? In early June 2012, D.C. legislators pushed back against Uber with the "Uber Amendment": a provision proposed by the D.C. Council[20] mandating that fares for Uber's sedan service start at five times that of a local taxi. The response from Uber was immediate. In an email to every D.C. resident who had used the service, Kalanick urged supporters to contact the council and voice their opposition.[21] As he argued, the provision was plainly an attempt to prevent "Uber from being a viable alternative to taxis."[22] Rather than encourage choice and innovation, the "Uber Amendment"—according to Kalanick's email—would accomplish the opposite. By protecting the local taxi industry from market competition, Kalanick added, the council was limiting consumer choice and blocking innovation. In short, the proposed legislation was antibusiness.

Kalanick's efforts proved fruitful. Over the next eighteen hours, the council was inundated with angry emails—more than fifty thousand of them—arguing against the minimum fare language. The provision, which had been introduced on a Monday at 4:00 p.m., was dead by that Tuesday afternoon.

This was what Kalanick called "Operation Rolling Thunder"—a reference to the aerial bombardment of military and civilian targets in the Vietnam War. The success of Uber's "operation" would reverberate, especially in those cities that dared to resist Uber's advance.[23]

The local impact was notable. In the years that followed, D.C.'s initially combative approach to Uber was marked by a stunning reversal. By the end of 2014—just two and half years later—the D.C. Council had not only yielded to Uber's continued expansion in the city but also approved legislation that made the city, according to libertarian think tank R Street, the "best place in the country for transport app start-ups."[24] Uber emerged victorious from the D.C. "taxi wars."[25] To quote Uber investor Shervin Pishevar, the company had offered a glimpse of "a new local politics"—one in which tech and Silicon Valley were "exercising newfound muscles at the policy level in real-time."[26]

What did Uber's victory in D.C. mean? What, if anything, was "new" about Uber's approach to local politics? What exactly was at stake?

In exploring how Uber and other tech companies shape the political life of cities, this book starts from the presumption that the events in D.C. represent one of many efforts by Uber to consolidate economic and political power. At its broadest, however, the goal of this book is to place those efforts in context and to offer a critique of Uber that takes the company's popularity and its ability to inspire allegiance just as seriously as its role in undermining democratic urban governance.

Rethinking the Gig Economy

The material developed in the following chapters draws from interviews conducted in D.C. from 2016 to 2022. These were interviews with gig workers, city legislators, transit planners, staffers at regulatory agencies, tech consultants, Uber lobbyists, journalists, and others either directly or indirectly connected to Uber and the debates that erupted in D.C. following Uber's entrance there. In drawing on these interviews to make an argument about Uber, tech, and the nature of urban politics, *Disrupting D.C.* finds common cause with other scholars who—in their attempt to make sense of the changes wrought by the gig economy—have, like us, seen value in starting with the voices and lives of real people in real places.

Perhaps unsurprisingly, a considerable number of these scholars have focused on questions of labor, particularly on what sociologist Alexandrea Ravenelle, in her book *Hustle and Gig*, describes as the "contradiction between the lofty promises of the gig economy and the lived experience of workers."[27] Companies like Uber, Lyft, Airbnb, and TaskRabbit have routinely pledged to provide workers a way to "be their own boss" or to "work when they want." A growing number of writers and scholars—Alex Rosenblat in *Uberland*, Sarah Kessler in *Gigged*, Juliet Schor in *After the Gig*, Trebor Scholz in *Uberworked and Underpaid*, Tom Slee in *What's Yours Is Mine*, and Veena Dubal in "The Drive to Precarity"—have shown how such promises have fallen short.[28] Rather than countering wage stagnation, underemployment, or economic insecurity, the actually-existing gig economy, they argue, represents "crowd fleecing"[29] or, worse still, a return to "the bleak employment and living conditions of the early industrial age."[30] The Dickensian mills of the industrial age, which once drew the scorn of everyone from Friedrich Engels to Jane Addams, have been transposed to city streets and thousands of glowing screens.

Yet the gap between the rhetoric and reality of the gig economy is, for many of these scholars, not the central concern. It is certainly worth noting that there are "contradictions between the lofty promises of the gig economy and the lived experience of the workers."[31] But this contradiction is just as concerning as the gig economy's role in "upending generations of workplace protections,"[32] "eviscerating a hundred years of workers' rights,"[33] and extending harsh free-market principles into ever more areas of people's social lives.[34] For many, the arrival of the gig economy simply marks the latest iteration of neoliberalism's four-decades-long assault on workers, the public sector, and the poor.

For others, the dangers of the gig economy intersect with the dangers of what sociologist Shoshana Zuboff calls surveillance capitalism.[35] Pointing to the growth of corporations whose profits derive from the accumulation and commodification of personal data, Zuboff cites the increasing risks such corporations pose to both privacy and democratic accountability. Whether as an expression of neoliberalism or as an expression of an emergent surveillance capitalism, the consequences of the gig economy are similar. Gig supporters promise consumer choice, entrepreneurship, and market competition. But behind the rhetoric, we find a society increasingly defined by inequality, the erosion of public institutions, and the consolidation of elite class power—whether measured by wealth or measured by control of data.

Many of the preceding criticisms of the gig economy are crucial to an assessment of Uber's role in catalyzing what one Uber investor described as a "new local politics" in D.C. Given the writings of Ravenelle, Kessler, Schor, and other scholars on the subject, it is easy to view Uber's promise of "choice" and "innovation" as an expression of a quintessentially neoliberal project: behind the pledge to boost the income of D.C.'s low-wage workers is a simple attempt to secure market dominance. And Uber's rollout in D.C. can be seen as a manifestation of Zuboff's new surveillance capitalism.

Yet, in the chapters ahead, we paint a more complex portrait of D.C.'s "new local politics." Most people we interviewed rarely spoke of class power, capital accumulation, neoliberalism, or the political ramifications of surveillance capitalism. More often than not, they seemed to see Uber through the prism of a narrower set of questions, such as these: "To what extent is Uber a solution to the city's transportation woes? In what ways will Uber redress D.C.'s legacy of racial discrimination, especially in the taxi industry? How might Uber build local economic capacity, encourage tech investment, or catalyze innovation?" And, for residents looking to supplement their income, "To what degree will Uber provide a solution?"

Few with whom we spoke held up Uber as a real solution to D.C.'s transportation, racial, economic, or employment challenges. Yet their expectations of the city and its democratic institutions were even lower. These people did not trust Uber to solve problems of racial polarization, stalled economic mobility, or concentrated poverty, but neither did they expect that such problems might be solved through public provision, urban public policy, or—dare we say—"politics." This is the foundation of the book's argument: that Uber's success in D.C. and elsewhere hinges on exploiting a political and infrastructural vacuum and, in so doing, redefining what people expect from cities and the urban public realm.

Uber's rise in D.C. was not simply a top-down imposition of its worldview on unsuspecting citizens. To see it as such fails to reckon with its popularity or to give full consideration to the many people we met for whom Uber was important precisely because it made sense. We met commuters frustrated with the Metro system and others long burdened by the inability to get a cab. We met drivers who were working for Uber to pay for an engagement ring, to monetize their commute to work, to afford their children's college tuition, or to arrange their schedules so that they could take care of their families. We even met people who drove for Uber because they professed having too much spare time or because they were lonely.

What we found is that Uber's growth in D.C. depended not only on its ability to exploit gaps in the city's social safety net but also on its appeal to "common sense." Common sense, here, refers to "the basic human faculty that lets us make elemental judgments about everyday matters based on everyday real-world experience."[36] Common sense is "plain wisdom." To quote media studies scholar Daniel Greene, common sense "emerges organically from practical responses to real problems in the real world."[37] Can't get a taxi? Call an Uber. Metro isn't working? Take an Uber. Struggling with work scheduling or underemployment? Drive for Uber. Uber is commonsense because it is a sensible, practical, and rational response to any number of urban problems. For individuals and cities alike, Uber's benefits "need no sophistication to grasp and no proof to accept."[38]

But to understand how Uber has reshaped cities around the world, it is worth invoking a different yet related meaning of common sense. Here, common sense resides in the realm of politics and ideology. It is shaped and diffused by institutions, political interests, and economic regimes. The prevailing common sense is both historically contingent and the product of political and class struggle. In this second meaning, Uber's rise to the status of common sense is less a product of "plain wisdom" than it is an impressive political achievement and the product of a political struggle to reshape expectations.

The central argument of this book starts from here. *Disrupting D.C.* argues that where Uber (and tech in general) have intervened to shape local politics, such interventions have not been limited to legislation or public policy. Uber has intervened in the realm of people's "commonsense" ideas of what cities can and should be. These ideas include where public transit goes, what constitutes a good job, how cities use data, and the nature of racial justice. Uber's success in D.C.—and the success of the "new local politics" it catalyzed—is evidenced not only by the sheer number of people who seem eager to look to anything other than formal democratic politics as a way of solving urban problems but also by how many look to Uber for those solutions.

Uber and the Urban Question

This book focuses on the growth and expansion of Uber in D.C. We hope it will speak directly to anyone interested in how something as broad as the gig economy shapes urban politics. The chapters that follow draw connections to the work of scholars in many areas, from those working at the intersection of labor and urban studies[39] to the full range of scholars now documenting the tech sector's role in reshaping both the physical structure and the cultural life of cities.[40] Most significantly, however, the arguments advanced in the book will be of special interest to those working in the area of urban governance.

Since the 1970s, the bulk of studies analyzing urban governance have focused on questions of economic development.[41] Often those analyses begin with some variation of the claim advanced by political scientist Paul Peterson in his book *City Limits*—namely, that "city politics is limited politics." Peterson argues that cities are "limited in what they can do" and that "the powers remaining to them are exercised within very noticeable constraints."[42] Many of the debates both within and across disciplinary approaches to urban governance have hinged on how scholars interpret those constraints and how much political agency cities still exercise.

There is, however, a broad consensus in urban studies about the need for cities to be entrepreneurial. Specifically, many scholars agree that globalization, federal devolution, and state retrenchment (in areas of social provision, deindustrialization, suburban capital flight, and the hypermobility of capital) have all, in varying ways, forced cities to adopt a more entrepreneurial approach to economic development. As geographer David Harvey noted, the rise of the "entrepreneurial city" has erased substantive political differences and produced "greater polarization in the social distribution of real income."[43] Other geographers, as well as political scientists like Peter Eisinger, have noted the same. In abandoning demand-side strategies to economic development, mayors and elected officials of widely different political orientations and cultural backgrounds have been forced to adopt the same suite of policies aimed at responding to interurban competition: aggressively courting real estate development through the use of tax abatements, enterprise zones, privatization schemes, and the selling-off of public property.[44] In this context, to quote Harvey, "even the most resolute and avant-garde municipal socialists will find themselves, in the end, playing the capitalist game, and performing as agents of discipline for the very process they are trying to resist."[45] The distributional effects of such policies are almost always regressive. Municipal resources are directed toward enhancing the local business climate and attracting capital investment. Meanwhile, social services aimed at supporting poor and working-class residents invariably take a back seat. In some instances, the active presence and visibility of the urban poor themselves become a problem and threaten the business climate. Here, the response is the cleansing of public spaces and the promotion of "quality-of-life" policing.[46]

Whereas studies of urban politics often begin by acknowledging the constraints on the development of more redistributive urban public policies, they differ in their treatment of the nature and extent of those constraints. In some instances, those constraints are unambiguous products of legal convention. It is generally understood that cities, as Peterson says, "cannot make war or peace; . . . issue passports or forbid outsiders from entering their territory; . . . issue currency; [or] control imports or erect tariff walls."[47] For the most part, these are activities that cities just cannot do. The nature of party politics, the power of local elites, and the internal class structure of cities all pose their own limits. Cities, as a result, face a profound set of *political* and legal limits.

For many people, the most significant constraints for urban politics are *economic*.[48] The fact that cities require revenue to provide public services means that local politicians are limited by the imperatives of economic growth. Political coalitions form and dissolve based on their capacity to attract and retain capital and people. But they direct public policy to those ends too. From broader transformations in the global economy to federal industrial policy, economic factors are decisive in shaping the outer limits of what types of public policies cities can and do undertake. Whether the focus is on deindustrialization in the Global North and suburban capital flight or the financialization of the municipal bond market, the consensus among scholars of urban politics is that the changes of the last fifty years have narrowed the options available to local policymakers, especially those seeking to prioritize the needs of their city's poorest residents.[49]

Earlier studies of the urban growth machine, the entrepreneurial city, and urban regime theory have been succeeded by studies of the neoliberal city, the post-democratic city, and the post-political city.[50] Added to this list are the now numerous works on planetary urbanism.[51]

Many of the central questions, however, have remained the same. Given the imperatives of economic growth and the pressures of interurban competition, are cities capable of enacting policies that redistribute real income or that mitigate income inequality? What limits and constraints do city governments seeking to increase public provisions for marginalized or working-class communities face? How do such limits and constraints shape what local politics can be or what city residents expect from cities and politics? If "proper urban politics," to quote geographer Eric Swyngedouw, "fosters dissent, creates disagreement and triggers the debating of and experimentation with more egalitarian and inclusive urban futures," then what sorts of "proper politics" remain viable?[52]

Consider how the rise of companies like Uber answers such a question. In 2015, before an audience assembled at a D.C.-based tech incubator, Uber strategic adviser David Plouffe touted the company's role in advancing the economic prospects of American workers.[53] As Plouffe argued, some of these economic benefits were indirect. He pointed to Uber's capacity to expand urban transportation options and provide service to communities that had long been marginalized. Noting the prevalence of "transportation deserts in every city in the world," Uber was well placed, he said, to "quite literally transport people out of poverty."[54] The days of transportation discrimination, he added, were over.

Plouffe claimed Uber offered a set of more direct economic benefits too. Citing problems of wage stagnation, student debt, and underemployment, Uber, he said, provided people a way of putting money "back in their pocket" and gave workers the "pay raise that they've been denied for years."[55] Uber offered a necessary and flexible solution that would help the many people still struggling to recover from the 2008 recession. Toward the end of his remarks, Plouffe made a special appeal to city leaders and city regulators who were skeptical of Uber. He argued:

> These are powerful economic effects—and by the way, they're economic benefits that require zero government funding. We are not asking for special tax breaks like those who want to build a factory or headquarters in a city often do. We're simply asking cities to allow their citizens to use their personal assets—their cars—to make money by driving their fellow citizens around their city.[56]

As a senior adviser to President Barack Obama, Plouffe had spent five years intimately involved in federal debates on economic policy. His arguments for placing Uber, rather than the government itself, at the center of debates on wage stagnation and economic mobility are as notable as they are ironic.

Plouffe's claims remain unsupported by evidence. Studies on Uber's impact on low-wage workers are just as likely to prove that Uber has contributed to lowering labor standards or driving down wages as to prove that—as Plouffe would have it—the company has generally improved the prospects of American workers.[57] But what is worth noting is *not* that Plouffe's claims are inaccurate. More important is that by making such claims, Plouffe is not just outlining a business model but advancing a political project. That project, to quote Uber CEO Travis Kalanick, is about "changing how cities work"—and doing so in the interest of securing market share, increasing shareholder value, and consolidating economic and political power.[58] It is also a project that reinforces the widely perceived limits on what urban politics can be.

In discussing the problems of economic inequality and transportation injustice, Plouffe began where scholars of urban politics leave off. The fact that "city politics is limited politics"—that the power afforded to cities is invariably constrained by the imperatives of economic growth and a competitive global economy— helps explain why city governments of all political stripes so often fail their poorest residents. For Plouffe, unlike scholars like David Harvey and Peter Eisinger, this reality is not an indictment of federal policy or neoliberal capitalism. Instead, for Plouffe, such a failure is an argument for allowing Uber to do what city governments and politics allegedly cannot. The following chapters explore how this idea—*to just let Uber do it*—has become common sense.

The imperatives of growth, federal retrenchment, and the pressures of interurban competition have all limited the policy choices available to city governments. And so it is not surprising that arguments like Plouffe's resonate. After all, Plouffe literally says it won't cost the city any money to let Uber operate. As city politics and policies have ossified in the face of ever more rapid global flows of capital, tech companies like Uber have flowed into the economic and political vacuum to offer market-based and technocratic solutions. People's level of trust in these solutions is low. But their belief that urban politics can do any better is even lower. Uber and similar companies benefit from these lowered expectations of city government.

Building on and extending scholarship about urban politics, this book maintains that lowered expectations are yet another constraint on policymakers seeking to secure a more egalitarian city. On the one hand, the truism stands that "city politics is limited politics."[59] On the other hand, city politics is never more limited than when people stop expecting politics, especially democratic politics, to do anything at all.

Every Person for Themselves, Uber for Us All

Part of the story we've told thus far about Uber's success concerns the erosion of public confidence in cities. In addition, the story of Uber showcases the language of trust and confidence that has long served as the currency of many gig-economy behemoths associated with Silicon Valley. Indeed, the language of trust underpinned the early days of "the sharing economy."[60] This language was powerful but was also criticized.

Writing for *The Nation* in 2015, journalist Doug Henwood penned a trenchant critique of what was then still being described as the "sharing economy,"[61] with a focus on Uber and Airbnb. Both companies, Henwood admits, embody the central appeal of the sharing economy—"the promise of using technology to connect disparate individuals in mutually profitable enterprise, or at least in warm feelings."[62] But he adds that these warm feelings are belied by significant social costs. Airbnb, for example, has "grease[d] the wheels of gentrification" and exacerbated the housing affordability crisis.[63] Media coverage of Uber's sexual-harassment and corporate-espionage scandals overshadowed its broader costs to cities—be they due to urban congestion, falling transit ridership, increased pollution, or indebted drivers.

For Henwood, perhaps the most irksome element of the sharing economy is the language itself. The constant use of the words "disruption," "revolution," "movement," "collaborative consumption," and "sharing" seems designed to mystify what, for many, is merely the continuity of the "race-to-the-bottom" capitalism that has defined the last four decades. The sharing economy, Henwood argues, is, at its core, "a classically neoliberal response to neoliberalism."[64] In addition to representing the continued push for market-driven and individualized solutions to all of society's problems, the leading sharing-economy enterprises consciously seek to take advantage of the postrecession economic instability. Henwood's core argument is straightforward: "The sharing economy is a nice way for rapacious capitalists to monetize the desperation of people in the post-crisis economy while sounding generous, and to evoke a fantasy of community in an atomized population."[65]

This book expands on many of Henwood's claims. In D.C., for example, Uber has attempted to monetize the post-2008 economic anxieties of people in many ways: from Black residents' frustration with a discriminatory taxi industry (chapter 2) or the anxiety of workers looking for extra income (chapter 5), to the harried attempts by elected officials to make D.C. appear either innovative (chapter 1) or smart (chapter 3) or invested in the future itself (chapter 4). Though *Disrupting D.C.* shares Henwood's criticism of the sharing economy, it endeavors to go beyond the "'simple Scooby-Doo Marxist' exercise of pulling the mask off the villain to reveal that, yes, indeed, it was capitalism . . . all along."[66] This means acknowledging how Uber speaks to people's real and genuine needs while also pointing to the dangers it poses to the democratic institutions that define our cities. The argument to *let Uber do it* is an argument that sacrifices democratic accountability for consumer convenience.

Few people expect Uber to completely solve problems of economic inequality, or even to offer a suitable alternative to something as vital as public transit. Still, the fact that even fewer people expect city governments to offer an alternative is a problem not purely for policymakers but for all people committed to the idea of self-government. After all, despite their problems and limitations, cities remain accountable to a polity in ways that companies like Uber do not.

For some observers, the rise and expansion of Uber and companies like Uber is further evidence of a decades-long process that has restyled citizens as consumers. As *n+1* contributing editor Nikil Saval has argued, such a campaign has always been a core part of Uber's strategy.[67] What Uber and other ride-hailing companies understand, Saval argues, is that "under capitalism . . . the figure of the consumer can be invoked against the figure of the citizen." Where consumption "has come to replace our original ideas of citizenship," the ultimate role of the state becomes offering citizens choices or stepping aside so that enterprises like Uber can do so.[68] The dangers posed by Uber are not merely the dangers of unfettered capitalism. They are dangers associated with control.

To what extent, Saval asks, "do we want an entire transportation order at the mercy of the ride-sharing companies?" Can the idea that we should control how we move through a city be made a matter of public policy? Since Uber seeks to push legislators to answer yes to the first question and no to the second, the lesson should be clear. What Uber wants "cannot exist alongside a democratic society."[69] This statement makes a rather bold claim, and many people with whom we spoke in D.C. might think it too bold. *Disrupting D.C.* not only offers a defense of this claim; it lays out what happens when the idea of *just let Uber do it* becomes common sense. This idea, we argue, leads to a politics of greatly diminished expectations. It also leads to cities where the "we" of politics is narrowed to the citizen consumer alone. In such cities, active political participation becomes indistinguishable from brand loyalty, democracy becomes little more than clicktivism, and the most important decisions facing voters are consigned to choosing between Uber and Lyft rather than choosing between policies aimed at improving transit and creating more living-wage jobs.[70]

The Case Study: Washington, D.C.

Washington, D.C., occupies a unique place in the history of Uber. It was in D.C. that the company "created a playbook" for how to deal with intransigent regulators.[71] It was also in D.C. where the success of "Operation Rolling Thunder" offered critics a glimpse of the company's political power—a power that would find expression in campaigns the world over.[72] As will become evident in subsequent chapters, in D.C. Uber trialed many of the tactics that it would later deploy nationwide in its efforts to stay exempt from

providing workers with employee benefits, such as its 2020 campaign for Proposition 22 in California and a copycat ballot initiative
in 2022 in Massachusetts.[73]

In the context of debates about urban governance, however,
D.C. is hardly unusual at all. Despite its status as a federal district—
and, thus, something of a jurisdictional anomaly—few cities offer a
clearer picture of the problems of income inequality, racial polarization, and municipal sclerosis, as well as the constraints on what
elected officials can do to resolve such issues. As in many North
American cities, decades of underinvestment have left our nation's
capital in a bind and with a stunning list of delayed infrastructure
projects. The shame of its crumbling transit infrastructure has
been particularly notable and was illustrated by the wave of track
fires that beset Metro in 2016—the target of the "Metro's a loser!"
protest with which we started this chapter.[74]

The historic dominance of the federal government has sepa-
rated D.C. from most American cities.[75] However, the relative
strength of D.C.'s service sector—which is largely a by-product of
this dominance—has made the capital a forerunner for the postin-
dustrial city.[76] The trajectory of local politics has been familiar too.
Irrespective of political orientation, every administration since
its founding—from the mayor down to the D.C. Council—has
placed the promotion of real estate development at the core of
its economic strategy.[77] A 1969 *Washington Post* article began by
noting, "What steel means to Pittsburgh, cars to Detroit, tobacco
to Durham, cattle to Kansas City, oil to Houston—that's what real
estate means to Washington."[78] On this score, little has changed.

At least since the mid-1990s, the specter of gentrification has
hovered over almost every policy debate—from those on education and charter schools, to those on housing and economic development, to those on bike lanes, coffee shops, and go-go music.[79]
After D.C. lost its designation as a majority minority city in 2011,
such debates have only intensified in a city that has, as scholar
Brandi Summers writes, long been a "fiercely and firmly recognized Black place."[80]

In short, D.C. residents face challenges similar to those in cities across the country, and they do so despite the city's distinct history and the particularity of its institutions. These are challenges directly related to the ever-familiar gap between what cities can actually do and the various crises they must work to resolve. Uber has succeeded in D.C. precisely by presenting itself as a solution to these crises. As such, the city is an augur for all those concerned about the quality and future of urban life across the United States.[81]

The Plan of the Book

Across five chapters, *Disrupting D.C.* traces Uber's political intervention into local debates over regulation (chapter 1), racial discrimination (chapter 2), data (chapter 3), automation (chapter 4), and labor (chapter 5). As we note in each chapter, Uber appeals directly to those seeking a ready fix to urban problems that are often structural in origin. While the chapters take up different topics, each builds toward the argument that Uber's intervention in local politics works at the level of public policy as well as at the level of people's commonsense expectations.

As we illustrate in chapters 1 and 2, to the extent that Uber has succeeded in pitching itself as a fix to an allegedly racist and archaic local taxi industry, it has reduced people's faith in the public institutions mandated to address such problems. And, even worse, it has advanced notions of racial justice and modernization that leave many inequalities intact. We show in chapter 3 that, for transportation planners and regulators (who view data sharing as central to solving various problems associated with traffic congestion), Uber has been both a resource and cause for frustration. While the expectation that data sharing will benefit the city has gone unquestioned, even less attention has been paid to the labor conditions under which that data is produced. Although many people expect D.C. to become a smart city, few expect that such a city will require giving workers rights to the data they produce.

In chapter 4, we look at Uber's promise of the self-driving car and its role in shaping drivers', venture capitalists', and city boosters' expectations. Irrespective of their feasibility, autonomous vehicles function ideologically to provide an outlet for investment capital and to ensure labor compliance. These fantastic promises relegate the concerns of present-day workers and residents to the figurative back seat. As we illustrate in chapter 5, Uber—especially in its appeals to flexibility—has played on workers' expectations. In addition, it has worked to structure the job in ways that limit collective action, that individuate work, and that lower expectations concerning what the job should provide. We show how the very strategies that Uber has employed to manage its workforce have also, at certain moments, unintentionally laid the groundwork for solidarity among workers.

In the book's conclusion, we explore what is required to raise expectations and to offer a new commonsense view of urban politics. The economic aftershocks of the global COVID-19 pandemic, we argue, pose new challenges and opportunities for those seeking to reimagine what cities and city politics can be—with or without Uber.

———

With the exception of the introduction and the conclusion, each of this book's chapters is adapted from material published or presented in other venues. Chapter 1, developed and written by Katie J. Wells, is adapted from "Urban Governance in the Age of Apps," a talk delivered at Data and Society in New York City in March 2020. Chapter 2, developed and written by Kafui Attoh, is adapted from "Uber's Racial Strategy and Our Own," a talk delivered at the November 2018 *Anti-Blackness and the City* conference in Baltimore. Chapter 3 was developed and written by Kafui Attoh and is adapted from "'We're Building Their Data': Labor, Alienation and Idiocy in the Smart City," published in 2019 in *Environment and Planning D: Society and Space*. Chapter 4 was developed and written by Declan Cullen and is adapted from "Taking Back the Wheel," published in *Dissent* magazine (online) in 2019. Chapter 5 was developed and written by Katie J. Wells and is adapted from "Just-in-Place Labor: Driver Organizing in the Uber Workplace," published in 2021 in *Environment and Planning A: Economy and Space*. While Katie J. Wells and Declan Cullen took the lead on the conclusion, Kafui Attoh took the lead on the preface and introduction. The appendixes and figures were developed by Katie J. Wells, with the cartographic help of Alicia Sabatino.

1

On Not Being a Dinosaur

> So, D.C., they adopted our view of the world, I think. And
> that's why it's one of the best models for us.
> —UBER LOBBYIST[1]

> There is nothing more difficult than to be a stepson of time;
> there is no heavier fate than to live in an age that is not your
> own. . . . Time loves only those it has given birth to itself: its
> own children, its own heroes, its own laborers. Never can it
> come to love the children of a past age.
> —VASILY GROSSMAN, *LIFE AND FATE*[2]

On January 13, 2012, Ron Linton, the chair of the D.C. Taxicab
Commission, ordered an Uber car from his smartphone. At the
time, Uber was operating in only five other American cities. Linton, an eighty-two-year-old man who had spent six decades in
local public service, including the police department, was frustrated. D.C.'s municipal government—the D.C. Council, the office
of the attorney general, and the mayor—had yet to confront
Uber about whether the company was breaking the law by offering a chauffeur service whose unlicensed livery drivers lacked

commercial insurance policies and charged by mileage (instead of time). So, Linton took matters into his own hands. He scheduled an Uber ride to a hotel downtown. At the end of the ride, and just as planned, taxi enforcement officials were waiting. They issued the Uber driver a $1,650 fine and impounded the vehicle.[3] Linton had set up and starred in his own sting.

Public debate arose immediately. While few denied that Uber's operations in D.C. violated the law, the question remained: What should D.C. policymakers do about it? Three answers emerged: (1) change Uber to accommodate the law; (2) change the law to accommodate Uber; and (3) whatever is done, make sure the city does not appear to be anti-innovation.

Linton argued for the first option. In making his case, he found himself on shaky ground. While attacking Uber for breaking the law, he stood at the head of an organization with its own legal issues and with a questionable public-relations record. In 2009, the commission had been caught in an FBI investigation of thirty-nine taxi drivers charged with conspiracy to bribe officials for taxi-company licenses.[4] Leon Swain Jr., Linton's predecessor, who notoriously carried a gun to taxi-commission meetings, was fired for unknown reasons in 2011.[5] Then, a few months later, the arrest of two journalists for taking photographs[6] at one of the taxi commission's supposedly public meetings added to the general sense that the taxi commission was corrupt.

Linton wanted Uber to agree to licenses, inspections, and other requirements akin to those for the taxi industry. "Regulations," he wrote, "make sense out of chaos."[7] But Linton's belief in the power of the government to regulate seemed old-fashioned. It made him not only a dinosaur in the age of apps but what author Vasily Grossman might call "a stepson of time."[8]

The second option for what to do about Uber was argued by David Alpert, a young Google retiree with a locally focused blog called *Greater Greater Washington*.[9] Alpert was sympathetic to Uber and advocated to change local laws to accommodate Uber. He wrote that his preference for Uber derived from a preference "to move the industry more away from regulation and toward an innovation model."[10] In a letter to the editor of the *Washington Post*, Alpert said that if Uber was deemed illegal, "then something is wrong with the law, not with Uber."[11] He, like many other residents, despised the way taxis worked in the city. Taxis in D.C. were old; they were outdated; and, for many, they were a symbol of urban dysfunction. The city had tried multiple times to change the taxi system (by adding medallions) but failed. For some, this history served as strong evidence that the city was powerless over its taxi industry. Taxis did not adopt metered pricing until 2008 (which had made it difficult for passengers to estimate a fare).[12] They did not have GPS trackers, often required cash payments (which irked the professional class), and offered only twenty wheelchair-accessible vehicles in the whole city. The mayor at the time reportedly joked that the uniform color for D.C. taxis was rust.[13] A senior policy expert and city employee talked about the taxi industry as antiquated: "We didn't *want* to drive the taxi industry out of business. But the taxi industry didn't have a mobile app."[14] From many current and former policymakers, as well as local stakeholders, we heard the same mantra about the incumbent taxi system's age and dysfunction: taxis were "ancient,"[15] "archaic,"[16] "backwards,"[17] "really bad,"[18] "terrible,"[19] "a complete disaster," "horrific,"[20] and "not functioning particularly well."[21] An economic development expert and former city employee who sympathized with this consumer resentment told us, "My favorite factoid is that D.C. taxis accepted credit cards within a few weeks of the taxis in Pyongyang."[22]

On top of this host of complaints, D.C. taxis were notorious for ignoring street hails from Black customers and for avoiding Black neighborhoods altogether (for discussion, see chapter 2). During the Uber debates in 2012, one Black councilmember said: "Uber does come east of the river [to the poorer neighborhoods, those with majority Black populations] without hesitation. . . . For the fact that Uber does come out, I really do support them."[23] A policymaker who was deeply involved in Uber's legislative battles in D.C. told us his spouse, as an African American, had similarly "absurd" experiences with taxis.[24] In sum, taxis were seen as resistant to change, overregulated, and racist.

Five high-ranking city employees and elected policymakers who spoke with us represented the third option in the debates. The real question about Uber was less *how* to regulate it and more *whether* any regulation would make D.C. appear to be antitech. Local policymakers, apart from Linton, were "nervous about crossing these companies."[25] One such policymaker explained to us the problem that Uber posed: "Uber had just been kicking our ass in the court of public opinion. . . . They had made the administration out to look like we were dinosaurs; we were anti-innovation."[26] He went on:

> The tech sector was really pushing this meme of disruption, regulatory disruption. And they weren't necessarily wrong in the notion that the regulatory environment as it existed didn't know how to accommodate these new innovations. But their answer was, "Throw it all out." And our answer was, "That's insane." Maybe the regulatory framework has to adapt, but that doesn't mean you throw it all out.

The lines of the debate had been drawn. On one side: the taxis, dinosaurs, legacy regulations, inefficiencies, and an outdated city. On the other side: Uber, innovators, efficiency, small government, the business community, and a city designed for the future. The Uber question became a referendum on innovation, the future of the city, and, fundamentally, regulation itself.

"Dawn of a New Local Politics"

When Uber arrived in 2011, the D.C. Council was already debating how, in its words, to "modernize" the local taxi industry. As a result, the question of what should be done about Uber was tangled up with the question of how to reform taxi services. The logic went like this: The taxi commission was bad. Taxi services were poor. Thus, Uber, which challenged both the taxi commission and taxi drivers, was, by default, good. If you were against Uber, then you were for taxis, you were pro-regulation, and you were an enemy of progress. At a hearing about Uber, a councilmember making the case for Uber said: "We should be embracing more of this technology. . . . If regulation meant high quality service at a good value, then D.C. would have the best service in the nation."[27]

In these debates, a different councilmember tried to add nuance. It was none other than Marion Barry, the septuagenarian who had served four terms as D.C. mayor. Barry was, as he would describe himself, "a friend of the taxi industry,"[28] which until the 1970s had been dominated by the local African American community but had since shifted to a niche occupation among first-generation immigrants.[29] At a hearing, he said that on a recent evening he had been unable to get a taxi to come to his address in the Southeast area of D.C. But he argued that chauffeur services needed *more*, not less, regulation to address these discriminatory practices. "How can you," he asked, "have a company [like Uber] that is unregulated" completely?[30] D.C. was about to find out.

In the summer of 2012, the D.C. Council debated several issues in preparation for a final bill on Uber. During this period, Uber negotiated with council staff about a ban on surge pricing, a requirement for 10 percent of Uber's fleet (and those of its competitors) to be wheelchair accessible, and the possibility of a price floor for Uber rides. But, on the evening before a hearing on the bill, in what would be a surprise for councilmembers, Uber shifted gears on a decision to support a mutually agreeable price minimum. Uber CEO Travis Kalanick said: "Look, price controls by governments, they don't always go well. In fact, I'd say 99 percent of the documented cases don't go well."[31] At the hearing, he also said, "When you tell us how to do business and you tell us we can't charge lower fares, you are fighting with us."[32] Through "Operation Rolling Thunder," the company mobilized its users—via in-app messages and direct emails—to ask the council to remove the price minimum. Kalanick sent an email titled "Un-independence" to every single Uber customer in D.C., with a request that they help prevent the price minimum by emailing and tweeting every councilmember.[33] Over the next twenty-four hours, a reported fifty thousand emails and thirty-seven thousand tweets with the hashtag #UberDCLove were sent to the council.[34] On Twitter, the term "UberDC" was used eight hundred thousand times in less than an hour.[35] And the tactic worked. The next day, the price minimum was struck from the proposal. The *Washington Post* described the action as a "rider revolt."[36] On its blog, Uber posted a write-up about its success in D.C., boasting, "Never underestimate the power of thousands of loyal supporters armed with email, social media, and a cause."[37] Brand loyalty had transformed into a new version of active political citizenship.

That same day, a venture capitalist and early Uber investor tweeted something similar: "What happened today with @Uber & DC is dawn of a new local politics: Tech/social exercising newfound muscles on a policy level in real-time."[38] *Bloomberg News* editor and author Brad Stone agreed: "Uber had flexed its political muscles for the first time, and won. A new tactic was then added to the playbook: when traditional advocacy failed, Uber could mobilize its user base and direct their passion toward elected officials."[39] This tactic represented a victory over the old local politics, which found no better representation than Linton. Officials had called Linton's sting "embarrassing," "silly,"[40] and "a huge black eye"[41] for the city. What made Linton's sting so embarrassing was not the operation itself but his belief that D.C. government might actually govern Uber.

In November 2012, Mary Cheh, the D.C. Council member who was shepherding Uber's proposed legislation—the Public Vehicle-for-Hire Innovation Amendment Act of 2012—urged the other councilmembers to adopt her committee's bill. In a letter to them, she wrote: "Through this legislation, we can support innovation in the public vehicle-for-hire industry by *decreasing regulation and encouraging competition, which will ultimately improve the quality and reliability of service for District residents.*"[42] The next month, D.C. policymakers unanimously passed the law, which created a new class of chauffeur services defined by "digital dispatch."[43] What was remarkable about the legislation was the exemption it created. Uber was awarded its own business category and exempted from existing taxi regulations and taxi commission oversight. As the *Washington Post* put it, Uber had won "the battle between sainted innovators and evil regulators and [successfully] pushed the idea that Uber should operate wholly free of government interference."[44] The new ride-hailing law would have, the *Post* continued, "little practical effect" on Uber's operations in the city. The *Post* described the outcome as evidence that "the system worked . . . grievances were redressed in a mutually agreeable manner. . . . Woo, democracy."[45] On Twitter, Kalanick used the hashtag #UberDemocracy.[46] Elsewhere he said D.C. had set "a standard for how other cities should be looking at this kind of innovation"[47] and "will serve as an innovative model for city transportation legislation across the country."[48]

To the libertarian-funded magazine *Reason*, Uber was the underdog that had almost been run over by Linton's "regulatory establishment."[49] In an eleven-minute documentary titled "Uber Wars: How D.C. Tried to Kill a Great New Ride Technology," which three local media outlets covered,[50] *Reason* characterized Linton as part of a big "embedded bureaucracy" that was "accidentally repressive" of new small businesses, meaning Uber drivers.[51] These arguments were not new. Hubert Horan—an early and, in retrospect, prescient observer of the ride-hailing industry—traces Uber's playbook to the taxi deregulatory campaigns launched in the 1990s by Charles and David Koch, who, not coincidentally, are funders of *Reason*.[52]

In "Uber Wars," when Linton is shown, he is in the corner of a poorly lit office. The video footage is grainy, there is no music, and Linton looks washed out, motionless, and every bit the gray, bureaucratic state functionary. In comparison, the narrator appears energetic as he quickly walks down a street under bright natural lighting. If the narrator was pushing D.C. toward the future, Linton was holding it back. A few years later, a *Washingtonian* obituary of Linton indeed described him as "the face of anti-innovation."[53]

Uber consultant Bradley Tusk, who claims to have written the D.C. legislation, described the 2012 victory in D.C. as a win about the broader notion of government itself: Uber "disrupt[ed] the status quo of governing."[54] Indeed, Uber officially became a "regulatory entrepreneur,"[55] a company for which rewriting laws, as opposed to simply currying favor through traditional lobbying, is a significant part of its development plan.[56] But something else took place too: Uber, in this first period of D.C. legislative debates, helped limit whose rights count.

Squandered Progress on Accessibility

In the years that followed, Uber's D.C. customer base grew exponentially. Then the company picked D.C. to be one of its first markets for UberX, a low-cost service to connect any regularly licensed driver of a private automobile with paying passengers. When UberX arrived, Linton did not stage another sting. He did, however, try again to single-handedly take on the Silicon Valley beast. Within a week of UberX's arrival in D.C. in the fall of 2013, he ushered in new regulations at the taxi commission to ban the service. The D.C. Council immediately came to Uber's rescue and used emergency legislation, the Livery Class Regulation and Ride-Sharing Emergency Amendment Act of 2013, to block the regulations, which, in the words of one councilmember, "were horrible."[57]

In response, Uber itself spent $300,000 to lobby the D.C. Council, resulting in at least eighty documented in-person meetings, eighty-seven email exchanges, and twenty-nine phone calls with councilmembers or their respective aides in 2014.[58] The council staffer most responsible for drafting the Uber legislation told us that he "had either a meeting, at least one phone call, or at least one email [with Uber lobbyists] probably every day."[59] A senior business improvement district (BID) official with whom we spoke was aware of this persistent lobbying: "D.C. had to sort of be pushed. . . . And it was an education process for D.C. legislators to understand what the rideshare economy meant."[60] A high-ranking policymaker described the legislative period as less of an education process and more of a battle: "I always found it ironic that after fighting D.C. for so long—and we've talked about this—[Uber] eventually started going around the country saying that D.C. was the model jurisdiction. Because, when we lived through it, it was extremely adversarial."[61]

During this second period of legislative debates in D.C., Uber's loudest opposition came from two sources: taxi drivers and local disability rights advocates. For taxi drivers, the primary issue was one of unfair competition. Whereas they were required to undergo regular inspections, pay registration fees, pass a sixty-hour training course that cost several hundred dollars, and maintain certain insurance coverages, UberX drivers faced no comparable hurdles. Taxi drivers, who hoped that new regulations would "level the playing field,"[62] made two sometimes-competing arguments about what should be done. On the one hand, taxi drivers wanted Uber drivers to do everything *they* did (e.g., submit to annual inspections, pass a deep background check, and report tip data) plus be limited to a twenty-hour workweek and have a price floor.[63] On the other hand, they sometimes argued that their own industry should be deregulated so that they could use surge pricing and reduce the number of annual inspections. To stress their points, taxi drivers twice blocked the roads outside the John A. Wilson Building, where the council meets. In addition, some drivers tried to form a union-like association with the International Brotherhood of Teamsters, plan a cooperatively owned dispatch app, and raise public safety concerns about Uber via a social media campaign called "Who's Driving You."[64]

FIGURE 1.1. Taxi drivers protest Uber, June 25, 2014. Reproduced with permission by D.C. Jobs with Justice.

In the end, taxi drivers were unsuccessful in these campaigns. This fact can partially be attributed to the nature of the local taxi industry, which for decades had been overwhelmingly made up of taxicabs owned by individual working-class drivers.[65] In the early 2000s Ethiopian immigrants made up almost a quarter of all D.C. taxi drivers, formed strong social networks, and served on boards for professional driver associations.[66] However, these ties did not translate into a unified political strategy. When Uber arrived in D.C., there were 116 taxicab companies. The four largest accounted for just 1,200 of the 6,500 taxis in the city.[67] This decentralized industry, made up of independent contractors, meant that there was not a set of large taxi conglomerates, as there were in New York City, that could quickly coordinate a response to newcomer Uber. Taxi drivers had little power.

For people with disabilities and their advocates, the timing of UberX's arrival could not have been worse. As part of the effort to modernize the taxi industry, the taxi commission had finally agreed, after years of pressure from disability rights advocates, to a requirement that companies with more than twenty taxicabs would make at least 6 percent of those cabs wheelchair-accessible by 2014 (and make 20 percent wheelchair-accessible by 2018).[68] At the time, only twenty taxicabs in D.C.'s entire fleet (about seven thousand cars) met such standards.[69]

The taxi commission had also agreed to organize an advisory committee on accessibility, which published its first reports in 2014. The problem with Uber, the reports explained, was that it helped squander the progress that disability rights activists had made with the taxi industry. Taxi services are required by federal law to not discriminate against disabled passengers—which means, for example, they cannot refuse to give rides to individuals with service animals—*and* to provide wheelchair-accessible service with any new vans.[70] The issue, however, is how many rides and wheelchair-accessible vehicles are available and with what frequency. A sting in 2013 by a local journalist and the American Council of the Blind found that nearly half the taxi drivers in D.C. ignored accessible service requests, overcharged passengers, or discharged passengers at the wrong location.[71]

By undermining the taxi industry, Uber inadvertently undermined the taxi industry's progress toward accessible transportation. As Terri,[72] a member of the advisory committee, told us: "Transit is hard for somebody who uses a wheelchair in D.C. The buses are often full, and they're allowed to pass you by if they're full. They don't have to make room. They can't kick off a person to make room for a wheelchair user. The elevators [at the Metro stops] don't work."[73] And so, in one of the first reports that Terri and other committee members authored for the D.C. Taxicab Commission Accessibility Advisory Committee, they recommended that companies like Uber be subject to the same minimum fleet requirements as every other taxi company in the city. The report recommended that Uber, if it failed to meet those requirements, pay into a fund that would support the purchase of accessible taxis or the development of training modules to expand accessible taxi service in the city. But, according to Terri, representatives from Uber and its peers said that "they didn't understand the laws [or that] accessibility was a requirement under the [Americans with Disabilities Act] and the history and all of that." As Terri explained, the D.C. Council's commitment to regulation around accessibility faded when Uber arrived:

> [Policymakers] just stop[ped] thinking whenever Uber and all that stuff was around. They were like, "Oh, we can be the leader, and all of this, innovation and blah blah blah, everybody will look up to us." Not thinking critically about any of it! None of it! Anything that Uber wanted. We could not out-lobby [Uber] to save our lives.[74]

Uber's regulatory wins in D.C. created sizeable barriers to wheelchair-accessible transportation and stymied years of progress toward that goal. In addition, they undermined the notion of public oversight as a social good, the practice of democratic policymaking, and the idea that innovation could be compatible with—and even benefit from—regulation.

A Wholesale Coup

The eventual legislation on UberX, The Vehicle-for-Hire Innovation Amendment Act of 2014, was a coup for the company and, apart from the recommendation that Uber drivers watch a short safety video on accessible transportation, a defeat for accessibility advocates. The law states that digital dispatch companies, such as Uber, shall (a) make sure that company websites and mobile apps are accessible to blind, visually impaired, deaf, and hard-of-hearing customers; and (b) provide a report to the council about how the company "*intends* to increase access to wheelchair-accessible public or private vehicle-for-hire service to individuals with disabilities" (emphasis added).[75] The law made clear that ride-hailing services do not need to purchase or maintain any wheelchair-friendly vehicles. All they must do is express *the intent* to increase accessibility.

To anyone who has focused on the rise of Silicon Valley and venture capital, this outcome may come as no surprise.[76] What is a surprise, and what does demand attention, is the cost of such outcomes for the possibility of democratic urban governance. Uber increasingly sells itself as capable of providing a public service but fiercely fights any regulation that would actually require it to do so.

One of the most galling representations Uber made in the years after its legislative win concerned wheelchair-accessible vehicles. In late 2014, Uber announced that it was taking steps toward offering the very services that it had vehemently sought to avoid being mandated to offer. The company said it was launching a partnership with a wheelchair-accessible-vehicle dealer to help drivers buy such vehicles.[77] That same month, Uber announced a new service, called uberTAXI, that would match riders with a wheelchair-accessible vehicle. A coauthor of the Americans with Disabilities Act celebrated the news: "Before today, people requiring wheelchair accessible vehicles lacked freedom to move around D.C. at their leisure."[78] A few months later, the company said it would allow deaf drivers to work on its platform.[79] It remains unclear whether any of these programs came to any kind of fruition. What we do know is that, to this day, Uber's only mandate from the D.C. government is to submit plans that detail its *intentions* to increase accessibility. Because of the way that Uber has been able to evade regulation and to shift expectations of regulatory oversight for its services, no outside entity knows how many requests on the Uber platform are for wheelchair-accessible vehicles, how long such riders wait for services, and whether those riders face discrimination.

A number of bills sought to change this bleak reality and bring Uber in line with accessibility standards. One such bill would have required the company to report the number of people who requested accessible vehicles, as well as the number of rides actually provided. Another would have required Uber to make 12 percent of its fleet wheelchair-accessible. But Uber convinced D.C. policymakers that these proposals and their "excessive regulatory burdens"[80] would decimate the industry, ultimately hurting the population of riders that the city sought to help.

Uber also contested the idea of regulated accessibility when the National Federation of the Blind and the U.S. Department of Justice filed a complaint against the company for discrimination with a federal district court in 2014.[81] When disabled individuals in D.C. who use nonfoldable wheelchairs sued Uber for systematic discrimination in terms of longer wait times and higher costs, Uber again argued that it should not have to ensure equitable transit access for disabled riders. But, in a statement that gives hope to disability rights advocates, then U.S. District Court Judge Ketanji B. Jackson said Uber has *not* shown that its services in the city fall outside the scope of the Americans with Disabilities Act or the D.C. Human Rights Act.[82] The case, though not yet settled, stands as a reminder of Uber's decade-long resistance to mandated accessibility and its limited conceptions of transportation justice.

The Aftermath: A Perverse Victory

In addition to eliminating the possibility of mandated accessibility, the 2014 Uber law divested the city of other regulatory powers by stipulating several kinds of oversight that the government *cannot* exercise. First, and most broadly, that law states that digital dispatch companies, such as Uber, are "exempt from regulation by the [Taxicab] Commission" and need not collect or transmit anonymous data about customer trips, even though the commission does so for taxis.[83] Second, the law says that ride-hailing companies cannot be required to provide any inventory of their vehicles or information about their drivers. Last, the law enshrines the ride-hailing companies' desires to keep secret the volume of their rides in the city. Whereas taxis pay the city 25 cents for each ride, thus allowing the city to calculate the number of trips each day, the new law allows Uber to instead pay 1 percent of gross receipts from trips that begin in D.C. By agreeing to this alternate arrangement, the drafters of the law created a significant barrier to policymakers' basic understanding of Uber's operations in the city.

What is most notable about ride-hailing companies' ability to shield their performance and footprint from view is a special clause in the legislation that makes data about ride-hailing exempt from the D.C. Freedom of Information Act (FOIA).[84] As journalists, policymakers, and researchers in D.C. soon found, documenting even the most basic information on the operation of Uber or other ride-hailing platforms was virtually impossible. One journalist sought information on a first-mile/last-mile partnership between the city and Uber, to no avail. Still, a reverse kind of information-sharing has taken hold. In D.C., Uber uses FOIA requests to track the actions of city agencies.[85] One high-ranking city employee, Alan, told us that he was no longer bothered by Uber's regular FOIA requests to the agency in which he worked and that he had learned to communicate only by phone about any policy proposals that might be construed as affecting the industry, because Uber "can't FOIA a phone call."[86]

In the landmark book *Uberland*, tech writer Alex Rosenblat documents informational asymmetries between Uber drivers and the company.[87] What we find in D.C. is a wholly different set of informational asymmetries, which in this case exist between the company and the city. An economic-development expert and former city employee pointed out to us the irony of this arrangement: "I frankly think it's hypocritical of Uber and Lyft to say 'We are partners of cities' while systematically undermining the ability of their elected officials to actually manage how these services fit into the milieu."[88]

Zack, one of Uber's lobbyists for D.C. with whom we spoke, described the 2014 law as "our foundational legislation."[89] When asked how D.C. ended up, in his words, with "the most welcoming and the most friendly" laws in the country, Zack told us: [D.C.] adopted our view of the world, I think. And that's why it's one of the best models for us." When probed on what that worldview was, he said it was one in which Uber would "set the standards." He went on, "We can do all those functions that a regulator would, but we can do it at the pace of business." He then said:

> We take on all the responsibility of making sure that all the people that we partner with are vetted. . . . Rather than kicking that over to a regulator, who then would spend a lot of time trying to vet each individual driver and might or might not do that with the best of intentions. Because traditionally, a lot of regulators were captured by the industry because they had a vested interest in protecting the traditional industry and protecting a lot of the jobs associated with regulating that industry.[90]

The idea here is simple: D.C. trusted Uber to regulate itself—because Uber, presumably, promised solutions for a city that craved innovation while struggling, as many do, to build and maintain adequate transit systems, including taxi services. Zack stressed to us that D.C.'s law conforms "pretty well to that view of the world, and that's what we've been advocating for across the country."[91] Uber's regional manager in D.C. similarly celebrated the city's legislative achievements as the result of a mutual outlook: "We've been fortunate enough to align with leaders who see what is happening in the future. The District and the state of Virginia have been innovators nationally and on this issue it is the same."[92] By presenting regulation as antithetical to innovation, Uber's political project to dissuade regulatory oversight in D.C. and elsewhere[93] speaks to a set of broader ideals, not just immediate questions of how policymakers should contend with new technologies that enable on-demand chauffeur services. In D.C., Uber raised a question not unlike the ones critical urban scholars have asked for decades (see the introduction to this book): What do we expect from our cities and their policymakers? Who should oversee what? Who should be accountable to whom? Does regulation as we know it (and as Linton tried to devise it) still make sense in the age of apps?[94]

A Solution

"On the East Coast, if you want to innovate, it's D.C."[95] These are the words of a former senior official at the D.C. Department of Transportation who explained to us why Uber's arrival in the nation's capital made sense to him. Before Uber entered D.C., local policymakers spent almost a decade exploring alternative transportation modes and represented the city as a paragon of twenty-first-century transit planning. In the early 2000s, the municipal government gave public space access to a car-sharing program, Zipcar, and, not long after, it launched the country's first bike-sharing program. Then policymakers began to heavily pursue new investments *from* tech companies and *in* technology (see chapters 3 and 4). They launched economic development programs called Digital D.C. and Smarter D.C. They spent $8 million to turn a former psychiatric hospital into an Innovation Hub. Most spectacularly, they mobilized D.C.'s Black history to brand the city as "the capital of *inclusive* innovation."[96] A former senior official at the Office of Planning explained to us the rationale for these efforts, which emerged alongside civic efforts such as Code for D.C., the volunteer hacker brigade. She said: "We wanted the city to demonstrate . . . that it was innovative and forward-thinking, and that innovation as a brand was going to be increasingly important. Because a lot of problems that we were trying to solve really couldn't be solved with the old way of doing things."[97] Innovation became inarguable common sense.[98]

In debates about Uber, the future of D.C. as an oasis of innovation was juxtaposed not only with regulation but also with an archaic and inconsequential past, which the stalwart taxi commissioner

Linton represented. A staff member of two mayoral administrations with whom we spoke framed the city's innovation strategies as not just exemplary but *new*:

> There's never been a business development strategy in D.C. at all until . . . I came down [from New York City] ten years ago, because it's a young city. It's sort of a city that's figuring out how to get one foot in front of the other after the disaster of [former Mayor] Marion Barry. To a large extent it's really only been a functional city for twenty years.[99]

Whether or not there is truth to this inflated claim, the story about D.C.'s past signals the extent to which many local policymakers agreed with Uber's view of the need for new approaches to urban development. In recent years, the D.C. government has worked with Uber to create promotional videos, hold ribbon-cutting ceremonies, and collaborate on transit plans. When long-overdue repairs to the Metro system caused massive service disruptions, Uber was permitted to use designated pick-up/drop-off zones at Metro stations and to offer customers a 70 percent discount on shared rides from those zones.[100] In addition, D.C. partnered with Uber to offer students free rides to meal sites in the summer of 2021.[101] More than once, Mayor Muriel Bowser has celebrated the city's close relationship with Uber. She said, "We're excited to be one of the early partners with Uber,"[102] and claimed that her elderly parents' use of ride-hailing apps helped them live independently.[103] A deputy for the mayor reiterated these points: "We are partnering with companies like Uber to help us use technology to move the needle on the intractable challenges faced by our communities."[104] A local alliance of transit policymakers and an urban density advocacy group (both outgrowths of Alpert's *Greater Greater Washington* blog) made separate arguments about the environmental benefits and traffic-reduction benefits of shared ride-hailing services in testimonies at D.C. Council meetings.[105]

At a ribbon-cutting ceremony for a new Uber drivers' center (in Uber-speak, a "Greenlight Hub") in a poor, majority Black

FIGURE 1.2. D.C. Mayor Muriel Bowser celebrates new Uber "Greenlight Hub," October 19, 2017. Reproduced with permission by Khalid Naji-Allah / Executive Office of Mayor Muriel Bowser.

neighborhood near Benning Heights, Mayor Bowser spoke to the labor implications of the ride-hailing service:

> A Greenlight Hub at East River Park means good paying jobs for Washingtonians, contracts for local small businesses, and easier access to supports for our residents who drive with Uber. . . . As we continue our focus on job creation and equitable development in all eight wards, we are excited to work hand-in-hand with Uber to spread prosperity and create more pathways to the middle class for D.C. residents.[106]

In interviews with more than thirty-five local government employees, business leaders, transportation experts, and elected policymakers in D.C. (see appendix B for a list of interviewees), we heard this refrain over and over: Uber helps low-wage workers have more control over their lives.[107] A long-serving, high-ranking elected official[108] said that residents are "making decent money on [the Uber platform], knowing when to hit the peak times . . . and [how to] manage their other work schedule around it."[109] For the vast majority of the policymakers and elite stakeholders who spoke with us, Uber was good enough for D.C. Though many differed in their estimation of the ride-hailing service, they were uniform in their assessment that Uber was a useful addition to the city. This is not to say that they saw Uber as having no drawbacks or short-comings. But, given their skepticism about regulation and their strong commitment to innovative growth, Uber just made sense.

Just Let Uber Do It

At the very beginning of our research for this book, we went to a meeting inside Uber's corporate office on Rhode Island Avenue Northwest in downtown D.C. There, in January 2016, we met with an employee who had joined the company two years earlier to work on its international expansion. He had agreed to speak with us about Uber's operations, though D.C. wasn't his area of focus. In that conversation, he used a phrase that we hadn't heard before. He explained that Uber's "playbook" for entering new markets involved removing "legacy regulations."[110] At first we weren't sure what he meant. By the end of the interview, the answer became clear: the old urban politics and its municipal regulations were relics of a bygone era. Uber promised a future freed from such constraints.

Urban governance in the age of Uber has its roots in outsourc-ing, public-private partnerships, and the broad shift toward decen-tralized and distributed governance.[111] But there is something else afoot. D.C. presents a slightly different model of the city—one that is less open and more opaque. In a public-private partnership, the city enlists the private sector to join efforts.[112] The case of D.C. is the opposite: Uber enlists the city, just as it does drivers, as *its* partner.[113]

Uber's power in D.C. has major implications for how urban governance is done, which publics are prioritized, and what kind of infrastructure gets created. The strategies Uber uses to advance its sovereignty undergirds a worldview in which the public good is of less and less import and in which regulation, as a safeguard for the public good, is seen as antiquated.[114] Uber's operations in the city lay bare a relinquishment of power from the city to this private entity. Low expectations of democratic governance, we argue, go hand in hand with this power shift and the constrained forms of urban governance it benefits from and contributes to. Moreover, these low expectations help transform the idea of *just let Uber do it* into common sense. Today's leaders hope that platform apps can deliver to individuals what they believe D.C. itself no longer can.

To ensure accessible transportation or enable governmental oversight of private corporations at an urban scale is far from easy. It is hard work to live among strangers on land that is contested, saturated with conflicting uses, and subject to a host of financial pressures.[115] That is, however, the task of living in urban spaces and governing them. Governance is a kind of unending practice, like teaching or parenting, with conflicts that require all sorts of negotiations, discussions, and renegotiations. To live with others, whether in a classroom, in a family, in a community, or at the scale of a city, necessitates collective agreements, rule-making, and ideally some kind of democratic principles. Linton tried to offer a warning about what lies ahead if we abandon those. In this regard, Linton is less a regulatory dinosaur than a canary in the coal mine of an innovation-obsessed city where *just let Uber do it* has become common sense.

2

UberKente

FIGURE 2.1. Uber billboard in Portland, Oregon, 2020. Reproduced with permission by Mark E. McClure.

If you tolerate racism, delete Uber.

—UBER[1]

CECIL GRAHAM: What is a cynic?

LORD DARLINGTON: A man who knows the price of everything and the value of nothing.

CECIL GRAHAM: And a sentimentalist, my dear Darlington,
is a man who sees an absurd value in everything and
doesn't know the market price of any single thing.[2]

In July 2015, the *Washington Post* published a punchy op-ed by
Cornell Belcher, founder of the polling firm Brilliant Corners.[3]
Belcher, an African American, recounted his experience as a
twentysomething-year-old waiter at an upscale restaurant in
the Georgetown neighborhood of Washington, D.C. His shift at
the restaurant routinely ended late, after the buses had stopped
running, and because Metro did not extend to Georgetown, he
often had difficulty finding a way home at night. Time and time
again, he noted, taxis would "blatantly swerve around me to pick
up white patrons, or my white colleagues."[4] Even to a child of the
American South such as him, Belcher added, such overt racism
was shocking.

Belcher's was only one of a flurry of op-eds in Uber's early years
that decried the racism of the taxi industry in D.C. and other major
cities.[5] In late 2012, *Washington Post* staff writer Clinton Yates, a
staunch opponent of initial attempts to regulate Uber, wrote that
"even in our 'post-racial society,' one of the realities of being a
brother is that hailing a cab is a nearly impossible task."[6] For Yates,
Uber was a dramatic improvement over taxis, and he worried that
imposing restrictions on Uber to protect the taxi industry would
do D.C. a disservice. Though Yates acknowledged there were "legal
kinks to be worked out," he said "it would be unfortunate if the city
managed to get rid of a useful company with a guiding principle
based on the color of the money in your pocket and not the color
of your skin."[7]

Personal anecdotes like Yates's and Belcher's voiced D.C. residents' deep resentment for the taxi industry. Belcher drew on his

personal story to introduce findings from a new report titled *Hailing While Black*. Published by his own polling firm and based on research in Chicago, the report attempted to quantify the experience of discrimination associated with trying to hail a cab as an African American.[8] As the report lays out, 48 percent of African American respondents reported that "it's likely that if they tried hailing a cab, the taxi would ignore them and continue driving."[9] Belcher concluded his op-ed by citing the importance of understanding racist incidents like these in the debate "between the legacy taxicab industry and new-school providers like Uber."

The most noteworthy aspect of Belcher's op-ed was neither the personal preamble nor the study's findings. Rather, it was the "editor's note" appended two hours after the original article went live on the *Washington Post*'s website: "[Editor's note]: The original version of this story did not mention that Brilliant Corners Research and Strategies' study was commissioned by Uber, which competes with taxi companies. The author did not disclose the relationship, and *Post* editors were unaware of it when the story published."[10] While going some way to undermine the claims in Belcher's study, the addendum failed to lay out other potential conflicts of interest—namely, that the *Post* was owned by Jeff Bezos, an early Uber investor.[11] More than anything, however, the "correction" hinted at Uber's interest in the race question.

In this chapter, we examine the role that race and narratives of racial justice have played in advancing Uber's operations in D.C. We argue Uber's entry into the city must be seen in the context of D.C.'s rapidly changing racial landscape, as well as the political and social anxieties that have accompanied such changes. Ultimately the chapter advances an argument for why op-eds like Belcher's should be seen as troubling for those with a commitment to racial justice. Apart from neglecting to mention the obvious conflict of interest, Belcher's op-ed offered an incredibly narrow account of racial injustice. Rather than seeing racism in D.C.'s paltry late-night bus service, or in the absence of a Metro stop in Georgetown, or even in the working conditions of waitstaff at the upscale eatery at which he was employed, Belcher's account of racial injustice begins and ends at the level of the interpersonal and focuses on one industry alone (i.e., taxi services).[12] In short, it is an account of racial injustice *just* broad enough to land an emotional blow but *just* narrow enough to seem eminently fixable—and fixable with only the right technology or the right incentive structure.

As will become evident in this chapter, this rather narrow account of racial injustice has real political pull. We argue that Uber's success in the city has relied not only on tapping into frustrations associated with the persistence of racial inequality but also on the company offering itself as a commonsense response to those frustrations—both for individuals who are rightly angry about racial injustices and for a political machine that has largely proved unable or unwilling to address those injustices. The focus here is less on Uber's legislative success than on its victory in the realm of people's commonsense expectations. Rather than exploring questions related to the importance of regulators like D.C. Taxicab Commissioner Ron Linton (see chapter 1), this chapter turns to the issues of race, racial discrimination, and the conditions that have allowed Uber to both cultivate and reinforce an impoverished view of what we should expect from the city when it comes to redressing long-standing racial divisions.

The Old D.C. and the New D.C.

In 2011, the same year that Uber started to operate in D.C., the city reached a "milestone." For the first time in fifty-four years, less than 50 percent of the population was Black. As a result, "Chocolate City," as D.C. was once known, lost its designation as a Black-majority city.[13] This dramatic shift in the city's racial demographics was paralleled by growing inequality (see appendix C). Although D.C. ranked third in median income growth among the nation's largest cities, significant sections of the city remained mired in poverty. In 2011, and in the midst of D.C.'s "renaissance," the census singled out the city's Ward 8 as having the nation's highest jobless rate.[14]

The politics of D.C.'s racial transformation played out electorally. Many people attributed Mayor Adrian Fenty's failed 2010 reelection bid to the anxieties surrounding the rate at which the city was changing. According to local pollster Ron Faucheux, "Adrian Fenty was perceived as the white candidate" in a city that was losing its Black identity.[15] Fenty, himself an African American, had enjoyed early support from both White and Black residents, but by 2010 his support among the latter had plummeted. In a *Washington Post* poll conducted before the 2010 Democratic primary election, only 19 percent of Black Democrats favored Fenty, while 64 percent favored his challenger Vincent Gray—an African American with a long history of public service who had previously chaired the D.C. Council. Among White Democrats, the figures were reversed, with 64 percent favoring Fenty and 28 percent favoring Gray.[16]

Fenty's problem was clear. In addition to his perceived mishandling of the city's struggling schools, he had become the candidate of dog parks, bike lanes, and the creative class—in short, the candidate of and *for* White-led gentrification.[17] If Gray's ascension to mayor marked a repudiation of Fenty, it hardly registered in the realm of public policy. Many of the initiatives that had so divided the city continued apace. Fenty's "Creative Action Agenda" became Gray's "Creative Economy Strategy," both touting the need for the city to attract young "creatives" in order to compete in an ascendant knowledge economy.[18] Gray embraced the school reforms that had been so controversial under Fenty, and Black unemployment remained in the double digits. Despite their ostensible differences, their approaches to urban governance were remarkably similar. The city continued to grow unequally. As urban scholar Timothy Gibson writes, the early 2000s "created a stark picture of 'two Washingtons,' split between newcomers and struggling old-timers and characterised by radically diverging fortunes and life-chances."[19] That stark picture came to shape both public discourse and various political campaigns. Yet, for all the talk of inequality or racial polarization, concern for bridging the "two Washingtons" seemed to begin and end on the campaign trail. Behind the mask of choice, voters found different forms of the same nonsolutions.[20] To quote one Ward 8 activist at the end of Gray's tenure in 2015, "We're still a city divided, the haves and the have-nots, the whites and the blacks."[21] When Uber arrived in D.C. in late 2011, the debate over ride-hailing apps reflected this broader context. By the time we began our research in 2016, the city's racial and economic divisions had become sharper, and those divisions and the political impasse surrounding them had been incorporated into Uber's messaging machine.

In 2016, we spoke with a recent college graduate, Zack[22] (introduced in chapter 1), who was working as a lobbyist for Uber. Zack's role involved working with elected officials in D.C., Maryland, and Virginia to make it as easy as possible for drivers to join the platform. As Zack admitted, by that time, as far as Uber was concerned, D.C. was in a "pretty good place."[23] Two years prior, the city had passed the landmark legislation that Uber would go on to tout to the rest of the country (see chapter 1). Yet Zack's work in the city continued. This work included maintaining relations with councilmembers and striving to be, in his words, the best "corporate citizen partner" possible. In addition, it meant "figuring out ways that we [Uber] can be helpful and can try to help solve problems." For him, these problems included not only a lack of public-transportation options in Southeast's Ward 8 and other parts of D.C. but also a general lack of connections between the communities themselves. And one of the things that made Uber special was its ability to facilitate those connections:

> What's unique about this tech company is that it's bringing people together, and it's very cool to see the old D.C. and the new D.C. bridging. And people having interactions . . . I don't know if there's any research done on that, but every time I get into a car, or people get transported around, there's just [these] vibrant exchanges that are happening with total strangers, and that's kind of a really cool thing that I think can engender a lot of stronger community values. That might just be platitudes. Or not.[24]

We asked Zack what he meant by "the old D.C. and the new D.C. bridging." Was he speaking in terms of race and class? Or did he mean something else?

> Yeah, all of those things. You have people going across the Anacostia River, you have people that are driving around new neighborhoods [that] usually wouldn't be there because they're isolated in some other community. You have a lot of other folks that . . . live in these affluent bubbles [that] get to interact with people that maybe aren't as well off. It's a really interesting dynamic. For me personally, I think that's important. I think if you all are just trapped in your little worlds, you can't [think creatively].[25]

In a city divided by geography, race, and income, Uber offered a way of bringing people together, according to Zack. Moreover, the car itself provided a venue for cross-class interactions and exchanges between people from different backgrounds and cultures. Even more interesting was how Zack interspersed this message with a more direct appeal to residents in poorer neighborhoods. The language of this appeal was less Jane Jacobs or other tributes to urban cosmopolitanism and more William Julius Wilson—an appeal to the employment needs of the "truly disadvantaged."[26] Here, Uber's offer was economic opportunity. Zack gave the example of the then-new on-demand food delivery service Uber Eats:

> Uber [Eats] . . . is a very interesting potential opportunity for us, because not only does it provide economic opportunities for people who maybe aren't good at driving passengers for whatever reason, or their cars don't comply because they're only two-door cars as opposed to four or whatever . . . But not only that, you're supporting local businesses by becoming a force multiplier and earning incremental sales on their food. And that can be really important in places like Northeast or Southeast. I think we're probably one of the only delivery options that's really reliable in Southeast. So things like that are important.[27]

And he was sure to mention Uber's role in ending the problem of "hailing while Black."

> What's most interesting to me about [Uber] is the way that it's granting access to people. There are tons of stories about folks who are African American can't get picked up in a cab. It's a well-known, well-documented phenomenon. And now we're doing trips, you can get picked up in a couple minutes in Anacostia [which is in the Southeast], regardless of where you are or the way you look. It's a game-changer.[28]

Having spent hundreds of hours with legislative staffers, executive managers, and public officials in D.C., Zack's message was attractive to policymakers seeking to solve what had seemed an intractable set of issues—from the city's racial polarization to the taxi industry's racial discrimination. Although Uber's solution may have seemed simplistic—Jane Jacobs for the "new D.C." and William Julius Wilson for the "old D.C."—to many D.C. policymakers, this technological solutionism[29] was enough.

What Is Progressive?

In 2016 we spoke with one high-ranking D.C. policymaker who took precisely this technological solutionist stance. As he admitted, in some ways, he was a perfect fit for Uber. He had entered public service committed to innovation and to sweeping aside laws that had long outlived their usefulness. As evidence of this approach, he had worked to revise the city's regulation of food trucks, which he argued was overly stringent:

> I had done a lot of work with food trucks to help [them] not be overregulated. In D.C. there was all these crazy regulations on food trucks, on where they could park, [and on] how they could operate . . . So, really early in my tenure here, I . . . worked on helping food trucks get good [with the law]. So I think the Uber folks knew I was somebody who was willing to

talk about a different thing, some kind of innovation that was not normal in the city. And so they came to me.[30]

Apart from his general interest in breaking (i.e., disrupting) conventions and excessive regulations, his support for Uber was personal. Having grown up in D.C., he was embittered by his experience with the city's cabs, which, when he was younger, had regularly refused to take him home. And he was White. When we asked him what accounted for Uber's success in D.C., his argument was notable. One reason was D.C.'s "strong mayor" system, which allocates the mayor significant discretion and power in setting policies. The second reason boiled down to race—and, more specifically, the racism of the incumbent taxi industry:

> I can't tell you how many of my friends growing up, who were African American, would ask me to hail them a cab, because they knew if they tried to hail a cab, they wouldn't actually get a stop. And then we passed all sorts of laws over the years saying you can't deny somebody a ride once they were in the vehicle, but there was never any enforcement of that.

He was not the only person to make this point. When we spoke with Tom, a young White council staffer, he reiterated this stance. Tom had been a legislative aide during Uber's entry into the city and witnessed the full force of Uber's popular support. For Tom, as well as the councilmember, Uber's success in D.C. was inseparable from questions of race. Although he admitted that Uber's ability to combat racial discrimination may have been overblown, the benefits were still considerable.

> I've had so much frustration with the taxicab industry in terms of discrimination against passengers. That media has done story after story about it . . . , and it's sort of a . . . my [spouse] is African American, and [their] anecdotal experience with cabs is absurd. And so, Uber in some way had seemed in a way to fill that niche. That was because it was somewhat blind in terms of acceptance and denials . . . and we had heard from people who

said, "My gosh, I love Uber . . . I live in Upper Northwest. Cabs don't just travel the street. When I call a cab to come, it doesn't show up. If I have to go to the airport and get an early flight, I'm on pins and needles about whether or not this cab's going to show up. And Uber comes. It shows up." Or "I'm Black—cabs pass me by all the time. [With Uber,] I can sit inside my home, order a car, it shows up, nobody's turning me away once I get to the car."[31]

Uber's appeal went in two directions. For residents of D.C.'s wealthy and White majority Northwest neighborhoods looking to catch an early flight, Uber was a marked improvement in terms of convenience. For D.C.'s Black residents, Uber's appeal was even clearer: it showed up. In short, Uber was good for the "old D.C." and the "new D.C."

For many policymakers, the political calculation was clear: Uber offered a straightforward answer to a real problem, and it was popular. For those concerned about the implications for labor, the reality was that the incumbent taxi system was hardly any better. To quote Tom, "It's not as if we're providing minimum wage or living wage to taxi drivers, or that we're providing them retirement benefits, or that we're providing them health care. They've always been 'independent contractors,' all along."[32] Raising expectations surrounding what either job might offer—whether driving for Uber or driving for an incumbent taxi service—was not on the policy agenda.

In 2019, we spoke with a policymaker who had deep familiarity with the activities of the D.C. Council Committee on Transportation and the Environment during Uber's entrance to the city. While much of the interview hinged on questions of legislation, we raised questions of equity too and asked about several studies showing that Uber's surge-pricing algorithm could facilitate discrimination.[33] Citing the city's antidiscrimination rules, the policymaker said that she had seen no evidence that such discrimination was occurring in D.C. Indeed, problems of discrimination had been the reason why Uber had been so "successful straightaway."[34] She then mentioned the current mayor, Muriel Bowser, who had been a D.C. Council member four years prior and was African American: "[Bowser] would always take Uber. She was in Ward 4, and even up in Ward 4, she had trouble getting a taxi to come up there."[35]

Many of these same policymakers also had criticisms of Uber. For Tom, the problem with Uber was the company's inadequate response to the demands of D.C.'s disabled community. For the high-ranking D.C. policymaker quoted earlier, it was the labor question. As a self-described progressive, he had supported living-wage initiatives and thrown support behind a paid family leave policy for city workers. He told us that he supported Uber because it promised to solve the problem of racial discrimination but that the company's reliance on independent contractors was worrisome. According to him, the challenge in pushing through progressive legislation was not simply combating the power of big business but discerning what counts as progressive. His support of Uber was a perfect example.

> I mean, when a new idea takes hold because it has a practical implication, then yes, it might seem progressive, because people want it to be taken on. It literally came down to that. The discrimination of taxis—it was really a reaction to the inability of the taxis to adapt to what we wanted. That allowed Uber to grow here. But the more that you find out that Uber's doing all these crazy things, it'll be hard—you watch—it'll be hard to back up and regulate them properly. And they should be [regulated]. I think they should be.[36]

The policymaker's point was well taken, but it seemed to miss a central paradox—namely, the extent to which the very issue (i.e., discrimination) that had compelled his early support for Uber might stand in the way of commonsense regulation. If Uber had come to symbolize "antidiscrimination," any attempt to regulate Uber would mean the opposite. Indeed, this was precisely the lesson of "Operation Rolling Thunder" four years earlier.

The Specter of "Operation Rolling Thunder"

As noted in both chapter 1 and the introduction, the 2012 "Operation Rolling Thunder" campaign marked a turning point for Uber in D.C. It showed the depth of Uber's popular support, and it highlighted the company's ability and willingness to mobilize that support to shape public policy.

Using the Freedom of Information Act, *Washington Post* deputy editor Mike Madden gained access to some of the fifty thousand emails Uber's D.C. customers had sent to councilmembers within a twenty-four-hour period as part of the campaign. The emails revealed general frustration with the city's taxi service, which was variably described as inconvenient, confusing, dirty, an embarrassment, and, most notably, deeply racist. Uber, in contrast, was described as convenient, straightforward, clean, and colorblind. The emails also revealed that the debate over the "Uber Amendment" was really a debate about the city's taxi industry, especially its alleged discrimination.[37]

In an email to a D.C. Council member, Shelton S. made exactly this case against taxi discrimination. Uber was welcome in D.C., Shelton argued, precisely because the city's current taxi system was so bad:

> The D.C. taxi cab system in this city is the worst I've encountered. As a young, African-American male, I can tell you that I've been passed by on NUMEROUS occasions while trying to get a ride home. If it were not for my White partner, he and I wouldn't be able to get around town at all. In addition to their discriminatory practices, the cabs are often dirty and smoky [*sic*]. The alternative being offered by Uber is a welcome change. . . . Think of the hard-working people in your Ward and the District as a whole that you purport to represent. Do not cave to the taxi lobbyist or whomever is driving this wrongheaded law and do what you know to be right.

In addition to Uber's progress on the racial issue, Alexis D. added the issue of safety, in an email to a D.C. Council member:

> I hope this email finds you well. I am a happy Ward 4 resident who is concerned about the new minimum fare language in the Uber Amendment. Uber happens to stop for me, an African-American female in her mid-20s, when taxis will not . . . I could wait on a taxi and take over an hour to try to get home, or I can wait on Uber who promises 15 and if it will take longer I know about it. I feel safe and secure.

Nick C., in yet another email to a D.C. Council member, offered an example of how inseparable race and geography had become. (Euphemisms are common in debates involving race; in D.C., those euphemisms are cartographic: Southeast is Black, Northeast is Black, and Northwest is White.) Nick C. wrote:

> I understand the D.C. Council will likely vote tomorrow on taxi modernization legislation (which I strongly support). I am, however, concerned about the inclusion of an excessive minimum fare provision in the so-called Uber Amendment. As an eight-year resident of Capitol Hill I know firsthand how difficult it can be to find taxi cabs in D.C. willing to take passengers to an address that ends in NE or SE. Never once, in my experience, has Uber applied such discrimination to riders. For this reason I ask that you work to strike the minimum fare requirement in the Uber provision or at the very least modify it to ensure it is no greater than a D.C. taxi cab's minimum fare.

In an email to all thirteen D.C. Council members, Bridgette D. clarified the extent to which class or professional status was no assurance against racial prejudice:

> Unfortunately, D.C. has a documented history of taxicabs refusing to pick up African-Americans. Being an African-American woman, I have difficulty catching a cab in front of my office on Capitol Hill. It is upsetting to stand in front of the U.S. Capitol,

in a suit, after a long day of public service and see cab after cab pass you by. With Uber, I call a car and it comes. I don't have to worry about the embarrassment and frustration of not being able to catch a cab because I am Black. I ask that you reconsider the language in the Uber Amendment. I can tell you that MANY [Capitol] Hill staffers are loyal Uber users, especially staffers of color, and we would hate to not have Uber available to us.

In yet another email to the council, Jimmy G. managed to combine, rather impressively, a criticism of racism in D.C.'s taxi industry, a defense of the creative class, and a paean to capitalist competition:

D.C. has been forced to deal with [a mishmash of] cab services who offer nothing more than poor cabs, poor service, generally a very poor experience. This is not to mention the cab drivers' blatant ability to discriminate where they will deliver a fare and more importantly who they will pick up based solely on looks. I think many of you would agree, it's appalling at best.

As D.C. has grown and begun to flourish in recent years, a new generation of residents have embraced the city with hopes of flourishing along with it. They have brought with them a new class of creativity, technological savvy, and entrepreneurship. Many of us welcomed Uber because it encompassed a technological spirit and values that many of our generation seek to embrace. It sought to improve the lives of residents by offering a service that enabled us to have a choice and bring much needed competition into a stagnant marketplace. Competition is a good thing, it lifts the standards and [it] forces sub[optimally] performing entities to improve or be left behind. It is capitalism at its best.

In a city (to quote Gibson again) "split between newcomers and struggling old-comers and characterised by radically diverging fortunes and life-chances,"[38] the one thing that everyone involved in debates about Uber seemed to agree on was that the incumbent taxi industry was terrible. Its antiquated meters were frustrating, but more significantly the system was racist too. Despite more than a decade of complaints to the city's taxi commission and multiple studies[39] revealing the extent of discrimination, little had changed. Uber's "Operation Rolling Thunder" was more than just a method of leveraging technology to intervene in local democratic processes; it tapped into people's deep frustration with the shortcomings of urban politics and city government. In addition to offering a lesson to municipal legislators on the dangers of crossing Silicon Valley, "Operation Rolling Thunder" demonstrated the power of a corporate campaign built on racial grievances.

On-Demand Racial Justice

The problem of racial discrimination was decisive for Uber's early success in D.C., but what were the outcomes? In 2015, Uber claimed in a press statement that its drivers not only provided "safe, reliable rides throughout Wards 7 and 8" (the neighborhoods with the densest Black populations) but also eased transportation difficulties created by "long bus wait times, far away metro stops, a lack of taxis, and the increasing cost of owning a car."[40] Apart from anecdotal evidence, to what extent was Uber really serving D.C.'s Southeast neighborhoods? What proof did the city have that Uber was not engaging in the same discriminatory practices that had defined the taxi industry? Might Uber be just as racist as the taxi industry it sought to supplant? Despite Uber's claims to racial progressivism, studies suggest that there is reason for concern. In a joint project between MIT, Stanford, and the University of Washington, researchers found that in Seattle, Black people who requested a ride using Uber or Lyft waited significantly longer than White people did. In Boston, they found, riders with Black-sounding names were more likely to have their pickups canceled.[41] Other researchers found evidence of racial bias in the dynamic pricing algorithms used by Uber and Lyft: in Chicago, ride-hailing fares tended to be higher for people requesting drop-offs in neighborhoods with large non-White populations.[42]

This pattern aligns with the experiences of the forty-three drivers we interviewed and surveyed intermittently over six years. Some drivers said they declined ride requests in certain neighborhoods to mitigate risk and increase their take-home pay. One White male driver explained to us, "I don't pick up in Southeast D.C. or [Prince George's] County because I don't know the area. It has nothing to do with racism, demographics, or anything like that."[43] He said he preferred Arlington (where he lived) and other neighborhoods where he felt more comfortable. Other drivers told us that they concentrated on wealthier neighborhoods because Uber provided them with opportunities to earn more there. Uber maintains that surge pricing reflects demand, which may well be the case, but its algorithmic pricing also shapes when and where drivers seek to work. Drivers' decisions about when and where to work, in turn, shape where ride-hailing services are available, raising questions about the veracity of Uber's claims that it uniquely serves marginalized neighborhoods.

Still, these findings—whether from the MIT study or from our interviews with D.C. drivers—fail to fully address the experiences or testimonies of D.C. residents who wrote to councilmembers in 2012 or the political calculations of policymakers eager to appear responsive to their constituents. For them, the debate in 2012 was not between Uber and some less discriminatory alternative or even between Uber and public transit. It was between Uber and what some people described as the worst taxi system in the country. Everybody concurred: D.C. had a problem, and Uber offered a solution.

This narrow framing of Uber as a solution to the problem of "hailing while Black" had consequences. Most notably, in public debates and forums, there was little discussion of D.C. taxi drivers themselves. While the 2012 "Uber Amendment" was decried for insulating the taxi industry from competition, the jobs it aimed to protect were largely held by Black or African-American workers.[44]

In fact, in the early 2000s, D.C. was the only city in the top seven U.S. taxi markets where a majority of drivers (53 percent) self-identified as Black or African American.[45]

Despite the many drivers from East and West Africa, the circumscribed discussion of Uber meant that the class and ethnic divisions *within* D.C.'s Black community were absent in public debates too. This absence was even more extraordinary given the real divisions between those Black residents who could afford an Uber and those who were necessarily reliant on public transit. If Bridgette D. and Nick C. were representative of Black D.C., the question was whom did they most represent—the African American on the bus, the Ethiopian taxi driver, or the Black lawyer? Or did such distinctions even matter? And what of Uber's impact on public transit—both in terms of its significant Black ridership and an equally significant Black workforce?[46]

Beyond D.C.

For some readers, the primary conclusion to draw from the previous sections may amount to little more than the following: Uber has been successful in D.C. because people in D.C. like Uber and because Uber is not racist. As sociologist William Whyte would say, "This might not strike the reader as an intellectual bombshell."[47] Our goal, however, has been to explain *why* people in D.C. might like Uber and to assert the role that race has played in making Uber so appealing. Uber's entrance into D.C. coincided with emerging concerns around gentrification, inequality, and the city's demographic transformation. In the context of a deeply divided city, Uber's popularity was understandable—if anything could bring the city together, it was mutual disdain for the city's taxi system.

Zack, the Uber lobbyist we quoted earlier, advanced a much larger claim: in addition to being a convenient and reliable alternative to D.C.'s taxi system, Uber offered access and economic opportunity to the very residents who were increasingly left behind. Uber's self-conception doubles as a political strategy, and the company has taken that strategy on the road in New York, in California, and elsewhere.

When New York City proposed a cap on Uber's fleet size in 2015 and again in 2018, the company employed the rhetorical tactics it had honed in D.C. As before, Uber offered a defense of its practices and its unrestrained growth on explicitly racial grounds. In 2015, for example, this defense took the form of a short commercial (uploaded to YouTube) in which, over the sparse and melancholic tinkle of piano keys, a voiceover narrates the plight of a diverse cast of working-class New Yorkers, each looking directly into the camera:

> You need to get to the night shift in the South Bronx. Get your baby to the doctor in Jamaica Queens. And get to the airport from Sunset Park Brooklyn. And while taxis often refuse people in minority neighborhoods, Uber's there, taking more people to and from communities outside Manhattan than anyone. But Mayor de Blasio is pushing the agenda of his big taxi donors to limit Uber cars and drivers, and vital service for thousands of New Yorkers may vanish. Tell Mayor de Blasio: don't strand New York.

Writing for the *New York Daily News*, journalist Errol Louis amplified this narrative. Not unlike Yates and Belcher in the op-eds mentioned earlier, Louis recounted his own experience of discrimination at the hands of New York City's yellow-cab drivers. As he argued, by supporting a cap on Uber's fleet size, local progressives were failing to take racial discrimination seriously: "The progressives say slowing Uber's growth is about protecting conditions for 'the workers,' meaning yellow-taxi drivers, some of whom deny service to vast numbers of New Yorkers. Personally, I'd like to hear a bit more about the customers, whose support for Uber is a clear repudiation of yellow-cab practices."[48] Although efforts to regulate Uber in New York City failed in 2015, they were revived in 2018—a year that saw a wave of high-profile suicides by taxi drivers. Some people attributed these suicides to the increasing debt of taxi drivers now facing competition from Uber and other digital-dispatch services.[49] In 2018, Uber employed the same rhetorical tactics it had used three years prior. This time, however, new voices emerged to defend Uber, on distinctly racial grounds. Both Al Sharpton of the National Action Network and Arva Rice of the National Urban League came out against the proposed regulations. While noting that Uber had donated to both organizations, each pointed to the persisting problem of "hailing while Black." National Action Network member the Reverend Dr. Johnnie M. Green said, "It's a racial issue," adding, "The people that champion the crusade against Uber do not have a problem hailing yellow cabs."[50]

At the height of its 2018 antiregulatory campaign in New York City, Uber hired award-winning film director Spike Lee to produce a series of short videos documenting the lives of five Uber drivers in Brooklyn. Lee explained his interest in the project: "I know a lot of people who drive on the Uber platform and it gives them the flexibility they need to pursue their dreams. That's how we do it in Brooklyn—that's the Brooklyn hustle."[51] Uber's efforts ultimately proved futile, and in 2018 New York City passed a groundbreaking law that both limited new licenses for for-hire vehicles and mandated a minimum take-home wage for Uber drivers and other app-based drivers working in the city.

New York City's 2018 legislation marked a win for Uber's opponents, but the November 2020 passage of California's Proposition 22—a ballot initiative that would make it easier for app-based companies to misclassify workers—reminded opponents that the fight was far from over.[52] Uber's appeal to racial justice had recently taken new and ever more extreme forms. Following the May 2020 murder of George Floyd at the hands of the Minneapolis Police Department, Uber announced its decision to waive all U.S. delivery fees for Uber Eats customers who ordered from Black-owned restaurants.[53] In August of the same year, Uber partnered with the National Action Network to give free rides to those attending the Get Your Knee off Our Necks March on the National Mall.

The event, which was held to protest police brutality, was set to coincide with the fifty-seventh anniversary of the March on Washington for Jobs and Freedom. During the event, Uber informed D.C. users how to participate in the protest and even provided a link to the American Civil Liberties Union's "Protestors' Rights" manual.[54]

In 2017, "Delete Uber" had been the rallying cry for protestors in New York City and elsewhere who were enraged at Uber's alleged complicity in President Donald Trump's "Muslim travel ban."[55] In 2020, Uber turned that same language to its advantage in an ad campaign, declaring "If you tolerate racism, delete Uber; Black people have the right to move without fear."[56] Billboards throughout California were plastered with this slogan as part of Uber's larger "Vote Yes on Proposition 22" campaign.[57] In addition, Uber mobilized support from a number of social justice organizations, including various NAACP chapters, the National Asian American Coalition, Black Lives Matter Sacramento, and the Baptist Ministers Conference of Los Angeles and Southern California. In a joint letter to the state legislature, these groups explained their support for Proposition 22. As they argued, platforms like Uber provided "an accessible, low barrier-to-entry way to earn income for those who often find traditional employment challenging—communities of color, seniors, disabled veterans and those formerly incarcerated."[58]

As with the examples from New York City and California, Uber's interest in the racial question, which debuted in D.C., did not stop there. In its pitch to cities, and its campaigns against regulation, issues of race and racial justice remained a key part of Uber's rhetorical and political strategy.

A Narrow Conception of Racial Justice

In many ways, it is easy to see Uber's routine discussion of racial injustice as cynical opportunism. Uber's commitment to addressing racial inequity often appears superficial and entirely instrumental—just like when, following the murder of George

Floyd, congressional Democrats donned kente cloth and took a knee for a photo op.[59] Such superficiality is only reinforced by the narrow conception of racial justice that so often is trotted out. As noted earlier, this conception of racial justice is just wide enough to accommodate the justifiable grievances of people like Cornell Belcher and Clinton Yates but conveniently narrow enough to exclude the interests of D.C.'s Black taxi drivers and the demands of Black independent contractors in California seeking employer-provided health insurance. It is a conception of racial justice that bemoans the problems of "hailing while Black" but has little to say about Uber's role in undermining local bus and Metro services, threatening the livelihoods of taxi drivers, or the racial implications of both. This rather narrow conception of racial justice—focused largely on the rights of consumers—appears especially limited in contrast with the more ample view of racial equity that once characterized a significant portion of the civil rights movement.

When in 1963 millions of people descended on D.C. for the March for Jobs and Freedom, the demand for civil rights was as much a call for political and social equality as it was a call for good jobs. In addition to demanding the full desegregation of all schools and the passage of comprehensive civil rights legislation, organizers demanded a "massive federal program to train and place all unemployed workers," a national minimum wage, and a broadened Fair Labor Standards Act.[60] Indeed, for many of the march's organizers, particularly Bayard Rustin and A. Philip Randolph, winning civil rights without a broader restructuring of the nation's political economic structure hardly constituted progress. To quote Rustin, "what is the value of winning access to public accommodations for those without the money to use them?"[61] What was needed, Rustin added, was an approach to civil rights that went beyond race relations to economic relations and that recognized that the economic problems at the core of racial injustice required more than "private voluntary efforts"; it required government action.[62] Rustin and other architects of the 1963 march translated these demands into the 1966 release of the Freedom Budget for All Americans—a document demanding "full employment for all who are willing and able to work," "decent and adequate wages," and "decent and adequate healthcare and educational opportunities."[63] For a whole generation of civil rights activists, the fight for racial justice was understood in terms that were inherently universalist in scale and scope. Martin Luther King Jr., in his foreword to the Freedom Budget, made this message abundantly clear: The long journey ahead required "that we emphasize the needs of all America's poor, for there is no way merely to find work, or adequate housing, or quality integrated schools for Negroes alone." We shall eliminate slums for Negroes, he added, "when we destroy ghettos and build new cities for all."[64] For Rustin, King, and many others, addressing the problems of racial inequality required a transformation of the economy itself and the *political* mobilization of poor and working-class people of all races and creeds.

In the late 1970s and early 1980s, D.C. itself adopted a similarly broad conception of racial justice. After a hundred years of control by the federal government, in the mid-1970s D.C. residents finally elected their own mayor and council. Of the first council, all but two of the thirteen members were Black, and the majority had ties to the Student Non-Violent Coordinating Committee.[65] "Nowhere else in the country," historians Chris Asch and Derek Musgrove write, "had a black protest organization so thoroughly come to dominate a city government."[66] City officials passed a series of anti-displacement and pro-tenant policies including rent controls, limited equity cooperative housing provisions,[67] a speculation tax,[68] and eviction restrictions.[69] The city became one of the first providers in the nation of all-day kindergarten,[70] policymakers built a brand-new government office at the site of the city's worst illicit drug market,[71] and Mayor Marion Barry started a popular summer youth employment program. When an economic recession hit and the federal government downsized its agencies, which employed a third of the city's working residents, the local government stepped in to alleviate rising unemployment.[72] During this period in D.C., racial justice was synonymous with the fight for good jobs, affordable housing, and civic investment. It was synonymous with a belief in "the power of government to do good."[73] This conception of racial justice was quite different from that promoted by Uber.

Given this national and local context, Uber's routine appeals to the problems of racial injustice seem insufficiently broad and entirely insincere. As this book has already intimated, however, questions of sincerity and of cynicism are the wrong ones. Whether or not Zack, the Uber lobbyist quoted earlier, sincerely believes that Uber can bridge "the old D.C. and the new D.C." is beside the point. No less immaterial is whether Uber's pledge to support Black-owned restaurants in the wake of George Floyd's murder stems from an ethical commitment or a purely instrumental one. These questions miss the point, because they focus attention on Uber itself rather than the conditions of urban life that have allowed Uber to grow and to claim the moral high ground. Uber's success is as much a testament to its marketing approach as it is a testament to the seeming abandonment of older conceptions of racial justice and civic authority. Whether those older conceptions are found in the Freedom Budget or the early campaigns around summer youth employment once touted by Marion Barry, Uber's investment in the racial question is also an investment in keeping those older, commonsense conceptions of social democracy at bay.[74]

3

The Work of Data

I made a comment, and Ron [Linton] started saying to me
something like, "Why are you always . . . going so easy on
Uber; why do you want to just give in to these assholes?"
And I got really mad and defensive because that wasn't what
I was saying at all. And what bubbled out from me was my
frustration [and] . . . what I said to Ron was, "I am not in
Uber's corner at all, but these fuckers are smart, and to beat
them, we've got to be smarter."
—D.C. POLICYMAKER[1]

It's not a positive partnership at all. From what I've found,
it's the driver trying to outsmart Uber and Uber trying to
outsmart the driver.
—JOE, AN UBER DRIVER[2]

[W]hatever "smart" actually is, it bears no necessary relation
to fundamental decency.
—RICK PERLSTEIN, *THE BAFFLER*[3]

In mid-May 2016, we met with Joe[4] at a Starbucks in D.C.'s Foggy
Bottom—the neighborhood just west of the White House. A White

man, he was twenty-five and burly. Originally from a small town in Virginia, he had moved to what he described as a "rough side" of D.C. a year prior.[5] Like many Uber drivers with whom we spoke, he had taken up work for Uber as a way of supplementing his income and covering his monthly car payment. Joe was the first in his family to finish college and had even earned a graduate degree. Even though he had a full-time job as an outreach coordinator for a local university, he spent roughly twenty hours a week behind the wheel for Uber in addition to working a part-time job in security.

The differences between Joe's three jobs could not have been starker. As an outreach coordinator and as a security guard he was "paid the same rate all the time," whereas with Uber it fluctuated.[6] He made $23 an hour at his university job, and between $12 and $13 an hour working security, but his earnings as an Uber driver could, depending on the day, range from a high of around $20 an hour to a low of just over minimum wage, which at that time in D.C. was $10.50 an hour. Unlike his other jobs, Uber was a "game of strategy," involving, in his words, the driver trying "to outsmart Uber and Uber trying to outsmart the driver." Joe reported using various strategies to make sure that he came out ahead—from avoiding rush hour and keeping tabs on big events like baseball games to timing the closing of bars on the weekends.

Joe worked hard to make Uber work for him, but it was a struggle. Toward the end of the interview, Joe's tone turned fatalistic. Given then-recent changes to Uber's commission structure and the introduction of a new shared ride service called UberPool—which Joe described as simply an attempt to get more work out of drivers for less pay—the long-term prospects of driving for Uber, he said, felt less and less feasible. It was not only the constant changes to the app that made working for Uber a dead end; it was the future of driving itself. As Joe argued, Uber was moving in the direction of the driverless car, and he and other drivers were complicit in helping make that future a real possibility:

I joke, people keep talking about driverless cars, which I still think [are] way off, but, honestly, if you look at it, *we're building their data*. . . . Where do people go, how do people travel, what roadways do they use? We're building their data. . . . Uber has monstrous data . . . to see what the trends are. What times of day are people driving? What roads are they using? What roads does the map recommend versus [the] way a driver would go? . . . So, when you think of the driverless car, [. . .] they're going to have that data to make it happen. And I joke with people, we're their guinea pigs now. We're building that data for them, and they have it. . . . The data of us driving around, the four hundred thousand Uber drivers driving around and dealing with the passengers, a million rides a day, is going to give them that data to figure out where people are going. So, it's a way off, but I tend to think like that. I'm building their database.[7]

Rather than simply producing a service called ride-hailing, Joe was building Uber's database. In short, he thought he was driving himself out of a job. Joe's conception of his role vis-à-vis Uber's data was insightful. He was not alone in this view. Only four months earlier, in an article for *Vice* magazine, journalist Jay Cassano pointed to a growing number of drivers and their advocates in New York City who had begun to consider Uber's data collection a "a new kind of wage theft."[8] As Cassano noted, their argument hinged on the simple observation that "even when drivers don't have passengers," they were still serving as data collectors. And such work was going uncompensated. As these same activists noted, Uber's data were a big deal. Not only were they central to Uber's day-to-day operations—from setting prices and directing drivers—they had become a business asset. Indeed, for some, Uber's trove of user data was a key reason for the company's stratospheric valuation.[9]

For drivers like Joe, however, alleged wage theft or unpaid labor was only part of the problem. Whether or not drivers were compensated for their role in producing Uber's data, the long-term prospects of driving for the company remained dim. As much as drivers like Joe might treat working for Uber like a "game of strategy," Uber's ever-expanding trove of data made "outsmarting" Uber a losing proposition.[10] The company had the data, and thus it had the power and control. Uber, in other words, had a monopoly on smart. As much as drivers were central to producing Uber's data, Uber was the one with the ability to aggregate such data, to commodify them as big data, and to put them to use—whether as a marketable asset or a tool to manage its workforce. Joe and other drivers thought about data as a product of their work. For policymakers and other stakeholders in the city, however, the view was different; data *did* work.

This chapter investigates the politics of how Uber's data is produced, interpreted, and put to work in D.C. The consensus among policymakers in the city has been that more data allows the city to be smarter. From this perspective, Uber's data are essential to addressing many of the city's transportation problems, from traffic congestion to declines in transit ridership. While the city has attempted to secure ever more data from Uber and other ride-hailing companies (sometimes referred to as transportation network companies, or TNCs), the conditions under which Uber's data are produced—specifically, the realities of the people who do the driving—have largely gone unquestioned. This impoverished view of how data are produced has only led the city to adopt an equally impoverished view of what it means to be smart. For Uber, the narrow conflation of data collection with being smart represents yet another political achievement.

Uber Movement

In 2017, Uber selected D.C. as one of four cities around the world in which to pilot Uber Movement—a free web-based service promising D.C. transportation planners unprecedented access to some of the data collected through Uber's app. Uber touted the new service as a tool for local policymakers as well as an expression of the company's commitment to working with cities to "crack their commute."[11] The explicit understanding was that good data made for good policy. Uber's new platform promised to be a game-changer in data-driven urban policy.[12] Despite the company's proclamations, for many of Uber's longtime observers the initiative reeked of a cheap "public relations" exercise. As *New York Times* contributor Mike Isaac suggested, Uber Movement was merely the company's latest attempt to use data as "a lure" to win over municipal critics.[13] Such critics were understandably chastened by the company's practice of running roughshod over local regulations and its ability to politically mobilize a consumer base. Isaac also questioned the quality of the data Uber planned to share. Two years prior, and as part of a similar effort at "data diplomacy," planners in Boston had discovered that much of the data Uber released had little practical value. Would Uber Movement be any different?[14]

In sharp contrast to Mike Isaac's skepticism, city leaders in D.C. greeted Uber Movement with a great deal of excitement. In particular, Mayor Muriel Bowser gave it a ringing endorsement:

> Smart technology and intelligent use of data are critical to the success of the nation's cities, and the District of Columbia is committed to using these tools to keep pace with the rapid growth of our neighborhoods. We're excited to be one of the early partners with Uber on this new platform. We want to employ as many data sources as possible to mitigate traffic congestion, improve infrastructure and make the streets safer for every visitor and resident in the nation's capital.[15]

In some ways, her enthusiasm was understandable. Like many cities, following the 2008 financial crisis, D.C. had invested heavily in what sociologist Sharon Zukin has deemed the "innovation complex"—a reference to the initiatives and infrastructure projects promoted by cities to attract investment in the technology sector.[16] In 2019 we spoke with a senior-level policymaker who had served under both Mayor Adrian Fenty and Mayor Vincent Gray. For him and others leading the city's economic development strategy, creating a welcoming business climate for tech was the clearest path to becoming what he called a "functional city."[17] Starting in 2012 with initiatives like Digital D.C., the city had created innovation hubs, tech incubators, and start-up districts.[18] In each case, the goal was the same: to diversify the economy away from "the federal government and business and professional services like law firms" and—again, in the words of this senior-level policymaker—to play to D.C.'s growing strength as "an attractive place to live for young, well-educated people."[19]

Mayor Muriel Bowser, who was elected in 2014, continued to place tech at the core of the city's economic development strategy.[20] For her, Uber Movement could not have come at a better time. Uber Movement spoke directly to her administration's latest tech-focused initiative, Smarter D.C., which sought to bring the benefits of smart-city technologies to ever more areas of the District. This initiative involved finding new ways of using the data collected and produced by Internet-connected devices—be they sensors, smartphones, or other objects—to improve the delivery of public services and encourage economic development. In D.C. this ambition had already taken the form of a project called Pennsylvania Avenue 2040—a partnership with the global networking company Cisco Systems to install Internet-enabled streetlights and trash receptacles along Pennsylvania Avenue Northwest. In addition to bestowing the "honor" on D.C. of being one of Uber's "early partners," Uber Movement was aligned with the city's commitment to data collection and employing as "many data sources as possible."[21]

Still, Bowser's embrace of Uber Movement revealed a troubling disconnect between rhetoric and reality. If Uber's entrance to D.C. (see chapter 1) had proven anything, it was that Uber was hardly the most scrupulous actor. Its role in D.C. had been that of a bully, not a company eager to work alongside cities. Uber had not only shown flagrant disregard for the city's laws but also proved willing to target local legislators who stood in its way. In addition, the mayor seemed to be ignoring the company's proven reticence with respect to data sharing. In early 2016, we spoke with a handful of planners at D.C.'s Department of Transportation (DDOT) who were developing a new congestion study. Although they expressed general optimism about services like Uber—especially as a way of increasing the number of modes of transport available—they told us that collecting data from the company had been a battle.

> We're working on a congestion study, and for that, we are reaching out to TNCs to get their data, but we haven't gotten far yet. . . . We've been working with them on some sort of [a memorandum of understanding] to perhaps get data from them, but it's a battle, so we haven't gotten far yet.[22]

For local blogger and early Uber supporter David Alpert (see chapter 1), the struggle with Uber over its data had been altogether foreseeable. In 2014, as the D.C. Council debated legislation to legalize UberX, Alpert took to the op-ed page of the *Washington Post*. He urged legislators to require Uber and other ride-hailing companies to provide regular caches of data to municipal agencies tasked with managing the city's transportation infrastructure. He argued that the ability to access data sets "with approximate origins and destinations of trips, wait times and fares" would not only have direct applications for local transportation planners but also ensure that ride-hailing companies complied with existing laws—especially those related to racial discrimination. Speaking as a resident deeply invested in improving the city and making it smarter, Alpert was clear: data transparency might "allow cities to legalize Uber, Lyft, Sidecar and others without giving up our ability to see and address problems."[23]

To Alpert's disappointment, the D.C. Council went in the opposite direction. While permitting the city to inspect Uber's records pertaining to safety, in 2014 the council passed a law that exempted ride-hailing companies from sharing data on much of anything else. Moreover, the new law exempted any information that the city might collect about ride-hailing companies from requests made through the D.C. Freedom of Information Act (FOIA) (see chapter 1 for discussion).[24] These injunctions on ride-hailing data remained in place even while Smarter D.C., Uber Movement, and other local initiatives championed the centrality of data in addressing the city's problems. Uber's data was still Uber's alone.

The City Bytes Back

The dissonance between the city's commitment to smart data and its approach to Uber partially ended with the passage of the Budget Support Act of 2018. The act, which drew considerable press attention for raising taxes on both alcohol sales and assessed commercial property, included new provisions with respect to ride-hailing data. It contained an amendment titled the Private Vehicle-for-Hire Data Sharing Amendment Act, which mandated that Uber and other ride-hailing companies submit quarterly reports to both of the city's transit agencies, the DDOT and the Department of For-Hire-Vehicles (DFHV). According to the amendment, such reports were to include information on the total number of ride-hailing operators in the city; the average fare and average distance for all trips; and the total miles driven en route to pick-up and drop-off locations. Even more importantly, the amendment mandated that ride-hailing companies share anonymized data on both the location and the time of all pick-ups and drop-offs originating or ending in the city. The budget legislation retained the FOIA exemption on ride-hailing data collected by the city, but both transit agencies were allowed to make certain data available to the public, with stipulations on privacy. In addition, the new budget act granted agencies the power to request data from Uber and other companies through a rulemaking process.[25] These new data-sharing parameters reflected a potentially meaningful shift in the city's approach to Uber.

What prompted this new approach? Between 2014 and 2018, two important changes had occurred. First, Uber's political power had become more open to contestation. Although in its earliest years Uber's popularity had made the D.C. Council wary of imposing regulations, those fears no longer had the same weight. Uber had been rocked by scandals,[26] including the #DeleteUber campaign of early 2017 and the decision by Uber CEO Travis Kalanick to serve on President Donald Trump's business council. Second, planners could now point to a series of studies that found ride-hailing companies were exacerbating traffic congestion and reducing transit ridership.[27] Transit ridership in D.C. had fallen precipitously between 2016 and 2017. Some of that decline was attributable to ongoing Metro track work, but many questioned whether Uber and other ride-hailing companies were to blame as well.[28] Concerns about ride-hailing's negative effects led to a behind-the-scenes mobilization of elite institutional actors outside the local government—specifically, stakeholders from a business improvement district, the D.C. Sustainable Transportation coalition (led by Alpert), and the Washington Metropolitan Area Transit Authority (WMATA). Data, this group successfully argued, were key to getting a clearer picture of Uber's impact on transportation in D.C.

At its core, the budget act codified a view of city streets and curbs as public resources that the city—not Uber—should manage. But the impact of the new provisions was less than local transportation planners had hoped. In fact, one transportation planner told us that her agency contracted with a third-party company for data precisely because what she "can get from [the ride-hailing companies] is not clean."[29] She also said there were problems with the data specifications, which were often too general to be useful:

Again, the level of specificity in the data that we got, we believe it may not be enough to make some policy decisions regarding use of curbsides, for instance, because they provide us data I think down to five decimal [places]. And with that level of specificity, if we wanted, for instance, to put a pick-up/drop-off lane, we need to understand where exactly the hotspots are.

And [with] five decimal [places] you can generally understand
what intersection, but you can't understand the direction. . . .
So, if you want to put in a pick-up/drop-off zone in public
space to ease congestion, to reduce pedestrian-vehicle conflicts, it's sort of impossible.[30]

She also spoke with us about the difficulties of obtaining data to
gauge the effectiveness of new regulations or planning initiatives:

We instituted one of the very first pick-up/drop-off zones for
TNCs in the nation a couple years ago . . . but one of the things
that we kept thinking about and talking through is that in the
absence of good data to evaluate the success of whatever program we put in place, there is no way that we can expand it.
How do we convince the general public . . . or, for that matter,
the different divisions inside of DDOT, that this is a good idea?[31]

While the 2018 data provisions seemed to mark a break from the
past, the reality was defined by continued frustration on the part
of policymakers, city employees, and transit planners.

Much of that frustration was associated with the persistent
intransigence of ride-hailing companies themselves: in some
instances, the data they provided to the city was either riddled
with mistakes or delivered in such a way that it required a great
deal of time and energy to make use of it. As James, an official from
the D.C. agency tasked with overseeing all taxi and ride-hailing
services (DFHV) noted, sometimes those issues were related:

Oftentimes the TNCs push a lot of data to us that is very raw. I
don't know if it's intentional, I don't know if it's out of malice,
but it's very raw, and it's up to us, the entity, to figure it out,
to crunch the data, to validate the data, and to make it into a
usable format. . . . I mean sometimes there's even bigger, glar-
ing data problems. For example, one company might have a
lot more rides than another, but that just doesn't make sense
sometimes. So then you go back to the company and make
them correct the data. Sometimes it's not always the perfect

data when we first get it. So you can't really analyze or make
decisions based off that in that first iteration of the form. You
have to go back and forth a few times in order to get that data
to a good spot.[32]

Beyond the labor, and the resources necessary to clean up the data,
what planners and policymakers in D.C. *really* needed was real-
time data. This, however, had never been "in the cards," according
to a different official at the same D.C. agency.[33] The challenges
associated with data specifications were compounded by the challenges associated with companies prone to litigiousness. As James
admitted to us, Uber and companies like it seemed eager to do
everything in their power to make things difficult:

> They always try to play off every city against each other. They
> say [to us], "Oh, well, the regulator in Massachusetts didn't
> ask that." . . . It's things on data reporting. On the accuracy of
> the data. And they'll say, "Well, how geographically accurate
> do you want it?" And they'll say, "Well, this city was okay with
> this thing, with like rounded-up data." Say, well, I don't really
> care what that other city says. We're not that city.[34]

The result was that the DFHV spent almost as much time negotiating with lawyers over what data could be shared or cleaning up
errors in the data as they spent on analyzing the data. The process,
according to James, was incredibly draining:

> It's always a battle trying to get more data. And even the stuff
> we think we're legally entitled to has been a little bit of a battle.
> It's why I dread every email. When I see one from Uber or Lyft,
> I'm like, is it their lawyer yelling at me?[35]

Despite their criticisms, for many planners and policymakers
in D.C. Uber's reluctance to share data was understandable. Data
sharing was, according to one city planner, a direct challenge to
Uber's business model. More to the point, sharing data meant
providing a potential opening for a competitor. Yet another city

planner offered us the same argument, albeit framed against the equally compelling desire for cities to learn about ride-hailing's impact on traffic patterns:

> I know a lot of cities are requesting data to look at how [TNCs are] affecting traffic and congestion, and where people are going. . . . So . . . there are all these questions cities have, but without the data, it's speculation. And [TNCs] regard their data as proprietary business information. They often are reluctant to give up detailed information because they say it violates their users' privacy, which is somewhat ridiculous . . . they don't truly believe that. That's not the argument they're making in good faith. They just don't want their competitors to know what they're doing.[36]

For D.C. planners and policymakers seeking to understand the impact of the ride-hailing industry on congestion and traffic, or inequities, the data provisions in the budget act generated more data but, in some instances, less clarity. Although the quantity of ride-hail data shared with the city had increased, the quality of data had not. Uber retained its monopoly on smart.

Micromobility, Macrodata

In late February 2020, D.C. transit officials brought renewed attention to issues around data after the city enacted a data-sharing requirement for dockless mobility providers. These included the bike and electric scooter services in operation, on which there were at least eight: Bird, Bolt, Lime, Lyft, Razor, Skip, Spin, and Jump (a subsidiary of Uber). Under the new rules, transit officials required that providers submit data using the Mobility Data Specifications (MDS) platform—a "digital tool" aimed at standardizing communication between cities and private mobility providers.[37] Although data requirements for providers such as Bird and Lime were not new in D.C., MDS marked something of an escalation. Under the new rules, dockless scooter and bike companies were required not only to provide data on the locations of scooters and bikes when parked but also to provide "real-time" data on their movement when in use. Though these new MDS requirements were not applied to ride-hailing services, the fear was that it was only a matter of time.

Not long after the city enacted the new data-sharing requirement for micromobility providers, a coalition of local and national civil liberties groups penned an open letter to D.C. officials, expressing their concern with the privacy implications of the new data protocols. Signed by the local American Civil Liberties Union chapter, the Center for Democracy and Technology, and New America's Open Technology Institute, it argued that the data collected "could reveal much about an individual's private life, including attendance at a political protest, a visit to a doctor or Planned Parenthood,"[38] or other kinds of sensitive information. Moreover, the letter added, the city had failed to communicate to the public how it planned to safeguard such personal information. The letter borrowed heavily from language developed by an ongoing campaign against MDS in Los Angeles, the first city to mandate that mobility providers use the MDS platform. That campaign had recently found expression in a federal lawsuit filed by Uber against the Los Angeles Department of Transportation, in opposition to the agency's demand that Uber—which operated both an electric-scooter and a dockless-bike service in the city— submit real-time location data.[39] According to Uber—named in the lawsuit as Social Bicycles LLC—such regulations constituted a violation of the Fourth Amendment and its prohibition against warrantless search and seizure. As the complaint also alleged, the ultimate goal of the people backing the new data protocol was to eventually extend such protocols to ride-hailing services as well as other forms of urban mobility, including driverless cars.[40]

In an article published by the Electronic Frontier Foundation, a nonprofit aimed at defending digital privacy, contributor Jamie Williams framed the debate over MDS as one between those pushing for "surveillance cities" and those advocating for what

he described as "smart enough cities."[41] Placing himself squarely
in the latter camp, Williams argued that MDS was a clear case of
government overreach. Alpert, in his blog *Greater Greater Washington*, disagreed.[42] MDS protocols allowed the city to collect data
on individual travel patterns, but such data, Alpert noted, were far
less sensitive than the data already collected by cities in the form
of public-housing applications, student records, city ambulance
call logs, and so on. For Alpert, the debate over MDS hinged on a
yet more abstract question: Whom do you trust with your data—
governments or companies?

For two policymakers who spoke with us, such an abstract
question belied the limited utility of the data in the first place. To
quote one of the officials:

> Sometimes I think the case for data, at the government use-
> fulness level, at least in District government, is overstated.
> And I've had off-the-record conversations with people within
> District government who have said that. Sure, you can give
> us all the data we want, but we get massive terabytes of data
> on a daily or constant basis that's in essentially an unreadable
> format. We don't have people who are equipped to analyze
> it. . . . And so that would involve probably hiring contractors to
> come in and do that for us, which is more money—and, while
> it might be useful, to what end? . . . And then when you put
> that up against companies who are very, very reluctant to want
> to give it, it can be difficult to make the case, I think, for us.[43]

For him, the issue was not simply one of capacity or lack thereof.
Nor was it simply about weighing the costs against the possible
rewards. It was also about translating data into policy. Even after
solving the technical challenges of wrestling data into a usable
format, the political challenge of making policy remains. He
continued:

> We have lots of mandates about reports and studies and all the
> rest of that . . . many of which are simply ignored, others of

which are done, but not in a way that's useful or satisfactory to a legislative body, which is how I come at it. Or they're done and they sit on the shelf someplace. And so at some point you have to say . . . to what end? What's the point? Is it likely to be useful to the government for the benefit of citizens?[44]

The necessary question was a simple one: Data, to what end? Beyond the costs associated with turning "massive terabytes of data" into something usable, there was no guarantee that more data would yield anything approaching a policy change. Whether the goal was to expand ride-hailing pick-up and drop-off zones or simply to add a new bus route, such policy changes required resources and politics. Yet another study backed up by data was insufficient. In many ways, the policymakers' comments were a direct challenge to the single-minded obsession with amassing ever more data—whether from Uber or from other mobility services. In D.C. that obsession has too often come at the expense of asking what is all this data for, anyway? Does more data translate to better policy? What questions can data answer? And what questions remain impervious to data?

Data as Work

Across various debates and legislative actions related to data in D.C.—whether in relation to the new data protocols in 2018 or in relation to the later introduction of more stringent protocols around micromobility—the central assumption has largely remained unchanged. That assumption, which has become common sense, is that data from companies like Uber can provide important insights to planners and policymakers seeking to better understand the cities they are tasked with improving. For planners and policymakers in D.C., questions around data have run the gamut. While many of those questions have focused on issues of technical capacity and the challenge of turning raw data into a usable format, the substantive task remains identifying and solving problems. Can Uber's data be used to address traffic congestion, to better manage public streets, or to restructure transit routes to better effect? Can such data ensure Uber's compliance with local laws or gauge its impact on congestion, idling times, or pollution? Indeed, what can Uber's data tell us about its own drivers' wages, working conditions, or challenges?

In many ways, Uber faces its own data questions. These are related to the role of data in securing market power, increasing profitability, and attaining a higher valuation. They are related to Uber's role in managing workers, improving its algorithm, or heading off political or legislative challenges. Such questions also include assessing the dangers that might arise—whether dangers to Uber's business model or dangers to its users' privacy—if such data were to be shared publicly. From the perspective of planners and from Uber's own perspective, all these questions begin and end with a focus on the work that data performs in either public policy or private strategy, respectively. However understandable and important they are, such questions are radically different from the questions that arise if we start with the experiences of drivers like Joe. When Joe told us he was building Uber's database,[45] he was recognizing his individual role. At the same time, he was clearly correct that when Uber and similar companies seek to leverage their data for economic and political gain, they are leveraging an asset produced by, to quote Joe, "the four hundred thousand Uber drivers driving around and dealing with the passengers."[46] In addition to the work that data can perform in various policy areas, data is a *product* of work. Where the focus is on "data as work," the questions shift markedly. What are the working conditions that make Uber's data possible? What types of labor are necessary, and how do the conditions of work map onto the types of data produced? As Cassano reminds us, "Data doesn't materialize out of nowhere—it is made by people simply driving around, trying to earn a living."[47]

Few drivers with whom we spoke were as explicit as Joe in identifying data as a product of labor. But many shared the broader sense that working for Uber was largely a dead end, and the only difference between Uber and other forms of low-wage work was the flexibility. According to one driver, Dwayne, Uber was little different from Walmart:

> What Uber's done is they've lowered the cost of cab rides, more or less. The money that they're making is at the expense of the cabs. Now, they would also argue that they're generating more rides because they think the millennial generation uses it more and they wouldn't have used a cab anyway. I think both of those things are true, but at the end of the day, they're driving prices down. They're becoming the Walmart of transportation . . . and all that it entails. So as long as they get low-paid people to accept jobs and do the driving, they're fine.[48]

For another driver, Zaki, a full-time IT professional, the flexibility of the job was one of its only true benefits: "That's one positive thing I'll say about it."[49] Otherwise, he added, the working conditions were often less than ideal. Uber's pricing model was in a constant state of flux, making it impossible for drivers like him to predict their earnings. Working for five hours one day might yield $60, while working for the same amount of time another day might yield $30. For Zaki, the inability to predict his earnings was compounded by the insecurity associated with Uber's approach to complaints by customers. As he explained to us, "The first thing Uber does when a customer has a complaint is kick you off . . . and then you have to fight your way back inside."[50] Without any appeals process or method of arbitration, the presumption was that a driver was "guilty before proven innocent." Given such conditions, the idea that Uber drivers were entrepreneurs was laughable to Zaki. If anything, he added, driving for Uber was more akin to "indentured slavery," especially for full-time drivers who "have to drive to keep money on the table" and who do so with no paid time-off or benefits.[51]

The working conditions of Uber drivers are not unlike the conditions facing many other workers in the gig economy. The authors of a study published by the Economic Policy Institute (EPI) in 2022 draw on data from a national survey comparing gig workers employed as independent contractors with traditional service-sector workers to show that the difference in the two groups' working conditions is stark.[52] Although service-sector employment in the United States is often defined by low pay, gig work by independent contractors falls in a category by itself. Because these workers are excluded from local, state, and federal regulations on minimum wage, overtime pay, and paid sick days, the study found that more than 25 percent of gig workers earned less than the state minimum wage that would apply if they had been traditional employees instead.[53] Per the EPI study, Dwayne was only partially right. Even if Uber was the Walmart of transportation, in many ways Walmart employees enjoyed far more rights and economic security than Uber drivers did.[54]

In the context of debates about Uber's data, comments like Dwayne's and Zaki's and the findings of the EPI study all function to direct attention away from questions of data access. They force us to see "data as work" and as tied to a set of working conditions that, for many workers, are far from ideal. These are working conditions that rely not only on unpaid labor—as evidenced whenever drivers produce data while not carrying a paying passenger—but also on insecurity and low pay.

Data and Expectations

In 2019, we published a short report called *The Uber Workplace in D.C.*[55] The report, which we presented to the D.C. Council at the John A. Wilson building, attempted to provide what we thought to be a needed picture of the challenges facing Uber drivers in the D.C. metro area: challenges associated with debt, lack of transparency, and health and safety. We ended the report with three recommendations for legislative action, one of which was new legislation mandating that ride-hailing companies share data on wages, dead miles, and workers' safety. Although the council had mandated data on transportation and congestion-related issues in late 2018, we pointed to the absence of data on the working conditions of Uber drivers. Several months after publishing the report, we presented a related paper at a think-tank event in New York. After our presentation, the organizer of the event pulled us aside and asked us a question that had somehow failed to emerge during the Q&A: Why exactly do you recommend that the D.C. government collect more data? What, she asked, did we *expect* the data to do or to show? Did we really need data on the working conditions of drivers in order to show the failures of the gig economy? How important, to borrow a quip from geographer David Harvey, was yet another "masochistic assemblage of some huge dossier on the daily injustice" of gig work?[56] Would it show us anything that we did not already know?

The questions stuck with us, and although we maintained our belief in the utility of data—especially on drivers' wages and safety—they were questions that forced us to think. We thought about the *idea* of data itself and its function, about the continual conflation of data with being smarter and the extent to which we, ourselves, had bought into the data fetishism that we thought we were condemning. How, in short, had the *idea* of data shaped our own thinking? In some ways, these questions forced us to reassess Uber Movement and the politics of data in the city.

In many ways, Uber Movement's impact on transportation planning in D.C. proved negligible. Many D.C. policymakers with whom we spoke in 2019 professed having never heard of the service. Others simply described it as redundant and especially so following the data-sharing mandates advanced in 2018. As one official stated in reference to Uber Movement, "We don't need their goodwill to do partnerships . . . and, given their history of not being totally honest, I'd rather do it on our own without them."[57] We heard a similar criticism from an economic-development expert and former city employee with whom we spoke in late 2019. As we learned during the interview, he not only had been involved in the launch of Uber Movement but had been one of its early boosters. He admitted that his initial enthusiasm for the initiative had proved entirely misplaced: "At first it was seen as this great data tool, and it was only later I realized, 'This is completely useless.'" Not only was it a "one-off data tool that doesn't do anything else," but also it failed to offer any "specificity of analysis."[58]

On the one hand, Mike Isaac's original description of Uber Movement—as recounted earlier from the *New York Times*—was not inaccurate.[59] Rather than a serious attempt at data sharing, Uber Movement was, in many ways, an exercise in public relations. On the other hand, as this chapter has made clear, Uber Movement was obviously more than a gimmick. As with Uber's campaign against taxi commissioner Ron Linton (see chapter 1) or its efforts to adopt the language of racial justice (see chapter 2), Uber Movement must be understood in political terms. It was an attempt to reinforce a commonsense view of data and of data's role in shaping urban policy. In D.C., those expectations were about data's importance to solving the city's transportation woes and to making the city smarter.

These expectations would reemerge in debates over MDS as well as debates among city planners on the future of local transportation. Uber Movement was not just an exercise in public relations. It was a political intervention, which aimed to sell Uber to cities precisely by selling the idea of Uber's data as something that cities desperately needed. The stakes of this intervention were not immaterial. Rather than merely a *thing* that is traded, exchanged, or simply handed over to planners, data are a *social relation* between people—drivers, customers, and engineers. When initiatives like Uber Movement treat data as a thing, they obscure the working conditions of the people like Dwayne and Zaki who produce that data.

At the same time, initiatives like Uber Movement shape how we think about urban problems and the politics of data. Rather than viewing traffic congestion, "transit deserts," and issues of new mobility providers as problems rooted in the broader political economy or requiring political persuasion, democratic institutions, or the mobilization of constituents, Uber Movement advances the idea that such problems simply require more data. At its best, the lure of Uber's data is the lure of improving city operations, mitigating congestion, or—to quote scholars Jathan Sadowski, Salome Viljoen, and Meredith Whitaker—simply treating the proliferation of behavioral data as a public good.[60] At its worst, however, the lure of Uber's data—and the lure of initiatives like Uber Movement—is the lure of escaping politics proper and shifting debates from the messy world of democratic governance to a more contained world. That more contained world may be a smarter and a more data-rich world, but, to paraphrase writer Rick Perlstein, it may not necessarily be a more decent, just, or democratic one.[61]

4

Flying Cars and Other Urban Legends

So: Why did the projected explosion of technological growth everyone was expecting—the moon bases, the robot factories—fail to materialize? Logically there are only two possibilities. Either our expectations about the pace of technological change were unrealistic, in which case, we need to ask ourselves why so many otherwise intelligent people felt they were not. Or our expectations were not inherently unrealistic, in which case we need to ask what happened to throw the path of technological development off course.

—DAVID GRAEBER[1]

By recognizing the promise of high-tech driving as illusory, we have our best chance of recognizing all that we can do.

—PETER NORTON[2]

In 2012, an early automated vehicle (AV)[3] prototype, a blue Toyota Prius operated by Google, took a spin on D.C. streets. The ride was part of a broad push by Google to promote the legalization of AV usage by state and city legislatures.[4] Inside the car were two "giddy" D.C. councilmembers who gushed about the benefits AVs would have for traffic, parking, the environment, and those unable to drive due to age, disability, or financial circumstance.[5] AVs, the councilmembers claimed, could dramatically change life in the city and they were eager to be among the first to usher in this promised transformation. The excitement that these councilmembers expressed about self-driving vehicles was almost ubiquitous in the 2010s, when endless images and news reports predicted not just AVs but flying cars too.[6]

Throughout that decade, Uber was a key protagonist in lifting largely unproven technologies from science-fiction obscurity and putting them firmly in the public imagination.[7] As this chapter will show, all kinds of people and institutions, from think tanks and corporations to city governments, investors, and workers have internalized Uber's futuristic view and, by extension, Uber's broader vision for the city. But the real question is *why* all these cities, actors, and institutions were so enthusiastic about a technology that remains a distant, if tantalizing, possibility.

To answer this question, we focus on the recurring historical gap between the wild promises and the reality of AV development in the decade since that Google-operated car drove around D.C.[8] That gap, we argue, suggests that AVs are not just an emerging technology. They are also a form of urban politics and part of an "automation discourse" endemic to modern societies.[9] Economic historian Aaron Benanav has argued that discussions about automation constitute a "spontaneous discourse of capitalist societies, which, for a mixture of structural and contingent reasons, reappears in those societies time and again as a way of thinking through their limits."[10] In a similar manner, we argue that companies like Uber and cities like D.C. engage in automation discourse because it allows them to appear responsive to a range of pressing limits and problems, from transit and infrastructure to equality and inclusivity. By circumventing a political process that has become defined by its constraints, automation discourse offers a superficial fix to all these problems and more.

We argue that automation discourse is generative in political terms. According to AV supporters, companies like Uber could, if given the right support and space to operate, generate solutions to urban problems that formal democratic politics simply cannot. AVs were proof that companies like Uber were on the right track. In a moment when national and city politics appeared more dysfunctional than ever and faith in democratic public institutions was eroded, Uber put forward an enticing vision of the city of the future.

Given a decade of Uber's lofty promises about AVs and the future they will bring, we might ask, "What has the technology accomplished for the city?" The answer, as this chapter will show, is "Surprisingly little." The promise of AVs seems especially empty in light of the changes at Uber, which was once the industry leader in AV research. In December 2020 Uber divested itself from AVs. Under pressure from shareholders, continuing financial losses, and growing uncertainty about the solidity of its business model, it sold its autonomous vehicle research unit, its scooter and e-bike division, and, most symbolically of all, its flying-car division.[11] The very same tech giant that sold the world a striking vision of the city of the future has resigned itself to trying to make a profit from ride-hailing and food-delivery services.

As argued in the previous three chapters, Uber's growth in D.C. and its decade-plus-long campaign to reshape the city have relied on the company's ability to shape legislation as well as on its success in reshaping expectations—from what we expect city regulators like taxi commissioner Ron Linton to do (see chapter 1), to where we look for solutions to racial injustice (see chapter 2), to which types of data are worth collecting and why (see chapter 3). In what follows, we show how AVs have similarly been part of a struggle to reshape expectations about the future of D.C. and the kinds of politics that could realize that future.

Uber Sells the Future

AVs have long been part of Uber's business strategy. In framing the expansion of AVs as a struggle against outdated legislation, industries, and modes of work, Uber strove to make its name synonymous with the future.[12] In 2016, Uber published an ambitious white paper titled "Uber Elevate," in which it outlined a future of on-demand urban air transportation.[13] As *Wired* reported, the company that had "redefined the idea of flexible labor," "gutted the American taxi industry," and "launched a fleet of self-driving cars in Pittsburgh" now promised flying cars.[14] Uber promised to revolutionize urban transportation and make cities more livable, giving residents back lost time and easing "the commute pain that citizens in cities around the world feel."[15] At its third conference to promote and celebrate the Uber Elevate idea, in D.C., Uber brought together a range of industry leaders and legislators to discuss the future of what it called urban air mobility. The conference's location in D.C. represented a coup for a city rebranding itself as a tech hub. The conference also pointed to Uber's eagerness for the attention of federal regulators. In opening remarks, U.S. Secretary of Transportation Elaine Chao observed, "Urban Air Mobility is joining autonomous vehicles, drones, and reusable rockets, in a wave of transportation innovation that may change the way we live, work, and travel."[16] At the conference, Uber unveiled plans for a fleet of car-sized quadcopters, accompanied by artists' renderings of sleek Uber skyports. Conference attendees crowded to get inside the cab of a prototype quadcopter that seemed to proclaim that Uber's aspirations were on the verge of realization.[17] But apart from artists' renderings and the user-friendly prototype, the plan was short on both details and rationale.

Precisely how flying cars would improve urban life was not obvious. Nor was it apparent how *more* cars—be they automated, electric, or airborne—might transcend basic constraints in transit and energy.[18] Essentially, conference attendees were asked to trust that the transition from a mundane world of traffic jams, transit issues, and decaying infrastructure to Uber's science-fiction world was imminent. The conference, and its associated campaigns, worked to convince policymakers and politicians of both the inevitability and the desirability of AVs and flying cars, and it bolstered Uber's position as an industry leader in such projects. Uber Elevate's farsightedness was one of the reasons why the company was reportedly "on its way to becoming the most valuable startup ever."[19] Such pronouncements about Uber were important for drumming up both public confidence and private investment. In 2010 Uber was valued at $5 million.[20] In 2019, when the company made an initial public offering and was floated on the stock market, it was valued at $82 billion.[21] This phenomenal growth was backed by a wide range of investors who, emboldened by historically low interest rates, gambled that Uber's vision of the future would eventually materialize.

Uber's vision of the future was central to its business model, which appeared to be based on three stages. First, Uber would monopolize cities' ride-hailing market through an expensive battle to eliminate competitors and change municipal regulations. Second, Uber would slowly begin to raise prices for consumers, on the strength of its market dominance. Third, the company would invest the resulting profits in AVs, thus promising investors a ground-floor buy-in to the future of transportation. That Uber had a plan for the future was clear; whether that plan was achievable was less so.[22]

One D.C. policymaker pointed out to us in 2019 that both Uber and its primary competitor, Lyft, charged fares well below the cost per trip—essentially subsidizing riders and operating at a financial loss, in a bid to beat the competition. Despite its astronomical valuation, Uber was not, in fact, a profitable company. This person noted that, thankfully, these companies "were burning through investors' money" rather than taxpayers' money.[23] Still, it was hard to see how the ride-hailing industry was sustainable. We live, the policymaker joked, "in this weird world where in a couple of decades we'll be telling our grandchildren that for ten years, billionaires paid for us to ride around in other people's cars."[24] In addition to a faith that Uber would eventually "do a capitalism and turn a profit,"[25] the company's success in raising venture capital rested on investors' faith in Uber's vision of the future. In the face of financial losses and eroding market share, AVs, flying cars, and other futuristic mobility technologies were important tools with which to recruit venture capital.

That the urban future can and should be built on automated technologies and operated by tech companies like Uber has become a commonsense proposition.[26] Objecting to such claims comes across as not just old-fashioned but mean-spirited, because what kind of person is against a better future? Like any technology, however, AVs anticipate a particular kind of future: they are a form of "world-making."[27] Conversations about AVs often occur in the realm of safety, regulation, congestion, or sustainability. Such conversations also make broad normative claims about what the future of cities should be and insist that tech companies like Uber can and should deliver it. As *The Economist* trumpeted in 2016, Uber was merely a harbinger of an economic revolution: "Whether Uber wins or loses" is essentially unimportant, the magazine said; what matters is that "we are all on the road to Uberworld."[28] The consequences of Uber's world-making strategy are visible in D.C. in the realm of work, legislation, and the built environment.

The Future of Work Is No Work

A plethora of studies, including this book, have emphasized the bleak reality of work under the imperatives of the gig economy (see chapters 3 and 5). Lurking behind this debate about working conditions, however, is a deep anxiety that the future of work is no work at all. Of course, this is not the first time such worries have emerged. These anxieties have resurfaced regularly throughout the history of capitalism.[29] Automation discourse is almost always associated with "a deep anxiety about the functioning of the labor market."[30]

AV discourse, as a variant of automation discourse, has similarly had a profound effect on workers in the gig economy. Since 2010 a wave of studies, popular books, and news reports have warned of labor's inevitable demise in the face of automation.[31] Uber itself has been a key player in these discussions. In its early days, Uber was explicit about its driverless endgame. CEO Travis Kalanick described Uber's investment in AVs as part of a plan to eliminate traffic, road fatalities, and billions of wasted hours.[32] Drivers, meanwhile, were subject to planned obsolescence. They remained necessary but for how long? Kalanick was reluctant to set a date. He told *Business Insider* in 2017: "I wish I had an answer for you on that one, but I don't. What I know is that I can't be wrong. Right?"[33]

When we first started interviewing Uber drivers in 2016, the company was just beginning to push the idea that a new data-driven age of AVs was on the horizon, and its publicity campaign was making headlines. In August of that year, in partnership with Ford, Uber began testing AVs in Pittsburgh. Unsurprisingly, drivers were the first to understand the stakes: "It feels like we're just rentals. We're kind of like placeholders until the technology comes out."[34] In D.C., the effects of automation were palpable. Discussions of drivers' current working conditions and the prospects for transforming them frequently ended with an appeal to the certainty that driverless cars were imminent. That year, ten of the forty drivers we interviewed brought up on their own the specter of automation. Though drivers could be excited about the arrival of such a marvelous futuristic technology on the streets of D.C., it was clear to them that it was a death knell for their work. The prospect of AVs lowered drivers' expectations regarding the current conditions and future existence of their work.

Olotun,[35] who had immigrated to the United States from Nigeria, was one such driver. He lived in D.C. with his wife and two young children. Like many drivers in Uber's early days, he had heard about the new ride-hailing service while working as a limousine driver. Uber's flexibility helped with his busy schedule, and the money was good at first. Olotun was studying psychology at the University of the District of Columbia. He also worked part-time as a security guard. His schedule was hectic. He slept intermittently and worked frantically, struggling to balance work, study, and family. He told us how he had been robbed while driving and, on another occasion, had fallen asleep at the wheel. After a year and a half of driving, the job became unsustainable for him and, as he would later tell us, he quit. Still, he remained upbeat about Uber's future. When asked what that future would look like for drivers, he brought up some immediate limits: "The world is getting into technology. . . . Pretty soon it will be flying cars!"[36] Another Nigerian-born driver and IT worker, Zaki (introduced in chapter 3), similarly talked with us about how Uber's economic prospects for immigrants were not endless. He said the opportunity was about to expire: "they're going to have automated cars in the future. That's the plan. It's always been Uber's plan."[37]

When news emerged in 2018 that AVs would begin limited testing on D.C. streets, some Uber drivers reacted immediately by piling into online forums like Uberpeople.net, where they discussed, like twenty-first-century Luddites, whether AVs should be sabotaged.[38] Others saw the writing on the wall, though they were surprised to see themselves made obsolete so soon. Many of the drivers who spoke with us concurred that the future was one of no work at all. One driver, Larry, a financial services worker, argued that the worsening conditions and declining pay rates for Uber drivers were sure indicators of a looming AV future. Driver burnout and turnover, he explained to us, must be a part of Uber's long-term business model: "I have to believe that Uber has done this analysis and said, 'At what point do we run out of drivers, and can we launch autonomous cars before we get to that point?'"[39]

For another driver, Hank, who had worked on and off in the automotive industry, it was only a matter of time before a driverless future materialized: "The technology is there already. It's the lobbying and the regulations that have to be figured out."[40] Jabari, an IT worker, saw AVs precisely in terms of driver obsolescence. He had started driving for Uber to help pay off his student-loan debt, but as drivers' pay rates declined, he began to see Uber only as a means of supplementing his income. Challenges to declining pay rates seemed futile in the face of a driverless future. As Jabari related, "I think it's inevitable that there [will] be autonomous cars, so I think within the next five years, that'll be here, and . . . each year or even every six months, Uber's going to keep doing the rate cut."[41]

Many of these drivers saw AVs as inevitable. Uber's own experience with the technology, however, shows they were anything but. The power of AVs lies precisely in this sleight of hand. In an AV world, conversations about workers' classification, pay, and surveillance become anachronistic. The only relevant labor question is what to do with workers once their jobs have been automated. Neither Uber nor D.C. had much to say about what would happen to the drivers replaced by AVs, beyond platitudes about retraining.[42] It is in this struggle for the future that AV technology truly goes to work, shaping the present in the process. Technology has not yet replaced drivers. In fact, Uber's driverless future has never seemed further from realization. However, the constant hum of automation discourse maintains the possibility that it can happen at any time.[43] To date, Uber's innovations have not been in labor-saving technologies but in labor-controlling technologies (see chapter 5).[44]

Not all workers have been convinced by Uber's vision of a driverless future. If, as driver Larry, pointed out to us, "The premise Uber is betting the company on is that they're going to be able to go autonomous before they run out of drivers," many drivers were furious and resentful at how the company was allegedly phasing them out.[45] According to Larry, "There's so much angst and enmity being generated by the things I'm describing, that its drivers are actively rooting for the company to fail."[46] In response, drivers have reiterated and reclaimed the very simple fact that they are still here and vitally necessary and that the prospects of automation-led redundancy remain far off. One driver, Sung-ho, a writer and stock-market analyst, spoke to us about the underlying issues with Uber's AV future:

> This whole thing about the automated cars replacing drivers? That is a laugh. Because Uber loses so much money. I mean, think about it. The drivers bear 90 percent of the expenses. I mean, the drivers have to pay for the maintenance of the cars, the gas, and all that stuff, right? What does Uber do? Well, they have one app. They have this crappy app that's not proprietary, because everybody and their grandmother has an app like this, you know? And Uber doesn't make money as it is. They still lose money while the driver's bearing 90 percent of the expenses. So now you're going to tell me that you have an automated car that you have to buy, you have to maintain, their insurance is going to go up, there's more expenses, they're going to maintain a fleet, gas, fuel, and they're going to make money because of that? You're out of your mind. You would think this is a great business plan, but the reality is I don't see Uber lasting. I really don't.[47]

Sung-ho reaffirmed the place of drivers at the center of Uber's business and relegated AVs to the status of the emperor's new clothes. Drivers, according to Sung-ho, take all the risk, do the majority of the work, and are indispensable to Uber. In other words, "data don't drive."[48] Nor, as we have seen, do data collect themselves (see chapter 3). Drivers are central, and talk of AVs works to mask this fact. In pointing out this central contradiction, Sung-ho brought Uber and AVs out of the realm of speculation and hinted at their political stakes.

These are stakes of which Uber itself is well aware. Not long after it sold its self-driving-car division in 2020, Uber, along with other gig-economy companies, spent more than $220 million to push a ballot initiative in California that would allow the company to continue to treat its drivers as contractors.[49] This move seemed to confirm Sung-ho's skepticism that Uber ever really believed in a driverless future in the first place. As *The Economist* forewarned, however, it is not essentially important whether Uber itself actually delivers AVs. Instead, it is "Uberworld," the company's vision of the future and its effect on politics of the present, that is transforming the fabric of urban life.

Welcome, Robot Overlords

Uber's view of the future has been convincing in D.C. If, as Uber lobbyist Zack stated, D.C. has "adopted our view of the world" (see chapter 1), the city also has embraced Uber's view of the future.[50] Uber and AVs offer D.C. a set of solutions that are consistent with its embrace of a "smart city" approach to urban governance.[51] For much of the past decade, D.C. has altered its regulatory landscape in anticipation of AVs. Not long after their 2012 ride in Google's AV, local legislators spoke about the ride's special permissions, as there was no regulatory structure in place to deal with AVs.[52] Predictably, the D.C. Council soon adopted The Autonomous Vehicles Act of 2012, which saw D.C. become one of the first jurisdictions in the country to authorize the use of Level 3, Level 4, and Level 5 autonomous vehicles.[53] Despite the act's relative ambition and novelty, some people criticized it for not giving *more* latitude to companies testing advanced autonomous technologies.[54] However, it allowed AVs to move beyond geographically limited test areas and onto city streets, provided the vehicles' autonomous control could be manually overridden.[55] Local news site *DCist*, citing national polling, outlined how the new set of regulations prepared city dwellers "for a terrifying yet inevitable future where self-driving cars roam the streets."[56]

At the time, the idea of AVs was still a relative novelty. Their media presence far outweighed actual road testing or commercial deployment. Unlike their driver-operated ride-hailing counterpart, AVs were legislated ahead of time in D.C. In this sense, AV legislation did not respond primarily to urban needs; rather, it was part of a broader discourse shaping and anticipating a new kind of city. At this early stage, the most important aspect of D.C.'s legislation was that it sent a message to tech companies and other cities that D.C. wanted to be a key player in the emerging AV landscape and the corresponding phase of urban redevelopment. Though policymakers may have harbored some reservations, these were trumped by a desire to be ahead of other cities in the innovation race. As one critic named Terri (see chapter 1) told us, the city was dazzled by the potential of being a leader on both Uber and AVs: "All those hearings. Innovation, innovation! I hated that word for the longest time. . . . There wasn't a single councilmember back then that didn't get little stars in their eyes."[57] When it came to AVs, as with Uber, D.C. was eager to show it was not a regulatory dinosaur.

From 2012 on, the D.C. government, in partnership with various interest groups, companies, and business improvement districts, implemented legislation that allowed automated technologies, including AVs, to operate as freely as possible. Here, the city's peculiar political geography allowed it to maintain some advantages. As one city official explained to journalists, "Because the District operates under a single governing structure, it doesn't need to navigate state, county and local regulations to test innovative projects."[58] Instead, the official explained, "to do any of these innovative kinds of things, it really just takes the council and our mayor, and sometimes just an agency, to make it happen."[59] D.C. responded rapidly to emerging technologies and swiftly adopted regulations, sometimes with national and transnational consequences. Such nimble governing was in direct contrast to the failure of federal attempts to legislate AVs.[60] When jurisdictions like D.C. passed prototype legislation, they were not only enhancing their territorial competitiveness; they were shaping the regulatory future of AV systems.[61]

D.C.'s AV regulation in 2012 marked the beginning of an urban strategy to place the city within a growing crowd of innovation-friendly cities. In 2017, for example, D.C. joined the Bloomberg

Aspen Initiative on Cities and Autonomous Vehicles, a global network of cities working on AVs. According to Aspen's press release, D.C., alongside Helsinki, London, São Paulo, and Tel Aviv, "would marshal cutting edge data and facilitate an innovation process that helps city leaders consider the many ways this technology could solve chronic urban challenges, and improve the lives of citizens."[62] Bloomberg Philanthropies had been a key player in smart cities and AV innovation, providing large grants to cities and tech startups to promote data-driven governance initiatives.[63] These institutional and organizational gatekeepers were important not just because they managed a "flow of ideas and money"; they also propagated smart-city ideas by "mobilising particular policy interventions and exporting them to other localities."[64] In the process, such interventions would shape new realities of urban and interurban governance by leveraging new connections among cities, funding institutes, businesses, corporations, and tech start-ups as well as new technologies, Internet-connected devices, smart sensors, data analytics, and ultimately new forms of governance.

The year 2018 was a critical one for observing the effects on D.C. of the new political forms enabled by both smart-city technologies and AVs. The symbiotic, if asymmetric, relationship between the entrepreneurial city and a Silicon Valley–driven capitalism was nowhere more evident than in that year's bidding war between cities to host Amazon's second U.S.-based headquarters (commonly called HQ2). D.C.'s failed bid included $1 billion in tax breaks for Amazon, one-day permits for all major construction projects, and a dedicated Amazon ambassador position within the mayor's office to "ensure that D.C.'s executive, legislative, and regulatory arms are thinking as big as Amazon is, and swiftly enabling Amazon to create and innovate in D.C."[65] Predictably, part of this innovation involved AVs. The bid emphasized the city's regulatory innovation and its role in the Bloomberg Initiative. It also promised to partner with Amazon to pilot and deploy an AV fleet on the Amazon campus as well as throughout D.C. In its pursuit of tech-led growth, D.C. hastily reimagined its urban fabric.

The eventual failure of the Amazon HQ2 bid did not necessarily change the city's growth strategy. Indeed, the city has retained the bid's #ObviouslyDC slogan and repurposed it as a catchall phrase to invite tech companies to take up residence in the city. At the opening of Uber's Greenlight Hub for workers in Northeast D.C. in 2017, the mayor posed for photos holding a cutout sign of this very slogan.[66] While the city used the Amazon bid to showcase its economic growth strategy and attractiveness to tech capital, the mayor's office pursued other avenues too. The year 2018 included a "jobs trip" to Silicon Valley, where Mayor Bowser pitched D.C. as an ideal location for tech companies beyond Amazon and promoted the city as "the capital of inclusive innovation."[67] The jobs mission included meetings with Uber, Lyft, Boeing, Yelp, Apple, Netflix, and Cisco. During the trip, Bowser traveled San Francisco in an Uber AV and visited the Center for Automotive Research at Stanford University.[68] On her return, Bowser announced a plan to establish an interagency AV working group that would "proactively prepare the District for AV technologies."[69]

The establishment of the group was soon followed by an "Autonomous Vehicles Principles Statement" that prioritized (using these headings) "Safety," "Equity," "Efficiency," and "Sustainability."[70] The statement promoted AVs as a democratic and inclusive technology. The *Washington Post* pithily announced that the AV working group "lays out the welcome mat for self-driving cars."[71] "The District's embrace of autonomous vehicles," the article continued, is "a continuation of the city's commitment to innovation." Bowser said, "we will keep the District on the cutting edge of autonomous vehicles and do so in a way that benefits our residents."[72] But whom was the city of the future being innovated for, and who would build it? Doubts that a tech-driven growth model would benefit all residents equally did not make it onto the meeting's agenda. That agenda was set by Uber.

For almost a decade, Uber has played an important role in framing D.C.'s approach to automation. D.C. Council lobbying reports show a steady stream of meetings between Uber representatives and lobbyists and D.C. officials and legislators, especially in the years 2018 to 2020.[73] Much of this activity concerned the city's proposed Autonomous Vehicle Amendment Act of 2019. This legislation updated the original Act of 2012 by establishing an expanded set of laws around AV testing, liability, and safety standards.[74]

In January 2019, the D.C. Council's Committee on Transportation and the Environment held a public roundtable to solicit feedback about the integration of AVs in the city and to assist the council in "preparing to make that future a reality."[75] At the hearing, Uber's testimony was brief and reasserted the company's close relationship with D.C. government. Uber's representative thanked the committee chair for her leadership in passing the 2012 AV legislation and for her "consistent embrace of new kinds of technology." The city's stance on AVs, the Uber representative continued, "has really positioned D.C. as an innovation leader throughout the country."[76] The committee chair, councilmember Mary Cheh—who, perhaps not coincidentally, had helped approve Uber's foundational legislation in 2014—jokingly responded, "With that kind of testimony you can, of course, have more time."[77] Through this friendly working relationship, Uber's representative objected to proposals contained within the law "that could limit deployment and access of the many benefits of this technology for District residents."[78] Uber expressed concerns that legislative changes might impede upcoming plans to start mapping the city for AV tests.[79] Uber's representative noted that Uber and the Self-Driving Coalition for Safer Streets, a trade association representing companies that develop AV technology, had submitted model legislation.[80] This new legislation would, Uber's representative said, unleash AVs' potential while protecting it from fastidious regulators. For Uber, the current system of light AV regulation was working. But, as one D.C. official testified, that system was patchwork.[81] Ford and Argo AI were the only companies then carrying out testing in D.C., yet city officials at the hearing said they had no clear idea of how the pilot was structured, where exactly it was located, who was in charge, or even how many AVs were out there currently mapping the city.[82]

A range of other criticisms emerged at the hearing. One line of criticism focused on safety. A witness, the chair of the Trial Lawyers Association, described Uber's approach to automated driving as "reckless or worse."[83] He pointed to the March 2018 death of Elaine Herzberg, who was struck by an Uber AV in Tempe, Arizona, as evidence that AVs were not about safety but were "a profit technology."[84] Others contended that AV developers were treating D.C. residents as "guinea pigs."[85] A different witness raised concerns about the lack of firm legislation that mandated accessibility for residents with disabilities, whereas a pedestrian advocate noted that though AVs were promising, "it is not unusual for technology not to fulfill its promise."[86] Rather than place our hope in AVs, the advocate argued, we should look to approaches "that can do far more to improve safety for pedestrians and everyone else far sooner, including expanded public transit, better management, [and] more walking-friendly infrastructure."[87]

Still another line of criticism focused on the kind of politics AVs generated. One witness noted that AV pilot projects lack "transparency and adequate public involvement."[88] The AV working group was, this person pointed out, composed exclusively of representatives from government agencies with "limited input by outside stakeholders . . . [which] is unacceptable."[89] These criticisms are important because they undermine technological solutionism. They push back against the idea that AVs are, or should be, a substitute for difficult political discussions about what kind of city we want to live in and how we practice for that future. Although it had heard the misgivings of members of the public, in 2019 the D.C. Council adopted AV legislation that failed to address these concerns and contained only basic requirements for permitting.

Despite AV's pretension to being an apolitical technological solution, important questions of why AVs and for whom persist.

Their position in the vanguard of technological urban growth seems to grant them power to circumvent deep political engagement. Indeed, they are rarely, if ever, seen in terms of politics. D.C.'s interagency AV working group's long-awaited Autonomous Vehicle Study, published in April 2020, is a good example of the framework through which AVs are seen and how AVs are used to map the city's future.[90] To carry out the report, the D.C. Department of Transportation contracted D.C. Sustainable Transportation (DCST), an organization largely consisting of business improvement district (BID) representatives who were focused on making D.C. "a global leader" in sustainable transportation and run by *Greater Greater Washington* (which we discuss in chapters 1 and 3). DCST, in turn, subcontracted engineering firm AECOM to outline technical scenarios of AV usage in the city and region.[91] The resulting report detailed four scenarios for AV integration—two for low government intervention and two for high government intervention.[92] It presented AVs as an engineering problem that could be solved by leveraging the right kind of data with the right regulatory touch.

At its most optimistic, the report argued that AVs in D.C. could reshape urban transportation, reclaim land from parking, and create more green space, affordable housing, and economic growth.[93] Here the report saw AVs and other "mobility options" as not just transportation solutions but tools for cracking the affordable-housing puzzle as well.[94] The report's recommendations ranged from transportation pricing studies and electrification to workforce retraining, zoning reassessments, and data-sharing programs. Despite its attention to the mundane world of regional congestion pricing and vehicle miles traveled, the report presented a model of the future too.

These models established some basic ground rules. First, the arrival of AVs was inevitable. Second, data analysis and modeling were the correct framework for understanding AVs. Third, their effects would be transformative. Finally, only the correct kind of government intervention could ensure all D.C. residents would benefit. Such recommendations seem sensible but also established a new kind of expertise and common sense, one that Uber was sure to cheer. Meanwhile, more basic questions around AVs hung awkwardly in the air: When are they coming? Who will own them? Who benefits from them? How, precisely, will they solve the city's housing crisis? Or why are we even talking about AVs in the first place?

Technology's Promise

It is worth asking, what is wrong with an AV engineer's view of the world? What if engineering can solve urban problems like transit and housing affordability? Improving urban life will surely require inventive technologies. The problem is what we lose when we see the city solely as a technical problem that can be solved by technological rather than political means.

An example of how automated technology powerfully reframes political problems as technical ones unfolded with D.C.'s delivery robots. In 2017, the city became the first in the nation to pilot food-delivery robots.[95] The city's specific abundance of sidewalks and residential neighborhoods made it an ideal candidate. More important than the city's layout was its inviting regulatory landscape and the ready availability of gig-economy companies like Uber, DoorDash, and Postmates with which it could partner. Council-member Mary Cheh, introducing the Personal Delivery Device Pilot Program, remarked: "I do want D.C. to be the first. . . . I want Washington to be known for innovation and progress."[96] The legislation, delivered to the D.C. Council by a robot that navigated a throng of journalists with the help of a young technician, allowed for the testing of delivery robots on city streets and sidewalks.[97] AV robots—white, knee-high, six-wheeled, and about the size of a picnic cooler—would carry out test delivery programs in two approved locations. "Cutting edge," "innovative," and "cute" was how Cheh described the robots to the press.[98] As a media event, the adoption of robot legislation was a resounding success.

FIGURE 4.1. Starship delivery robot on a D.C. sidewalk, 2017. Reproduced with Attribution-ShareAlike 2.0 Generic license (CC BY-SA 2.0) by Elvert Barnes.

Starship Technologies, a company led by Skype's cofounders and whose tech credentials ran deep, operated the robots. Starship championed a commonsense view of urban problems that was not much different from that of Uber. As Starship's chief operating officer told the *Washington Post*: "You can engineer yourself out of any situation. That's the philosophy of this company."[99] Supporters echoed that sentiment, suggesting that robots could solve a range of urban issues. Robots could address sustainability issues arising from costly and polluting automobile delivery though "clean, efficient, green robots."[100] One tech website went as far as to suggest that delivery robots could offer a solution to the entrenched problem of "food deserts" in D.C.'s economically and racially segregated landscape.[101] The article followed D.C. resident Yvonne Smith, who was priced out of her Capitol Hill home when rapid gentrification saw rents soar. Smith moved across the river to Ward 8, where she found herself bereft of healthy food options within walking distance.[102] But, the article claimed, Starship's delivery robots would make Smith's move less disruptive and eliminate food deserts across the city. The idea is not a unique one; it has persisted through media reports, think-tank documents, and city-planning roundtables that treat technology and the gig economy as meaningful portals to food access.[103]

In recent years, companies like Starship have targeted college and corporate campuses and not, in fact, neighborhoods like Yvonne's.[104] An engineering solution to "food deserts" remains blue-sky thinking. Still, D.C. has become a regulatory model in the robotic realm. Two years after it approved the original pilot program, the D.C. Council adopted the Personal Delivery Device Act of 2018, which removed geographic limits and opened the city to a "robot invasion."[105] Starship's U.S. head of public affairs, David Catania, a former D.C. Council member, pointed out that six states had recently passed legislation that "all have their genesis in this District statute."[106]

In some respects, the appeal of robotic-delivery legislation is understandable. Robotic delivery seems like a practical, commonsense solution to precisely the problem facing residents like Yvonne: get food to where it is needed, efficiently and cheaply. Yet we do a disservice to Yvonne to frame her problem as simply one of access to food. It is a problem connected to housing affordability, to gentrification, to public transit, and to decades of disinvestment in neighborhoods where food access is only one of many issues. Robotic delivery is a post facto solution to problems that extend into the realm of public policy. How, for example, might a technological solution have intervened to make Yvonne's life better *before* she was priced out of her home? These questions lie outside the realm of engineering, in the messy realm of urban politics.

Robotic legislation is low-hanging fruit that generates good publicity. It allows issues like housing affordability and food access to be approached as technical problems, an inefficiency in a system that has absentmindedly located people too far from food. It doesn't have to be this way. We have other tools available. As historian Peter Norton argues, "When we rescue innovation from the technofuturists and recover the tools they have dismissed, we will find that we can do today, at far less cost, what they have promised to deliver for unlimited dollars at an ever-receding future date."[107] We can prioritize food provision, public transport, public housing, and, so much more. To do so, however, requires that we raise our expectations regarding what democratic politics can accomplish.

In many ways, technology's most seductive promise is that it allows us to escape from politics. Tech companies like Uber promise to deliver that future, the same way they deliver everything else, and city governments have doubled down on this promise. As a result, there is a democratic deficit in technocratic policymaking processes, which has been described as "the crisis of consensus."[108] Automation discourse in D.C. can be seen as a variety of what political theorist Langdon Winner calls "technological somnambulism": the way that "we so willingly sleepwalk through the process of reconstituting the conditions of human existence."[109] Winner suggests that we develop a thoroughly democratic version of technology, one in which we go beyond the idea of arguing about whether technology needs *more* regulation and instead see technology itself as a form of regulation, as a politics. This view of technology as politics is helpful when we are thinking about what AVs do in D.C. The dominant approach to AVs is to frame them as apolitical, as a solution that elides politics. That view is not "sleepwalking" precisely, nor is it apolitical, though it may present itself as such. AVs are a very real type of politics that prioritize certain types of growth, certain types of practices, and certain types of solutions. The result of automation in cities is policies that privilege "technological needs, capacities, and priorities in urban governance."[110] Those policies have profoundly uneven geographies, as people, problems, and places that lie outside technology's scope get left behind.

The City of the Future, Today

AV discourse in D.C. claims that AVs would create a safer, more equitable, more efficient, and more sustainable city. In this sense, AVs contain a promise to create a better city and constitute a social expectation. Such claims shape urban applications, steer public and private investment, and influence the construction of markets and forms of regulation.[111] But how do we evaluate such future claims, especially in a realm where our ability to judge their success is continually deferred to the next technological improvement? Automation's futuristic urban imaginary must inevitably be grounded in the messy complexity of the actual cities with which it interacts.[112] One way to assess what AVs do is to look at how such technologies currently function across a range of geographic places and scales. The question that AV projects must answer is, according to urban scholars Rachel Macrorie, Simon Marvin, and Aidan While, whether they are "enabling metropolitan transformation across urban geographies" or leading to "enclaves of experimentation and premium service delivery."[113]

To see how and where AVs interact with D.C.'s material landscape, we turn to a 2018 announcement about a pilot project from the mayoral administration of Muriel Bowser and the Southwest Business Improvement District (SWBID). The project was on 10th Street Southwest in an area called the Wharf, which is a multibillion-dollar waterfront redevelopment project and a flagship of the city's twenty-first-century development plans.[114] In an announcement for the new project, the head of the SWBID described the area as "in the midst of a renaissance."[115] The goal was to use AVs to connect the area to the National Mall. Because the Wharf lacked a Metro stop, the project was framed as a first mile–last mile solution. The SWBID's stated hope was to use AVs to create "mobility solutions," ultimately creating "an interconnected, sustainable community."[116]

A year later, the SWBID announced another forward-looking project: a Mobility Innovation District, which would position the business improvement district as a local and national leader for transportation innovation.[117] According to the SWBID, what differentiated the Mobility Innovation District from other projects was its "focus on the transition between today and the future."[118] Projects like this one hinted at the multi-scalar way in which futuristic transportation options were mobilized in D.C. Both within the city and between cities, AV policy reflected a fight to attract investment.

AVs, like all kinds of existing or proposed forms of transit, are closely linked to a particular kind of urban real-estate development.[119] Rather than transforming the city's fabric, automated services are part of D.C.'s amenity wars, "a high-end arms race between developers to see who can offer the most enticing perks for would-be residents."[120] In D.C., those perks have meant rooftop pools, gyms, gleaming common areas and party rooms, dog-walking services, and yoga studios. As the city's demographic and socioeconomic transformation continues apace and competition increases in the luxury rental market, technology is increasingly a means of cornering rent.[121] The results are automated grocery stores and smart apartments but also Uber waiting rooms[122] and, in the case of The Yards, a dedicated, if ultimately unsuccessful, AV transport system.

In February 2021 and in partnership with The Yards luxury apartment buildings, AV developer Optimus Ride debuted its driverless vehicles.[123] Optimus Ride's service was exclusively for apartment residents. In essence, though the company carried out some public relations during the pandemic by delivering food supplies, Optimus Ride was a privatized, tech-driven transport system in a rapidly transforming part of the city. Less than a year after they had begun, however, the rides stopped; Optimus Ride suffered a fate similar to that of Uber's AV division and was sold off.[124] Optimus Ride's experience raises an important question about the fate of privately operated transit options when the operating companies are shut down or bought: Who is responsible for maintaining the service?

The limited reality of these experiments is a far cry from Uber's vision of AVs seamlessly filling gaps in the city's public-transport network. If, as sociologist Sharon Zukin and architectural critic Michael Sorkin famously claimed, gentrification leads to the Disneyfication of the city, then AVs are the ultimate theme-park ride.[125] When viewed in the light of D.C.'s rapidly gentrifying urban landscape,[126] it is hard to avoid the conclusion that automation is not transforming the city but reinforcing its geographically uneven development.

Urban Utopias

Utopia has, as social theorist Fredric Jameson wrote, always been a political issue.[127] It has also been a geographic issue. Utopia is a translation of two Greek words meaning "not" and "place"—essentially nowhere—referring to an imaginary perfect society and place in Sir Thomas More's sixteenth-century text *Utopia*.[128] The utopia of the automated city, however, is resolutely somewhere. In this case, that somewhere is D.C., a city with its own history, geography, struggles, and inequalities. In D.C., a city built on a nineteenth-century utopian plan, AVs are part of a long line of urban utopian projects proffered up by new forms of economic organization.[129] They stand as the newest harbingers of a utopian urban program for the twenty-first century. Automation discourse fuels speculation both figurative and financial, rearranges governance, and creates new sites of technical, social, and political experimentation in D.C. In other words, the visions of an automated future, as varied and ambiguous as they sometimes appear, do heavy political work.

Uber's utopian vision, as deployed and embraced in D.C., has been a resolutely abstract one and characteristic of general smart-city narratives. This abstractness has been a result of the speculative nature of much of the technology, but it has also been a result of how automation discourse understands technological progress and its impacts on cities. For geographer David Bissell, popular automation discourse tends to reinforce a technologically deter-minist account of progress "where the location and operation of power is typically displaced to the technologies themselves, with-out due consideration of the possibility of a more complex range of forces at play, including the institutional interests which might be guiding these developments."[130] As a result, automation initiatives, and the smart city with which they are fundamentally linked, are characterized by a utopian form of abstractness.[131] Cities are con-ceived of as blank slates onto which these data technologies can be applied.[132] The automated city becomes a universal imaginary, where powerful actors and institutions seek to "plug their model of smartness into existing places, produce a type of 'generic space' and push a common narrative of the smart city."[133] If cities are seen as generic, then urban solutions and policies also become generic. AVs, like smart cities, are universalized as utopian strategy.

AVs, as utopian vehicles, manifest as an abstract technical solu-tion, a free-floating set of expectations. But AVs must be viewed firmly in the realm of politics and place. As much as they propose certain visions of *the* city, they work to change *a* city. They focus our attention on certain processes and people at the expense of others, all the while attempting to smooth rough edges to make cities more amenable to new and ever-expanding processes of urban growth and real estate development. Smart-city projects and Uber itself have generated publicity and immense goodwill by framing themselves as utopian answers. In this sense, perhaps the ultimate fix offered by automation is a utopian one: a reassurance that cities can solve long-standing issues and usher in a new world in one fell technological swoop. The tech utopia of Uber promises us a city of the future, but it seeks to hide the messy urban politics of the present.

Buying into Uber's utopian vision of an automated city has con-sequences for people and for democratic urban life. This "utopia" is one without politics and without accountability. Though it offers the ability to transcend politics and remake the city, it reflects and strengthens current inequalities. And Uber's vision involves seeing things like food deserts not as symptoms of structural inequality that can be addressed through the political process or by mobilizing those affected but as simply a glitch that can be repaired with the correct application of technology. As enticing as it is for so many people, this vision must not be accepted unthinkingly. The stakes for life in the city are too high.

5

The Uber Workplace

"IT JUST IS WHAT IT IS"

> The pressures of life in a capitalist urban environment leave less time for nurturing bonds with family and friends, let alone creating new ties with strangers. Yet in order to change the balance of power in the contested urban environment, what is precisely needed is to create networks with people who were once strangers but could become allies and even friends.
>
> **—GEOGRAPHER AMANDA HURON**[1]

> I've never met another Uber driver face-to-face . . . I see them on the streets, and I see them in the airport lots, but I don't have any real interest in socializing with other Uber drivers. Partly I think that—and I don't know this—but partly I think that I'm, hm, how to say this? Overqualified for the job.
>
> **—MARK, AN UBER DRIVER**[2]

When we first met Joan[3] in 2016, she was hardly new to the "side hustle." Single, college-educated, and a mother in her late forties, she had left a decently paying job in video production to be a public-school bus driver. Even though it paid less, she needed a more stable schedule to care for her young son. Being a bus driver meant that she wouldn't have to hire a babysitter whenever work ran late into the evenings. And it came with medical and dental insurance. As she explained to us: "I think that's what sucked me in, what kept me. The benefits. Because the benefits are excellent."[4] Her paycheck covered her mortgage in a D.C. suburb but not much else. To supplement her income she often collected free items from Craigslist on weekends and resold them on eBay or at flea markets. She could usually make $75 each week, which was enough to pay for groceries or to put gas into her car.

Though Joan liked her schedule as a bus driver, her income was unpredictable. She had to be on-call during the school day but was paid only for the specific shifts she actually worked, which often totaled as few as twenty-five hours per week. For years, her income oscillated between $32,000 and $38,000. So in 2015, when she heard radio commercials about working for Uber, the new ride-hailing giant, she was curious: "Hmm, turn on the app and work whenever you want? Hmm, okay. . . . So that's why I decided to try it."[5]

Joan's seven-year-old sedan initially qualified for Uber, which was good news. But, within a year of working on the platform, she hit a pothole and damaged the car's suspension. Then came the bad news. She didn't have enough money to fix the car. If she continued to drive for Uber, she worried, the car's condition would lead to bad ratings from passengers worried about safety. Enough bad ratings would result in her being suspended from the platform (or "deactivated," in Uber-speak). As credit-card debt and late fees on her utility bills began to pile up, she signed up for Uber's leasing program and started leasing a new Nissan sedan.[6] Although the Uber leasing program had lower credit barriers compared to traditional lenders, the payments that the company automatically deducted from her paychecks were significant.[7] Each week, she paid Uber $138, more than the national lease average of $100.[8]

She also had to pay monthly commercial auto-insurance fees of $200, which meant that her monthly expenses for this side hustle totaled $752—*before* other expenses like gas, cleanings, and Uber's booking fees and 25 percent commission.

Joan began to drive for Uber on the weekends and after her regular job (making for sixteen-hour workdays). She focused on parts of the Maryland suburbs where she knew the bus service was "lacking."[9] But, after driving six or seven days a week, she realized she was barely covering the lease, was behind on other bills, and was exhausted. She quit Uber, returned the car, and described a feeling of relief: "Once I did that, I kind of felt free."[10]

Still, Joan spoke highly of gig-economy work and the ride-hailing industry. She never had illusions about her job as an Uber driver or expected it to be more than a "side hustle." When her son, who worked part-time as a shuttle driver for an office complex, signed up to work for grocery-delivery service Instacart in 2020, she didn't try to stop him. The gig economy was certainly not above criticism. But she was more critical of those workers who had outsized expectations about the jobs. As she explained to us: "I feel like the people who make a career out of the gig economy are messing it up. . . . If you made it your nine-to-five, then sometimes I think you should just kind of accept what happens . . . *It is what it is.*"[11]

During the COVID-19 pandemic, Joan's views largely remained the same. As someone who had traveled as a union delegate to Boston in 2018 for the fiftieth anniversary of the Memphis sanitation workers' strike, issues of workplace safety were important to her. But, for her, gig-economy work was different. If Uber drivers were taking on exposures to the coronavirus, at least they were getting paid. What other choice did they have? Joan said, "It's a trade-off. Are you going to risk your health to pay the bills, or are you gonna sit home and wait for some [government aid]?"[12] The forty-three drivers we interviewed and surveyed for this book frequently painted the workplace much as Joan did: Uber might not be great, but neither were the other jobs they had or thought they could get.[13] For one driver, Ajay, working for a gig-economy company meant squaring his expectations with his reality. He said:

> I have two boys. I'm divorced. And [Uber] gives me a chance to kind of be [around] for them—during the summers, for example—and work around the schedule that is more amenable to being a single dad. . . . The only thing that's lacking is the kind of transparency in how they determine fares in your pay. So, in that way, they're doing the same thing as every other employer in the United States, which is wage stagnation for the sake of Wall Street, you know what I mean? There's no raise that I've seen . . . I wasn't expecting to make the kind of money that I did in consulting. So, it didn't fail my expectations. . . . *It just is what it is* . . . I think, though, that Uber is probably symbolic of a lot of the kind of work environment we're in now. I see it increasingly moving toward that, even with professional services: you do things on a contract basis and have your own health insurance and not much job security.[14]

Another driver said that complaining about this job was like "going to work for Chuck E. Cheese and expecting them to buy [you] a car."[15] A second driver echoed this belief: "If you don't understand what it means to be an independent contractor, don't do it, and don't complain about it if you *do* do it. I find that those people are . . . I think it's weak to complain about that sort of issue."[16] Wishing for a minimum wage, a third driver suggested, was "greedy and kind of lazy."[17]

In our previous chapters, D.C., its policymakers, and their policies have been the protagonists in the stories we tell about regulation, racism, data, and automation. Here, the city and its policymakers are largely offstage. This chapter is about workers in the gig economy, their conceptions of work, and where those conceptions lead. Drivers provide a window into how Uber contributes to, and benefits from, a set of lowered expectations about work. They also provide a window into how those committed to a different kind of city might attempt to raise such expectations.

As the comments from people like Joan and Ajay indicate, drivers come into the Uber workplace with deeply held convictions and beliefs about fairness, power, and justice. These expectations are shaped by a variety of factors, including broader shifts in the bargaining power of workers. Though the Great Recession (2007–2011) provided key ingredients for the rise of Uber—mass unemployment and underemployment, fiscal austerity politics, increased inequality, and a shrinking middle class—the platform's wide adoption can also be traced to decades-long trends in wage stagnation and the repression of organized labor.[18] Since the 1970s, the retreat of the welfare state, attacks on the public sector, and the adoption of neoliberal policies like outsourcing and privatization have contributed to the increasing flexibility of labor and the long-term evisceration of workers' rights.[19] This assault on workers (accomplished by both governments and private companies) has given rise to a contingent workforce—including Uber's—that is accustomed to having little power in the workplace and little hope for improving the situation.

Low Expectations of This Job and Each Other

If the Uber drivers who spoke with us expected little from the job, they expected even less from their peers. Suzanna, a widowed Uber driver, had worked for years as a freelance writer and editor of a financial news service. During the Great Recession, she was laid off and then was shocked that she could not find other employment. She spent the next few years taking care of her sick father and helping her mother run, and then close, a kids' furniture store. As a single parent of a child with special needs, she appreciated the flexibility that Uber offered. At the same time, she told us she would be terrified if Uber were her only source of income; on weekdays she was a contract inspector for home foreclosures. In describing the Uber workplace, she talked as much about herself as she did the plight of other drivers. She said:

You'd be better off working at McDonald's. . . . Unless you're smart enough to work the rules that [Uber has] laid out. . . . People that are not smart are really getting taken advantage of, and they don't think about the expensive operating costs. Somebody that is buying a car to do Uber has already lost money. If you don't need the car anyway, don't buy it for this. I resent that they're encouraging people to lease cars to do Uber. I really resent that they're taking advantage of people in that way. And they're taking advantage of these non-English-speaking drivers who go through all the trouble of getting on the system, get a car to get on the system, and then they're out in a week. I really resent that they're taking advantage of those people. It pisses me off. It doesn't affect me, but it pisses me off. I don't know how you prevent that. . . . They can't really have a test to allow people to drive. It's not practical. But I resent that they're encouraging all these people to do it when they're not going to make it.[20]

Though Suzanna felt pity for other drivers, especially immigrant drivers, it didn't necessarily come from a place of solidarity. Drivers like Suzanna repeatedly discussed other workers on the Uber platform not as fellow workers with something in common but unknowing pawns to be pitied.[21]

This lack of mutuality expressed itself not only in the form of pity but also in the twin sentiment of superiority. Forty-five percent of the drivers who spoke with us mentioned specifically how intelligent *they* were—intelligent enough, each said, to defeat Uber's complex and ever-changing maze of rules and outcompete other drivers. One driver, Rick, who worked full-time in sales and reported a household income of $180,000 in 2018, demonstrated this perspective:

I don't want an hourly wage, because I think I can do better than the average driver. Because I consider myself smarter and more efficient with my time. I don't want somebody to say,

"All right, we're going to pay for your gas and give you $20 an hour base," because I'd rather take that gamble.[22]

Drivers acknowledged many risks involved in the Uber workplace but described themselves as somehow exceptional: they believed that they had figured out how to make money while, they suspected, many others had not. Unlike other drivers, they were smart. The language of smart went to work in the driver workplace (see chapter 3). This smartness meant minimizing dead miles, calculating expenses, tracking hourly pay, and driving when fares were surging—most often when demand for rides was high and the supply of drivers was low.

The inability of many drivers to see other drivers as more than victims who lacked the intelligence to make Uber work for them, or competitors to beat, reinforced the reality of a workplace defined by isolation. As one driver, Joe (introduced in chapter 3)—who, when he first spoke with us, had worked on the Uber platform for more than a year—noted: "There's not a lot of camaraderie among Uber drivers. When you're out here, they'll cut you off just as quick and easy as a taxi driver will. There's not really a community. . . . You'll see that, for the most part, there's nothing that really brings them together."[23]

For some drivers, isolation and the lack of camaraderie in the workplace was a perk. Mark, who lived in a wealthy suburb of northern Virginia, said:

I've never met another Uber driver face-to-face . . . I see them on the streets, and I see them in the airport lots, but I don't have any real interest in socializing with other Uber drivers. Partly I think that—and I don't know this—but partly I think that I'm, hm, how to say this? Overqualified for the job.[24]

Three years later, we spoke with Mark again, and he was still working more than twenty hours a week on the platform to supplement his $100,000 salary from another job. When asked whether he now knew any other drivers, he again reiterated his preference for isolation:

> I don't need friends. I'm not looking for friends in the Uber driver community. But I've helped a number of them out. Sometimes I've been in the [airport parking] lot and they've come over and talked to me and asked, "How are you doing? What are you finding?" And I always try to help them out.[25]

For Mark, the atomization of the Uber workplace was not a problem. Perhaps unsurprisingly, his views on unions and other worker actions followed from that fact. When asked whether he thought Uber drivers should unionize, he told us: "It seems like the age when unions had power is gone, and I don't see it ever coming back. So trying to form a union and get power for drivers collectively—I just don't think that makes much sense."[26]

Even if Mark were open to building relations with other drivers, the lack of a centralized location in D.C. (like a factory floor or a bus hub) posed a barrier by making it difficult for drivers to connect with each other. Though Uber once operated a service center for drivers in downtown D.C., in 2016 this office had moved fifteen miles away, to Forestville, Maryland. In late 2017, a new office for drivers, called a Greenlight Hub, opened near the Northeast D.C. neighborhood of Benning Heights (see chapter 1). This hub, which the company says is useful for drivers to get answers to questions, might have seemed like a place where Uber drivers could connect with each other. But our visits to these sites suggest otherwise: surveillance (in the form of security cameras) was heavy, and peer-to-peer conversation was minimal.

Little about the Uber platform seems designed to physically bring drivers together or socially foster collaboration. Indeed, all evidence suggests the opposite. As our research found, Uber drivers not only do not know peers on the platform when starting out[27] but also do not meet peers in the course of everyday work. Seventy-eight percent of the forty drivers we interviewed in 2016 said they had *never* had a meal or drink with another Uber driver. They did not chat with other drivers in online forums. They did not text them. They did not say hello if they saw another driver at a gas station. We found a similar situation three years later, in 2019: Thirty-three percent of the drivers who spoke with us still did not know any other current or former Uber drivers. Another 27 percent knew only one current or former driver.

Uber's algorithmic management of workers also entrenches physical and social distance between drivers through its dynamic pricing schemes that pit drivers against each other and reward drivers differently based on a complex and often invisible system of sticks and carrots.[28] Where drivers are required to engage in a zero-sum competition for passengers, and where they are rewarded for being the quickest to respond to an incentive scheme, Uber drivers are less likely to see each other as coworkers than they are to see each other as competitors or, in some instances, as naïve casualties. One driver, Noam, claimed that the resulting isolation of drivers was precisely Uber's goal. When we spoke with Noam, he had just moved to D.C. from Penang, in Malaysia. According to him, D.C.-based Uber drivers were especially isolated. This atomization, he argued, was intentional:

> Well, in the United States, here's my cynical theory about this. In the United States—because to be an Uber driver is to be kind of exploited by Uber—to have them all connected like in Penang would probably cause them to be easier to unionize, create lawsuits, and put more pressure on Uber to create employees . . . and so I think that's probably something they foresaw when they were planning, when they brought Uber to D.C. or to Baltimore. They said, "Yeah, we gotta make sure they don't know each other, that we just keep funneling them through the farm, so to speak."[29]

Although it is hard to verify Noam's account of Penang, his larger point is an important one. To the extent that the company can make sure its drivers "don't know each other," Uber invariably limits the possibilities for collective action.[30] Mark, whom we quoted earlier, expanded on this point. Although virulently anti-union, he was quick to admit that the very structure of Uber's work made such efforts difficult. The problem was not simply America's culture of "every man for himself," as he put it, but the platform itself:

> [There] have been attempts at informal strikes, even in the D.C. market. There was one organized, and they promoted the heck out of it everywhere, trying to get a strike. But no one, no other driver, knows if you go online or not. It's not enforceable, you know what I'm saying? In a steel plant . . . you have to scab, you have to cross a picket line.[31]

As Mark argued, the nature of the work, and the ability of drivers to log in and log out anonymously, militates against the very types of collective actions that have long defined unions and long been central to winning improved working conditions. Rather than picketing a factory, fighting Uber requires picketing an algorithm.[32]

The socio-spatial isolation of the Uber workplace seems to have two related goals: to keep Uber drivers as strangers to one another and to keep them in the dark. Not all the drivers who spoke with us fully understood the rules or policies of the platform, a fact that in itself represented a significant barrier to worker power and solidarity. Of the drivers we interviewed, 38 percent said they did not know how Uber determined the amount of pay they took home on a single fare (whether, for instance, the booking fee is removed before or after Uber takes its commission). A majority said they did not know whether they were required to buy commercial insurance or how to report their pay and expenses on their tax return. One driver, Enrique, said:

> If you ask any driver—if you ask any Uber driver right now— when they signed up, did they know how much they were going to get paid per mile? They will say, "No." . . . They actually don't know the terms. They don't know how much they get paid per mile.[33]

Another driver put it this way: the Uber workplace is a system of "smoke and mirrors."[34] The fluctuating algorithms on which pay is based and the numerous expenses drivers must deduct made it difficult for all the drivers who talked to us to make sense of their overall compensation. One expert on the ride-hailing industry estimates that calculating drivers' earnings requires no fewer than twenty pieces of information.[35] But the rules and details of work for Uber change, sometimes hourly. Since it has been operating in D.C., Uber has reduced its base rate for drivers several times, added a rider safety fee (and then increased it, calling it a booking fee), raised the commission it takes from new drivers, and then eliminated the commission structure altogether. Today, there is no clear relationship between a passenger's fare and a driver's pay.

In the Uber workplace, there is no break room or water cooler to serve as a gathering place. Drivers are inaccessible and often invisible to one another. There are no visual markings beyond small stickers or dashboard lights, because most drivers use their own cars. The lack of physical space in which platform workers meet or congregate creates a material barrier to forming collective identities and deeply shapes possibilities for meaningful notions of collective consciousness among workers.[36] Suzanna, whom we quoted earlier, explained to us: "It's really, really difficult to organize a group of drivers like this. Because, even with all the online resources . . . there is no place you can go, like a workplace, where you can reach people."[37] Put differently, there is no obvious place where you can turn a stranger into someone for whom you do the hard work of caring, trusting, and building collective expectations. She continued, "If someone really wanted to organize and had the money and the time," then they could "hang out in the parking lots at the airport."[38] To build any sense of solidarity, she said in a separate interview, "you have to go to places where drivers hang out."[39] And, in D.C., finding other Uber drivers means hanging out at the airport.

Agency at the Airport

Since Uber's arrival in D.C., the only place where drivers in the region have regularly assembled en masse is the city's airport (which, technically, is located in Arlington, Virginia, on the other side of the Potomac River). In 2016, ten of the forty drivers with whom we spoke brought up the uniqueness of the airport parking lot as a place where they could actually see and sometimes speak with other drivers. In 2019, a similar story emerged among six of the thirty drivers we reinterviewed and all three of the new drivers we interviewed. In 2020, even with COVID-19's impact on the city, the airport remained important to how drivers discussed the workplace with us. How the airport came to be a site of worker agency and struggles over power in the Uber workplace begins with the spatial strategies of a related set of workers: taxi drivers.

After Uber won permission to pick up passengers[40] at the D.C. airport in late 2015, taxi drivers, who had priority access to ride requests at the airport, went on the offensive. They argued that ride-hailing drivers should undergo the same inspections and pay the same permit fees that taxi drivers did. They also argued that ride-hailing drivers should have to wait off-site for passengers. The airport and Uber acquiesced on the latter issue, added a $4 per-trip fee for Uber rides (which later rose to $5), and designated a parking lot for ride-hailing cars. While taxi drivers get to wait for rides in two lanes outside the baggage-claim level of the airport, platform drivers wait in an off-site lot. This "For Hire Vehicle Staging Lot" was moved in 2017 to a new site and in 2018 to a different site,[41] which saw more than three hundred cars enter the parking lot each hour. The number of daily vehicle trips was nearly eleven thousand, which prompted the county to install, at a cost of $45,000, a traffic signal just outside the wire-fenced lot. Notably, the triangular lot was sandwiched between two major roads and a budget hotel. These material contours make the lot an island of sorts, just the kind of space that could allow unsupervised and uninterrupted alliances between workers to blossom.

To manage the queue of drivers at the airport waiting lot, Uber adopted a geospatial data tool called geo-fencing. Geo-fencing is a virtual boundary for a real-world geographic area—in this case, an airport parking lot. This algorithmic management tool serves as a way of keeping track of and sorting data—in this case, spatial and temporal information about how ride requests should be dispatched. Uber uses a first-in, first-out (FIFO) system to create a *virtual queue* so that it can keep track of which drivers have been waiting the longest. What this virtual queue means is that drivers can park, get out of their cars, stretch, and not lose their place in line. Geo-fencing also is a key means of allowing Uber to control what drivers do and, most importantly, *where* they can be.

For some drivers, geo-fencing also created opportunities. One driver, Enrique, an immigrant from South America and a father of four without a college degree whom we quoted earlier, told us he liked to go to the geo-fenced airport parking lot. By parking in the same physical space—the airport—hour after hour and day after day, he could loiter in the lot and share strategies. Many drivers felt there was much to discuss and commiserate.

Over time, Enrique felt tricked by the company into working for lower and lower pay. And he was angry about it. Soon, he and the other drivers realized that Uber's dynamic pricing[42] could be "gamed from below" in the geo-fenced airport parking lot. (Gamification-from-below is a refusal of the ordinary rhythms for labor control.[43]) This strategy rested on understanding what makes the Uber workplace unique. When a customer requests an Uber, a driver appears not only "just in time" but also "just in place."[44] At the airport, Uber's reliance on a "just in place" labor regime was obvious and, eventually, subject to contestation.

Enrique and dozens of his peers would regularly turn off their Uber apps just as a large flight was arriving to the airport.[45] Though he and his peers would lose their place in line for ride requests, they hoped to secure higher pay by artificially manufacturing a mismatch between the demand for rides and the supply of available drivers.[46] To "rebalance" its system, Uber's algorithms and its

analysts would offer bonuses—sometimes as high as $30 a ride—
to encourage more drivers to head toward the airport waiting
lot.[47] Through this strategy, Enrique told us, he had been able to
increase his pay on a regular basis. Despite the extreme isolation
of the Uber workplace, the waiting lot fostered the connections
between drivers that formed the beginnings of worker agency.

It is important to note these practices of worker agency were
undertaken largely by workers of color. We found evidence that
the waiting lot is frequently seen as a place for non-White drivers.
One White driver, Dwayne (introduced in chapter 3), referred
to the space as a "refugee camp."[48] Sung-ho, an immigrant from
South Korea (introduced in chapter 4), said it was often filled with
"a lot of Muslim guys" who "wash each other's feet."[49] Discussions
in the online forum UberPeople.net reinforce these representations, with frequent derogatory comments about the lot being a
"Pig Pen."[50]

The airport is not only unique as a racialized and contested
place. It is also a situated and highly differentiated place where
persistent, voluminous demand for chauffer services has merited
coordinated operations with airport authorities. Had Uber drivers
not been cordoned off and geo-fenced, and had they not managed to rework Uber's dynamic pricing system, it is unlikely that
drivers—like Enrique—would have come together in 2019 in a
historic strike.

The Strike

On the evening of May 8, 2019, drivers around the world—in Nai-
robi, Lagos, Paris, Glasgow, São Paolo, Dayton, Brisbane, and tens
of other cities—demonstrated against Uber's poor working conditions. It was the eve of the company's initial public offering on the
New York Stock Exchange. At D.C.'s National Airport, roughly
forty drivers disrupted inbound traffic. For about twenty minutes, they slowly circled the airport's arrival lanes in their vehicles
while honking horns in unison. About twenty-five supporters and

FIGURE 5.1. Airport protest against Uber, May 8, 2019. Reproduced with permission by Jordan Pascale.

reporters, including two authors of this book, gathered nearby with signs ("Honk for living wages, overtime pay, benefits!") and cheers. Building on ongoing media coverage and political debate[51] on the nature of work in the gig economy, drivers' messages juxtaposed Uber's alleged $82 billion valuation with stories of drivers making below minimum wage, living in their cars, and burdened with predatory auto leases. Airport police, who unsuccessfully requested help from protestors to coordinate the protest (via Facebook messages), eventually diverted the striking vehicles.

A taxi driver later called the event a "fake strike."[52] To some extent, he was right. The driver action was not a work stoppage in a traditional sense.[53] Even those Uber drivers in the D.C. area who participated did so with limited commitment. Indeed, at the end of the rally, several striking drivers turned on their apps to pick up their next passenger. The workers' action did not create a visible picket line whereby workers could shame those who broke rank (though there was online evidence of customer shaming). The action did not erect a notable barrier to traffic on the city's main thoroughfares, as taxi drivers did when they protested the local government's lackadaisical regulation of Uber in June and October 2014 (see chapter 1). Neither did the action directly confront Uber at its company offices or disrupt the operations of any of its regulatory bodies.

On the other hand, the strike was remarkable in several ways. It was last-minute. It was well-covered in the media. And it overcame one of the fundamental conditions of the Uber workplace: the socio-spatial atomization of workers. The Uber rally was evidence of drivers exercising agency—and raising expectations—at new scales and places.[54] To Enrique, the strike was a step in the right direction: "What we accomplished, it was not big. But it sent a message."[55] The airport parking lot became a workplace where the "just-in-place" worker could, at least for a time, challenge such emplacement and exercise collective agency by reworking Uber's dynamic pricing system and protesting Uber's IPO.[56] The strikes were first initiated by San Jose's Gig Workers Rising, Los Angeles's Rideshare Drivers United, and New York's Taxi Workers Alliance, but they far exceeded those cities. Technology—in the form of Facebook advertisements, Twitter posts, text messages, and emails—allowed immense, last-minute coordination from places as varied as Toledo, Ohio, and Wellington, New Zealand.[57] The drivers' action linked together disparate workers from separate geographies around a set of collective grievances and hopes.[58] In D.C., organizers had decided (in a WhatsApp group) to participate just five days prior to the day of action. It was the first—and so far, only—action by the fledgling group, a mix of Latino and immigrant drivers and young, mostly White professionals from the D.C. chapter of the Democratic Socialists of America.

Perhaps the best evidence that the strike was successful or had potential was Uber's response. Prior to the workers' action, the Washington Metropolitan Airport Authority police generally came to the ride-hail waiting lot in small groups of three or four to make sure that drivers' cars had platform stickers displayed, as required by local regulation.[59] More importantly, these police would ask to see drivers' phones so that they could check to make sure a ride-hailing application was turned on. Such a surveillance tactic, which may seem odd, is the way airport police had decided to monitor drivers in the lot and ensure that individuals were not loitering. Following the action, D.C.-area Uber drivers noticed a change in the policing of the airport parking lot. The number of police seemed to double. And the police seemed to linger. As Enrique reported, one evening, six officers showed up at six o'clock and stayed for forty minutes. At eight that evening, a different set of six officers arrived. This time they stayed for an hour and a half. At eleven, the officers who arrived stayed even longer.[60]

What happened a few days later was more significant: a local journalist arrived with cameras to ask drivers how they had manipulated Uber's dynamic pricing system. Enrique and other drivers told us they believed that Uber had tipped off the journalist in an effort to turn back the goodwill that Uber drivers had amassed in the preceding week from the global strikes. Several drivers—some of whom would later regret it—showed the journalist how they could turn off and on their apps in unison to increase earnings.

The journalist's story about the collective manipulation of surge pricing aired just eight days after the strike, on May 16, 2019. Immediately, Uber put a cap on the amount that drivers could earn through a surge in the airport parking lot.[61] The local media, in lockstep with the company, turned drivers—who, only the prior week, had been seen as heroic—into greedy villains. Uber then used one of its favorite tactics: it fired two of the drivers who had spoken with journalists. These drivers were told that Uber had found new problems with their background checks. Through media attention, police presence, and digital technologies, Uber disciplined its embedded workers, reimposed its power over the socio-spatial relations of the waiting lot, and, for many, lowered their hopes of changes in the Uber workplace.[62] Enrique, fearing deactivation, switched to meal-delivery platforms and stayed away from the lot for a time. Local organizers stayed away, too.

Though we have no evidence that Uber tipped off the journalist, the timing is suspect.

The Uber workplace seems to be place-less ("You can work anywhere!"), but Enrique's experience revealed that being in place mattered and was fundamental to building worker power.[63] Some scholars have documented how online spaces, such as Facebook groups, can provide meaningful avenues for people to share information.[64] They have not, however, found evidence that online spaces can serve as an effective place for building workplace communities. Our book supports this conclusion. Of the fourteen drivers we spoke to who visited Uber forums on a daily or weekly basis, several mentioned the need to be wary of "fake" advice, either from fellow drivers or from suspected Uber decoys. In 2016, an infamous member of the UberPeople.net site named UberSaur regularly posted snapshots of enormous earnings. Some drivers said they believed these earnings to be impossibly large and suggested that company employees were creating the posts, though we have no evidence either way. Monthly meetups in the D.C. area organized on the UberPeople.net forum in 2016 and 2017 often brought together fewer than fifteen drivers. Facebook ads to recruit drivers for Drive United, the local labor-organizing effort for ride-hailing drivers, similarly brought together fewer than twenty-five workers at in-person meetings in 2018 and 2019 and on Zoom calls in 2020. We do not preclude the notion that technology and online forums can be useful places to cement or expand relationships among drivers, as has been the case in D.C. and Los Angeles.[65] The point is simply that the online forums *in and of themselves* have not yet fostered worker-organization efforts in the D.C. area. Only places like the airport parking lot have done that.

Collective Power

At the time of writing, the future of driver organizing in the Uber workplace in the D.C. area is uncertain.[66] The D.C. airport again relocated its waiting lot for Uber drivers in September 2020, this time making it slightly closer to passenger terminals and more visible to airport security patrols. Meanwhile, some drivers have said they believe that automated vehicles will render all these platform workplaces obsolete, and they are hesitant to make an effort to better a workplace that may be slated to disappear. Why organize the engine room while the *Titanic* sinks?[67] Other drivers have said they are not sure how much longer they will work on the platform, and they are reluctant to commit to improving a workplace that they may soon leave. Of the forty-three workers we followed for years, only eight were still working on the Uber platform after three years. After four years, the number was similar. The pattern is unmistakable, as are its effects: workers move in and out of platform workplaces frequently, creating a barrier to drivers' efforts to build relationships and a shared vision of the future. Local organizers felt the impacts of this turnover, too. When they stopped their formal efforts in early 2021, they lamented that their lists of active drivers (those who expressed interest in a collective campaign) were good for only six months.

What became clear to organizers and drivers like Enrique was that transforming the workplace requires collective action. This observation has long been clear to those involved in political organizing and asserting worker agency. Agency, broadly understood, is the capacity to act, intervene, or exert power in and on space.[68] In its most robust form, agency concerns an ability to reshape dominant structures and forge alternative futures.[69] According to geographer Cindi Katz, resistance—acts intended to subvert or disrupt exploitative conditions—is possible only with a critical consciousness, something that emerges collectively when "a nondominant group does not simply recognize the conditions and social relations producing them as such, but also the means through which these social relations are obscured or naturalized in their society."[70] In other words, counterhegemonic power requires a collective or a group made up of individuals who not only see one another but care for one another. Geographer Amanda Huron agrees:

The pressures of life in a capitalist urban environment leave less time for nurturing bonds with family and friends, let alone creating new ties with strangers. Yet in order to change the balance of power in the contested urban environment, what is precisely needed is to create networks with people who were once strangers but could become allies and even friends.[71]

This process, as feminist theorist Heather McLean has detailed, can be messy. So too are the difficult conversations that workplace organizing necessitates, especially conversations about intersectional inequalities and power imbalances.[72] This is because solidarities across sites and scales do not exist a priori. They are, as McLean reminds us, something that must be made, maintained, and struggled for.

For those of us concerned with predatory conditions in the Uber workplace and the anxiety of workers who navigate such conditions, the challenge is not just imagining other futures; it is finding the space in which to build relationships and expectations that are prerequisites for any sort of collective action.[73] Katz argues convincingly, "We cannot understand oppositional practice or its possible effects if we consider every autonomous act to be an instance of resistance."[74] Agency can be exercised on a collective scale by a group of workers or on a micro-scale by a single worker.[75] But collective action that subverts or disrupts material conditions of life is qualitatively different from other kinds of agency, like resilience (focused on daily survival) and reworking (concerned with materially altering conditions of people's lives but not challenging hegemonic powers). To practice for better futures and develop political consciousness, we must do it together. If workers in the D.C. area want to offer an answer to the problem of the future that is different from Uber's answer, they could do worse than stake out new political spaces in the city.

A New Common Sense

Expectation (ɛkspɛkˈteɪʃn): A preconceived idea or opinion based on what a person has hoped for or imagined regarding a future event, situation, or encounter.
—THE OXFORD ENGLISH DICTIONARY[1]

We changed again, and yet again, and it was now too late and too far to go back, and I went on. And the mists had all solemnly risen now, and the world lay spread before me.
—PIP, IN *GREAT EXPECTATIONS* BY CHARLES DICKENS[2]

While we were writing this book, our friends, family, neighbors, and colleagues would often ask us, "So, should I stop using Uber?" Given the company's very public record of violating labor standards and clogging our already congested streets, the question is a good one.[3] But the goal of this book has not been to persuade readers to avoid the Uber platform, either as a way of earning money or as a means of getting around town. Instead, we have sought to convince readers to think more broadly about Uber's place in cities and to ask *how* and *why* Uber has been made a commonsense solution to a range of urban problems, and to what effect.[4] We have sought to dislodge, in the words of political theorist Iris Marion Young, the "assumption that what is given is necessary."[5] The rise of Uber was not, after all, preordained but the result of politics.

Someone once joked that gig-economy companies like Uber do what moms used to do: meal preparation, chauffeuring, laundry, and errands. There is some truth to the quip. Gig companies do help us perform the work of social reproduction, albeit through the market. We take the point further and argue that gig companies also try to do what cities ideally do: write regulation, provide transportation, address racial inequalities, prepare for the future, and provide work opportunities. Across the United States, gig companies like Uber have presented themselves as solutions to actually existing problems of urban austerity—from underemployment in the wake of the Great Recession and decaying mass-transit systems to deep-seated racial inequities and ever-increasing anxieties about global economic competition. Drawing on geographer Ruth Wilson Gilmore's understanding of prisons as "a consequence of state failure," we argue that companies like Uber are "geographical solutions to social and economic crises."[6] These companies understand the present urban crisis and benefit from it. They know that economic crises, widespread alienation, and an urban landscape in disrepair provide them both a workforce and a consumer base. Though Uber is an inadequate response to these problems, it is a response nonetheless. And it is one that we must take seriously.

The preceding chapters illustrate how Uber appealed to those seeking an immediate fix to urban problems that were often structural in origin. Chapter 1 contends that Uber's regulatory successes in D.C. depended on convincing city leaders that Uber could deliver to the public what that the city was unable to. This convincing went hand in hand with framing governance as ineffective, byzantine, and embarrassingly outdated. Uber's impoverished view of government ran parallel to its narrow conception of racial justice, which chapter 2 explores. Just as Uber's worldview holds that governance is best left to the market, it sees racial injustice as a problem that can be solved by an app. We explain that Uber's consumer campaigns against racial discrimination evaded questions about how the platform may reinforce racial inequalities and work to foreclose more structural approaches to the problem of racial injustice. In chapter 3, we trace Uber's role in shaping debates surrounding data. While Uber often presented its data as a technological fix to transportation-policy stalemates, we make clear it was anything but. Chapter 4 challenges Uber's automation discourse and its utopian visions of cities teeming with automated vehicles. We show how D.C.'s policies around automation advanced Uber's limited vision of the future. Uber's appeal to workers who need flexible schedules, extra income, or both, take center stage in chapter 5. We explore how workers navigate, contest, and seek to transform the limits of the Uber workplace.

Throughout the book, we argue that by responding to the actual needs of individuals and of cities like D.C. over the past decade, Uber helped rework and reinforce a new set of expectations. These expectations concern everything from the kind of transportation options available in a city and the nature of regulation to how racial justice should be pursued, which data should be produced (and by whom), where (if at all) automated vehicles should roam, and what rights workers should demand. Still, it helps to think of Uber as more than a manager of expectations. Uber's greatest achievement in D.C. has been not only to lower expectations of what urban life should look like but also to codify those expectations into a new common sense in which the answer to all problems is, alarmingly, *just let Uber do it*. The low expectations that have made Uber and the broader gig economy seem like commonsense solutions to urban problems suggest a bleak future defined by social atomization, consolidated corporate power, persistent racial inequalities, inaccessible data sets, weak worker rights, and unmet promises related to automation. For some D.C. residents, such as Diana,[7] that future has already arrived.

For years, Diana, who has lived her whole life in the D.C. area, took jobs at fast-food restaurants even though she hated the work. The managers at McDonald's and similar businesses were willing to accommodate her schedule as a part-time student at the University of the District of Columbia. When she started to drive for Uber in 2016, she told us she was enthusiastic about its potential to free her from a reliance on fast-food jobs: "I love driving Uber . . . I set my own hours. It's stress-free . . . I have no boss."[8]

Diana was conflicted about Uber, however. She wondered whether the rise of Uber would endanger investments in the public-transit system, which she had used since she was eight years old. She also wondered whether Uber's presence in the city could mean fewer unionized jobs in the transit system, where she could imagine working one day.[9] As an Uber driver, she found herself rooting against Metro and cheering on what local radio stations called the "Metropocalypse," a proliferation of closures, delays, and track fires that had beset the ailing system.[10] "It's great. It's bad . . . because you're taking Metro people out of work. But at the same time. . . . It's going to be a lot of rides out there, a lot of customers. I like it when Metro [doesn't] work. That's how I make my money."[11]

Two years later, Diana stopped working as an Uber driver. She had graduated from college and, for the first time, was employed full-time. She was a police officer for the D.C. Housing Authority—a job with a salary and some benefits. Diana told us she loved the work:

> I get to interact with people from different parts of the city . . . I work in a lot of the [public] housing projects. And I get to see the struggle, and I get to make a difference. And I have a lot of communication with the younger kids. . . . It's an amazing feeling to do something that makes you feel like you're helping.[12]

Still, Diana didn't write off the gig economy. In fact, she was effusive in her defense of it. Uber, she said, "helps people at their time of need."[13] She felt this way despite running into occasional problems with the platform. These included problems where she did not get paid for completed rides, she incurred $1,200 worth of damage to her steering wheel, and she was sexually assaulted by a passenger. Diana was clear with us: If she lost her job as a police officer or needed extra income, she would sooner go back to working for Uber than return to the fast-food industry.

And go back she did. Three years later, she was still employed as a police officer for the housing agency, but her $53,000 salary no longer went far enough. Her rent had gone up, and so had her bills. And now, at age twenty-nine, she had a newborn baby. She took maternity leave, as mostly unpaid time off. To get by, she applied for food stamps and signed up to deliver for Uber Eats.

When we last spoke, Diana was averaging forty-one hours a week on the delivery platform, in addition to the forty hours she spends as a police officer. She does the Uber Eats delivery work on the weekends or after she finishes her job at the housing agency, where her shifts run from either 11:00 p.m. to 7:00 a.m. or 6:00 a.m. to 2:00 p.m. Her godmother or a friend watches her son while she works. She says that meal deliveries are easier than ride-hailing work, where there is the threat of physical violence: "I don't have to worry about people being behind me."[14]

Diana doesn't sleep much, and she drinks cups upon cups of coffee. She appreciates that she doesn't have to deliver for Uber Eats on days she doesn't want to, but she wishes there were more stability in the platform's pay, especially in the face of inflation. A minimum wage, she said, "would be so lovely, because when I think about gas . . . and how much time it takes to drive and pick up and drop off and everything like that, to have a set minimum would be great."[15] She also wishes she could qualify for rental assistance from the city or extend her food-stamp qualification, which expired once she returned to a full-time schedule at the housing agency. She earns too much to qualify for public-assistance programs but not enough to get by on an income from a single full-time job.

In the capital of one of the world's wealthiest countries, people like Diana should be able to survive without working eighty hours a week. The fact that Diana cannot is a reminder that the reason why U.S. workers do not earn enough to survive *is also* the reason why Uber is wildly popular. We do not pay people enough and do not take care of each other enough. Over decades, neoliberal retrenchment and austerity policies have warped American cities and the kind of lives we make possible within them. The reality is that companies like Uber invariably benefit when public institutions, welfare programs, and existing labor markets fail to address the needs of people like Diana.

In imagining alternatives, we ask "What would need to change in D.C. so that Uber no longer serves as a default solution for Diana?" Or "What sort of city would make Uber's solutions to public-transportation woes and racial injustice obsolete? What kind of politics, investments, or expectations might make a world where Uber no longer appears as common sense? What is required to raise expectations and to offer a new commonsense view of urban life?"

————

Disrupting D.C. has tried to identify the conditions that have made Uber a commonsense solution and to make those conditions visible. These conditions are structural, but they encompass feelings, values, hopes, and expectations too. How do we understand the seemingly intangible and emergent changes to what we expect from cities in the age of Uber? For cultural theorist Raymond Williams, emergent formations are best thought of as changes in the "structure of feeling," an incomplete and ever-hazy configuration of values, meanings, social experiences, and political arrangements.[16] In any historical moment, Williams explained, various structures of feeling vie for dominance. The age of Uber is no exception. In describing the emergent structure of feeling that has accompanied Uber's rise in D.C., this book finds common cause with a range of individuals, groups, and events that are building a new common sense not defined by Uber's narrow worldview.

In D.C., Green New Deal proponents have taken seriously the question of climate justice and have proposed policies that would transform the city in ways that would benefit people like Diana. Drawing on the work of the national Climate and Community Project, D.C. Council member Janeese Lewis George has proposed affordable, green social housing for the city, as well as a program to eliminate lead pipes; both initiatives would employ a unionized workforce.[17] The proposals have drawn support from an array of social movements—labor activists, housing and racial-justice advocates like Empower D.C., environmentalists, and socialists. Perhaps more importantly, these bills are testament to explicit attempts to resurrect an older common sense and restore confidence in the public realm—projects associated with Franklin D. Roosevelt's New Deal and Lyndon B. Johnson's Great Society.

For years, groups in the D.C. area, especially the Action Committee for Transit and the Washington Area Bicyclist Association, have pushed visions of safe, robust, and environmentally sustainable transportation infrastructure. Advocates have demanded not only protected bike lanes and grade-separated crosswalks but also more frequent bus services and adequate funding for Metro. Labor organizers and disability rights activists have called for Metro's paratransit service cuts to be reversed, its outsourcing systems to be discontinued, and its drivers to be fairly compensated. In 2022, for instance, drivers for MetroAccess[18] and the D.C. Circulator each staged successful multiday strikes to fight for decent working conditions.[19] That year, D.C. Council member Christina Henderson proposed a pilot program for fare-free transit on two bus lines, while councilmember Charles Allen advanced a bill to give D.C. residents $100 a month for Metro services and make all bus lines fare-free.[20]

These efforts to build a more just and sustainable city have emerged alongside proposals to improve conditions for D.C. workers. In 2022, councilmember Elissa Silverman introduced a bill of rights for domestic workers.[21] Voters overwhelmingly approved an extension of the city's $16.10 minimum wage to tipped restaurant waitstaff.[22] And, in the spirit of the late Mayor-for-life Marion

Barry's summer jobs program, D.C. Council member Robert White proposed a full employment guarantee.[23]

For those seeking to undertake such alternatives and reimagine what cities and city politics can be (with or without Uber), the economic aftershocks of the COVID-19 pandemic pose opportunities as well as challenges. At the beginning of the pandemic— in 2020—popular support for eviction moratoriums, free food resources, and accessible health-care services was palpable. In 2021, a wave of strikes swept the nation, on a scale unprecedented in forty years.[24] The right to strike and the right to take a bathroom break became newsworthy subjects. In 2022, organizing campaigns at Starbucks, Amazon, Trader Joe's, Chipotle, and Apple workplaces won stunning—and, again, unprecedented—victories. Gig workers, too, have been mobilizing in greater numbers and with greater successes through campaigns supported by Rideshare Drivers United in California and Los Deliveristas Unidos in New York City, among other organizations.[25] Though recently only one in ten American workers reported belonging to a union,[26] support for labor power reached an all-time high in 2022, when 71 percent of Americans said they approved of labor unions.[27] The pandemic gave way, in the words of *The Atlantic*, to a "revolution in worker expectations" and renewed a long-dormant common sense about the importance of organized labor.[28]

Decades of urban austerity and constrained political choices have trained us to expect little of urban governance and less from each other. Uber's disruption has exacerbated these trends toward political despair and social atomization. The task confronting those of us concerned about the future of D.C., or the future of cities more generally, is to collectively resist those lowered expectations. This task is especially important because the contemporary city is simply one iteration among all the possible ones we can—and will—forge together. If we are to build a city that serves human needs, we must raise our expectations for the possibilities of urban politics and overcome the democratic ennui that laid the groundwork for Uber's rise in D.C.

ACKNOWLEDGMENTS

A coauthored book, by definition, is a collaborative endeavor. But it is still a bit of a farce to suggest there are only three authors here. A tremendous number of colleagues, friends, families, and institutions made this book happen.

George Washington University's Department of Geography, City University of New York's School of Labor and Urban Studies, and Georgetown University's Beeck Center for Social Impact & Innovation provided collegial and supportive environments. For funding, we thank the Ewing Marion Kauffman Foundation (and the Washington Center for Equitable Growth for introducing us), Georgetown University's Tech & Society Initiative, the Georgetown Global Cities Initiative, and, most especially, the Urban Studies Foundation.

From the very beginning of this project, Shoshana Seid-Green created impeccable transcriptions of our recorded interviews and provided us with keen observations. We are grateful for her hundreds of hours of labor.

Ben Platt saw something in this work before we could, and he taught us to develop that something into a story worth telling. We are thankful for his editorial magic, his patience, and his listening skills.

At Princeton University Press, we thank Meagan Levinson, Erik Beranek, Will DeRooy, Natalie Baan, and the entire team of staff who smoothed rough edges and saved us from any number of potentially embarrassing errors.

In honing our arguments, we benefited from the comments of two reviewers whose feedback was as incisive as it was encouraging. The book, we believe, is better for it. Thank you, Kevin Ward, and thank you, Juliet Schor.

This book also benefited from the careful eyes of scholars whose work has long drawn our respect and admiration. For their humbling generosity, we are grateful to Sofya Aptekar, Johanna Bockman, Patrick Dixon, Desiree Fields, Josh Freedman, Amanda Huron, Jamie Kelly (who also introduced us to Princeton University Press), John Lauermann, Penny Lewis, Stephanie Luce, Aman Luthra, Dillon Mahmoudi, Jamie McCallum, Ruth Milkman, John Mollenkopf, G. Derek Musgrove, Joe Nevins, Jathan Sadowski, Samir Sonti, Joel Suarez, and Taylor Woods. Special thanks also go to Kate Coddington, Sandra Greene, and Carol Tyson for years of advice and path-shifting edits.

Conversations with our friends and mentors Mona Atia, Uwe Brandes, Veena Dubal, Sarah Edelman, Hannah Johnston, Mimi Kirk, Mike Mann, Brian McCabe, Eugene McCann, Galey Modan, Marie Price, John Russo, Joe Shaw, Jacob Shell, Alex Taliadoros, Cristina Temenos, and Joaquin Villanueva were essential to various stages of the project's development (as well as our own).

This book benefited from workshops and presentations with the American Association of Geographers; the American Sociological Association; the (anti)Blackness in the American Metropolis Conference; City University of New York Graduate Center's environmental psychology program; the D.C. Area Labor and Working-Class History Seminar; Data & Society; George Washington University's Department of Geography; Georgetown University's Department of Sociology; Georgetown University's Kalmanovitz Initiative for Labor and the Working Poor; Georgetown University's Worker Justice Alternative Spring Break; Georgetown University's Office of Government Relations and Community Engagement; Metro D.C. Democratic Socialists of America; Metropolitan Washington Workshop on Immigration and Race; Mount Holyoke's Department of Geology and Geography; Maintainers; Reboot; the University of California at Berkeley's Department of City and Regional Planning; the Urban

Studies Foundation; Vassar College's Earth Science and Geography Department; and the Working-Class Studies Association.

For the tangible stuff (churning out comments on draft upon draft) and the not-so-tangible stuff (inspiring each of us to think and approach the world in the way that we do), we remain joyfully indebted to Don Mitchell and Jamie Winders. Cheers to Eggers 155.

Our informants—workers, policymakers, and community leaders—gave substantial time not only to this project but also to each of us. Their willingness to let us bother them over the years gave way to relationships and, in some cases, meaningful camaraderie.

To our families—especially Angela DeFelice, Sofia Greco, and Michael Satin—we owe it all. Writing a book with graduate-school friends during the first few years of the Zoom era might not have seemed like the greatest of plans, but you made us feel wise anyway and more loved than we could have imagined.

For the little ones in our lives—Liam Cullen, Ronan Cullen, Izzy Satin, and Ora Satin—may you find the kinds of comrades and coconspirators that the three of us found in one another.

APPENDIX A

A Methodological Note

With almost all research projects, moving from the realm of proposals and initial questions to the realm of fieldwork and real human beings can present challenges. In our case—and, given our primary focus on capturing Uber drivers' experiences—the first big challenge was driver recruitment. The challenge was both practical (How do we get drivers to talk with us?) and ethical (How do we get them to talk with us without putting them in danger?).

To recruit these participants, Declan Cullen took thirty-five short Uber rides in busy areas of D.C. in February and March 2016. During these trips, Declan told drivers about our research project and distributed business cards with the URL for an online survey. He did not collect personal information or conduct interviews or surveys while he was a passenger in an Uber ride, in order not to skew a participant's answers by the promise of a good rating.[1] Nearly all the drivers he contacted during this initial recruitment process expressed interest in the study, but only two filled out the survey. The disparity between the number of drivers who expressed interest in the research project and those who completed the survey raised several questions.[2] Were drivers expressing interest in our proposed project because we would ultimately rate them? Since all Uber drivers are rated after each trip, and since drivers can be kicked off the platform if their rating falls below 4.5 out of 5 stars, the possibilities for coercion are numerous. Were drivers reluctant to participate for fear that Declan, who is a White man with an Irish accent, worked for Uber (though he told them he did not)? One driver who had tried to organize his peers said to us: "And you know, people don't want to even talk to you. . . . If you have any paper or recording device or flier, they're going to say, 'No, no, I don't want anything to do with it.'"[3] Other researchers who had similar difficulties with recruitment concluded that many drivers feared surveillance.[4] The fact that there were, and still are, no publicly available data about who drives for Uber in the D.C. area, how many drivers there are at any time, or where drivers live (be it inside or outside the region) only added to our recruitment difficulties. So we turned from in-person to another means of recruitment.

In May 2016, we shifted course and enlisted research participants through UberPeople.net, an online forum with a separate section for D.C.-area drivers. We posted a message about our research, which led us to connect with twenty-five self-identified Uber drivers. We conducted hourlong interviews with these individuals, as well as two drivers from the recruitment rides and thirteen others whom we met through snowball sampling or personal connections. These forty interviews were completed almost entirely in person ($n = 38$) at public libraries or coffee shops in the D.C. area. All drivers received a gift card for their participation.[5] Our questions for these drivers ranged from the broad to the specific. In addition to exploring drivers' motivations, work histories, and feelings about Uber as a company, our questions explored the more quotidian elements of the job—from daily routines and strategies for making money to the basic nature of the labor process itself. To triangulate data from interviews and expand our understanding of drivers' finances, we collected demographic, education, and financial information from thirty-four of these same forty drivers through a short online survey. Of all forty drivers, only 20 percent said they relied on Uber for their primary source of income; 65 percent had worked on the Uber platform for at least six months.

In 2019, we reconnected with thirty-one of these workers. About 40 percent of them were still working on a ride-hailing platform in some capacity; of that subset, only five drivers relied on platform work as their primary source of income. We repeated in-person, hourlong interviews and ten-minute surveys about employment histories and household finances with twenty-nine of these individuals. Two research participants, who had moved out of town, emailed us brief updates. In addition, at this point, we interviewed three more drivers who either contacted us as after hearing about our project or were involved in driver-organizing efforts.

In mid-2020, as the COVID-19 pandemic upended life in the United States, we reconnected via email or text messages with thirty-one of the original forty drivers in this study, several of whom we had not interviewed since the first round of interviews. We also reconnected with two of the three drivers new to the study in 2019. When we started to schedule interviews with these study participants, we thought the first few responses—all agreeing to interview so quickly—were just a coincidence. Joan said she was free to talk anytime. Dwayne said he could do a call tomorrow. Sung-ho said tonight was good. Before COVID-19, it would have taken us weeks to track down these individuals and schedule a time and place for our interviews. For others, it seemed the opposite was true. Working a full-time job plus two on the side, Suzanna never reconnected with us for a third interview. Certain periods of the pandemic made data collection about contingent labor in the digital age more, rather than less, accessible. In other instances, the effect of the novel virus on recruitment was less notable.[6]

In the end, we were able to conduct interviews with twenty-four of the forty original participants, in addition to one of the drivers who was new to our research project in 2019. These thirty-minute interviews were conducted remotely, over Zoom. All twenty-five of these interviews were audio recorded and transcribed. Our interview questions for this round were broader in nature. We asked drivers to tell us about their work situation, but we often focused on how the pandemic was shaping their life. This set of interviews felt different. The stories were rawer. They included stories about chemo treatments, denied unemployment-insurance claims, and an uncertain future.

Then, in 2022, Katie J. Wells reconnected via text and email with eighteen of the original workers for a related research project about grocery and meal-delivery platforms in the D.C. area. She reinterviewed five of these workers, who had left Uber for other gig-economy companies like Uber Eats. The transcripts of those conversations inform this book.

The demographics of our Uber driver participant pool ($n = 43$) largely mirror estimates found in other studies of the ride-hailing industry.[7] Fifty-two percent of the drivers we interviewed self-identified as people of color. Drivers' ages ranged from twenty-three to sixty, with an average of forty-one. About three-fourths of the drivers were U.S.-born. The remainder had emigrated from Ethiopia, Nigeria, Cameroon, the United Kingdom, Peru, South Africa, Venezuela, or South Korea. The drivers lived across the three jurisdictions of the region, with 47 percent of drivers residing in Maryland, 34 percent in Virginia, and 19 percent in D.C. There were two notable geographic concentrations of drivers: one in Arlington, Virginia, and the other in Silver Spring, Maryland. Eighty percent of drivers in this study were male, and most were highly educated, which we suspect is a function of the region's high concentration of college graduates. Only seven drivers had not completed any college. And, strikingly, fifteen had attended or completed graduate school. (For a list of these workers who participated in the study, see appendix B.)

The drivers who spoke with us, of course, are not representative of all drivers everywhere or even all drivers in the D.C. area. Nonetheless, our data are instructive for mapping the structures of work that Uber drivers navigate and the kinds of agency they exercise.

For this book, we also collected data from two sets of interviews with local stakeholders, whom we contacted through snowball sampling, cold calls, or personal connections. In 2016 and early 2017, we conducted a total of twenty-nine hourlong interviews (twenty-two of which were conducted in person at public venues in the D.C. area), with three current policymakers; two journalists; three Uber employees, including a lobbyist; one disability rights advocate; eight labor organizers and labor-policy experts; one taxi-industry representative; one taxi-company owner; one taxi-policy expert; two economic-development experts who were former city employees; and seven transit-policy experts, the majority of whom were current or former city employees.

In 2019, we conducted repeat interviews with five stakeholders. We also interviewed twenty-four additional local stakeholders. This second set of informants (twenty-nine in total, twenty-seven of whom we interviewed in person) was composed of one disability rights advocate; one regional safety expert; one gig-economy company employee; three taxi-policy experts and current city employees; ten transit-policy experts, some of whom were current or former city employees; five labor experts and organizers; four current or former policymakers; and four economic-development experts, some of whom were current or former city employees. Each roughly hourlong conversation focused on the same questions as the first set of interviews and was recorded and transcribed.

To contextualize these data about the rise of Uber in D.C., we drew on analyses of policy documents, testimonies made at hearings, lobbying reports, media reports, and conversations with local labor-advocacy groups. We conducted field observations around the region, including at Uber's Greenlight Hub (in September 2016) and airport ride-hailing lots (in February 2018 and May 2019), and participant observations in the form of email communications, phone calls, and Zoom sessions with local driver-organizing group Drive United (from 2019 to 2021).

Participant Summaries

Summary of Stakeholder Interviews

1. Disability rights advocate, 6 January 2016; 16 July 2019
2. Economic-development expert and city employee,
   17 July 2019
3. Economic-development expert and city employee,
   17 July 2019
4. Economic-development expert and former city
   employee, 27 September 2019
5. Economic-development expert and former city
   employee, 25 October 2016
6. Economic-development expert and former city
   employee, 3 August 2016; 30 July 2019
7. Former policymaker, 31 July 2019
8. Journalist, 6 January 2016
9. Journalist, 15 July 2016
10. Labor organizer, 1 February 2016
11. Labor organizer, 1 February 2016
12. Labor organizer, 6 December 2016
13. Labor organizer, 7 December 2016
14. Labor organizer, 14 July 2019
15. Labor organizer, 14 July 2019
16. Labor organizer, 18 July 2019
17. Labor organizer, 3 August 2016; 30 July 2019
18. Labor-policy expert, 12 July 2016
19. Labor-policy expert, 12 July 2016
20. Labor-policy expert, 18 October 2016

21. Labor-policy expert, 17 July 2019
22. Gig-economy company employee, 19 July 2019
23. Policymaker, 19 October 2016
24. Policymaker, 19 October 2016
25. Policymaker, 15 July 2019
26. Policymaker, 30 July 2019
27. Policymaker, 4 January 2017; 30 July 2019
28. Regional public-safety expert, 16 July 2019
29. Taxi-industry representative, 10 October 2016
30. Taxi-company owner, 18 January 2017
31. Taxi-policy expert and city employee, 8 February 2016
32. Taxi-policy expert and city employee, 17 July 2019
33. Taxi-policy expert and city employee, 19 July 2019
34. Taxi-policy expert and city employee, 19 July 2019
35. Transit-policy expert, 2 February 2016
36. Transit-policy expert, 11 February 2016
37. Transit-policy expert, 13 July 2019
38. Transit-policy expert, 25 July 2019
39. Transit-policy expert, 1 November 2019
40. Transit-policy expert, 15 July 2019
41. Transit-policy expert, 16 July 2019
42. Transit-policy expert, 18 July 2019
43. Transit-policy expert, 18 July 2019
44. Transit-policy expert, 19 July 2019
45. Transit-policy expert and city employee, 8 February 2016
46. Transit-policy expert and city employee, 8 February 2016
47. Transit-policy expert and city employee, 8 February 2016
48. Transit-policy expert and city employee, 8 February 2016; 18 July 2019
49. Transit-policy expert and former city employee, 26 October 2016
50. Transit-policy expert and former city employee, 17 July 2019
51. Uber employee, 7 January 2016
52. Uber employee, 13 January 2016
53. Uber lobbyist, 1 February 2016; 28 July 2016

Summary of Workers

TABLE A.1. A Summary of Workers

	Pseudonym	Age & gender at time of first interview	Highest level of education	Race/ethnicity	Job(s)/area(s) of employment in addition to Uber at time of first interview	Year(s) interviewed 2016	2019	2020
1	Aiden*	29 M	Less than 12 years of school	White or Caucasian	None	x	x	x
2	Ajay	48 M	Completed graduate school	White or Caucasian	Urban planning consultant	x	x	x
3	Aman	35 M	Not reported	Black or African American	None	x		
4	Anh*	33 F	Completed graduate school	Asian or Pacific Islander	Human resources manager; catering assistant	x	x	x
5	Anthony	38 M	Completed graduate school	White or Caucasian	High school teacher	x	x	
6	Arthur	29 M	Completed graduate school	White or Caucasian	Retail employee	x	x	x
7	Beatrice	44 F	High school	Black or African American	Asbestos removal	x		
8	Ben	41 M	Some college	Black or African American	Information technology	x		x
9	Bert	61 M	Graduated from college	White or Caucasian	Courier	x		x
10	Carol	59 F	Some college	Black or African American	None	x		x
11	Curtis	56 M	Completed graduate school	Black or African American	U.S. Postal Service	x	x	x

Continued on next page

TABLE A.1. (*continued*)

	Pseudonym	Age & gender at time of first interview	Highest level of education	Race/ethnicity	Job(s)/area(s) of employment in addition to Uber at time of first interview	Year(s) interviewed		
						2016	2019	2020
12	Diana*	27 F	Graduated from college	Black or African American	Security officer at a fast-food restaurant	x	x	
13	Dominic	26 M	Graduated from college	Black or African American	Security officer	x	x	x
14	Dwayne	54 M	Completed graduate school	White or Caucasian	Information technology	x		x
15	Enrique*	37 M	Some college	Hispanic	None		x	
16	Gary	52 M	Graduated from college	White or Caucasian	Catering	x	x	x
17	Hakim	55 M	Not reported	Black or African American	Taxi driver	x	x	
18	Hank	39 M	Some college	White or Caucasian	Stay-at-home parent	x	x	x
19	Ivori	37 F	Some college	Black or African American	Customer-service representative	x	x	x
20	Jabari	29 M	Graduated from college	Black or African American	Information technology	x	x	x
21	Jasper	34 M	Completed graduate school	White or Caucasian	Middle school teacher; coach	x	x	x
22	Jerry	58 M	Some graduate school	White or Caucasian	Self-employed entrepreneur	x		
23	Joan	51 F	Graduated from college	Black or African American	Bus driver	x	x	x
24	Joe	28 M	Completed graduate school	White or Caucasian	Security officer	x	x	

	Name	Age/Sex	Education	Race/Ethnicity	Occupation			
25	Jordan	37 M	Graduated from college	Black or African American	Information technology	X		
26	Kristen	38 F	Graduated from college	White or Caucasian	Graphic designer	X	X	
27	Larry	51 M	Completed graduate school	White or Caucasian	Entrepreneur; university staff	X		
28	Marco	34 M	Graduated from college	White or Caucasian	Religious institution	X	X	X
29	Mark	63 M	Completed graduate school	White or Caucasian	Manager	X	X	X
30	Mateo*	34 M	Graduated from college	Hispanic	Information technology	X	X	X
31	Noam	27 M	Graduated from college	White or Caucasian	None	X		
32	Osiris	45 M	Some graduate school	Black or African American	Courier	X	X	X
33	Olotun	30 M	Some college	Black or African American	Security officer, part-time	X		
34	Patrick	46 M	Graduated from college	White or Caucasian	Real estate	X	X	
35	Randy	31 M	Graduated from high school	White or Caucasian	Grocery clerk	X	X	
36	Rick	30 M	Graduated from college	White or Caucasian	Sales	X	X	X
37	Samuel	50 M	Graduated from college	White or Caucasian	Hotel manager	X	X	X
38	Sung-ho	48 M	Graduated from college	Asian or Pacific Islander	Writer; stock-market analyst	X	X	X
39	Suzanna	58 F	Completed graduate school	White or Caucasian	Field inspector; freelance writer	X	X	
40	Trent	33 M	Completed graduate school	Black or African American	None	X	X	X
41	Trevor	52 M	Some college	White or Caucasian	Sales	X		
42	Yoni	52 M	Not reported	Black or African American	None	X	X	
43	Zaki	32 M	Completed graduate school	Black or African American	Information technology	X	X	X

*These informants were also interviewed in 2022 as part of a related research project about delivery work in the gig economy.

Maps

MAP A.1. D.C. Quadrants and Landmarks

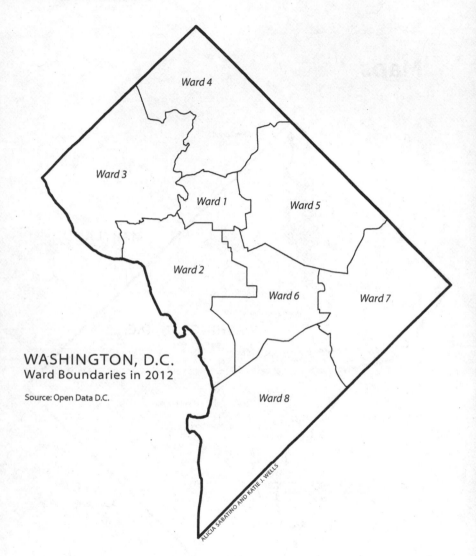

WASHINGTON, D.C.
Ward Boundaries in 2012

Source: Open Data D.C.

MAP A.2. D.C. Ward Boundaries (2012)

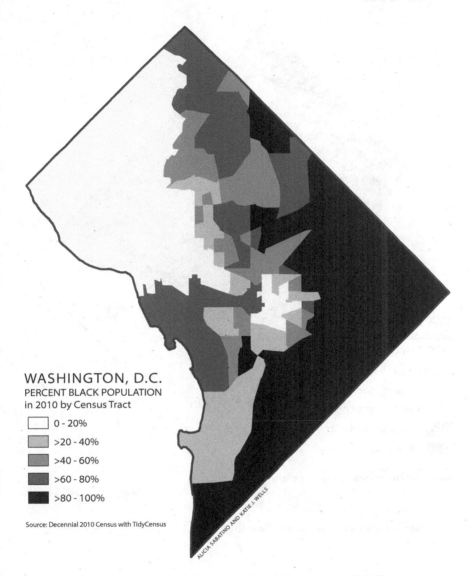

WASHINGTON, D.C.
PERCENT BLACK POPULATION
in 2010 by Census Tract

☐ 0 - 20%

▢ >20 - 40%

▢ >40 - 60%

▢ >60 - 80%

■ >80 - 100%

Source: Decennial 2010 Census with TidyCensus

ALICIA SABATINO AND KATIE J. WELLS

MAP A.3. Percent Black Population, by Census Tract, in D.C. (2010)

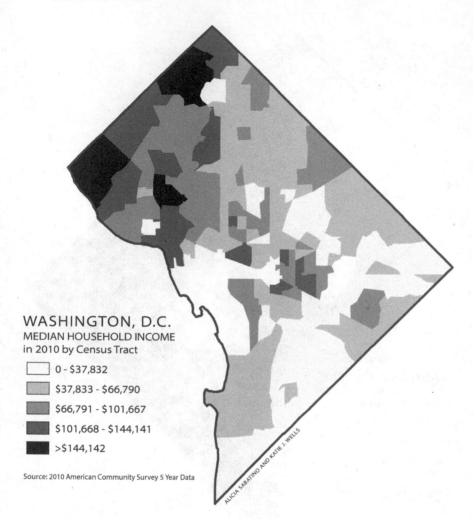

WASHINGTON, D.C.
MEDIAN HOUSEHOLD INCOME
in 2010 by Census Tract

- 0 - $37,832
- $37,833 - $66,790
- $66,791 - $101,667
- $101,668 - $144,141
- >$144,142

Source: 2010 American Community Survey 5 Year Data

MAP A.4. Median Household Income, by Census Tract, in D.C. (2010)

Time Line

2009 Uber is founded in San Francisco.

2010 Incumbent D.C. Mayor Adrian Fenty is defeated by Vincent Gray.

2011 **Uber launches operations in D.C.**

D.C. loses its status as a Black-majority city.

D.C. Taxicab Commission carries out a sting against Uber.

2012 Uber successfully campaigns to exempt Uber from D.C.'s taxi regulations.

D.C. adopts autonomous vehicle (AV) legislation.

The *Washington Post* gives Uber "verbification status."

2013 **UberX launches operations in D.C.**

2014 Uber hires David Plouffe to be its senior vice president of policy and strategy.

Taxi drivers unsuccessfully protest D.C.'s new Uber legislation.

Incumbent Mayor Vincent Gray is defeated by Muriel Bowser.

2015 **UberPool launches operations in D.C.**

A series of Metro track fires cause disruption.

Uber drivers are approved to pick up riders at D.C.'s airport.

Uber funds Brilliant Corners' *Hailing While Black* study.

2016 The Smarter D.C. program begins.

Uber Elevate is launched.

2017 **Uber Movement is announced for D.C.**

A new Greenlight Hub for D.C.-area Uber drivers opens.

The national #DeleteUber campaign begins.

2018 D.C. adopts data-sharing amendment and new tax for Uber rides.

A new waiting lot for Uber drivers opens at D.C.'s airport.

Mayor Muriel Bowser is reelected.

2019 **Uber becomes a public company.**

Uber drivers go on strike at D.C. airport.

2020 Uber sponsors the 57th anniversary of the March on Washington.

Uber sells its AV and Uber Elevate units.

D.C.'s AV Study is released.

2022 The Uber Files are released.

Mayor Muriel Bowser is reelected.

NOTES

Preface

1. Interview with Jim Fallows and Travis Kalanick at Washington Ideas Forum, Washington, D.C., 2013, CSPAN, video, 18:06, https://www.c-span.org/video/?316217 -3/travis-kalanick-washington-ideas-forum.

2. Interview with the authors, 28 July 2016.

3. Cory Doctorow, "The Big Lie That Keeps the Uber Bezzle Alive," *Medium*, 11 February, https://doctorow.medium.com/the-big-lie-that-keeps-the-uber-bezzle -alive-8d6e8c0ccde7.

4. John Kenneth Galbraith, 2009, *The Great Crash, 1929* (Boston: Houghton Mifflin Harcourt).

5. Gerrit de Vynck, Faiz Siddiqui, and Nitasha Tiku, 2022, "Inflation Is Helping Gig Ecompanies Like Uber and Hurting Their Workers," *Washington Post*, August 7, https://www.washingtonpost.com/technology/2022/08/07/gig-economy-inflation.

Introduction

1. Alyse Mier, 2016, "'Metro's a loser! We took an Uber!' Protestors Chant in Dupont," *Borderstan*, 19 July, https://www.borderstan.com/2016/07/19/metros-a -loser-we-took-an-uber-protesters-chant-in-dupont.

2. Kara Swisher, 2014, "The $17 Billion Man: Full Code Conference Video of Uber's Travis Kalanick," *Vox*, 8 June, video, 35:29, https://www.vox.com/2014/6/8/11627734 /the-17-billion-man-full-code-conference-video-of-ubers-travis-kalanick, at 1:41.

3. Bradley Tusk, 2018, *The Fixer: My Adventures Saving Startups from Death by Politics* (New York: Portfolio), 115.

4. Raye Weigel, 2016, "Mystery Group of Young People Protests for Metro Privatization," *Washington City Paper*, 20 July, https://washingtoncitypaper.com/article /328687/mystery-group-of-young-people-protests-for-metro-privatization. The style and demographics of the protest were reminiscent of the 2000 Brooks Brothers riot in Miami. See Josh Mound, 2020, "Republicans Don't Want the 'Wrong Kind of People' to Vote," *Jacobin*, 3 November, https://jacobin.com/2020/11/republicans-voter -suppression-trump-election.

5. Mier, 2016, "'Metro's a loser! We took an Uber!' Protestors Chant in Dupont."

6. Zachary Schrag, 2006, *The Great Society Subway: A History of the Washington Metro* (Baltimore: Johns Hopkins University Press), 283.

7. Ibid., 2.

8. Ibid.

9. Robert McCartney and Paul Duggan, 2016, "Metro Sank into Crisis Despite Decades of Warnings," *Washington Post*, 24 April, https://www.washingtonpost.com /local/trafficandcommuting/metro-sank-into-crisis-despite-decades-of-warnings /2016/04/24/1c4db91c-0736-11e6-a12f-ea5aed7958dc_story.html.

10. Weigel, 2016, "Mystery Group of Young People Protests for Metro Privatization."

11. For a comprehensive list of terms for the on-demand economy and their differences, see April Rinne, 2017, "What Exactly Is the Sharing Economy?" *World Economic Forum* (blog), 13 December, https://www.weforum.org/agenda/2017/12/when-is -sharing-not-really-sharing; Juliet Schor and Steven Vallas, 2021, "The Sharing Economy: Rhetoric and Reality," *Annual Review of Sociology* 47 (July): 369–389.

12. See Mark Andreesen, 2011, "Why Software Is Eating the World," *Wall Street Journal*, August 20, https://www.wsj.com/articles/SB10001424053111903480904576 512250915629460 (last updated 1/26/22).

13. Nick Srnicek, 2017, *Platform Capitalism* (Cambridge, UK: Polity Press), 21.

14. Ibid.

15. Ibid.

16. Karl Marx, 1967, *Capital* vol. 1 (New York: International Publishers), 667.

17. For discussion of "principled confrontation," see Andrew Anthony, 2014, "Travis Kalanick: Uber-Capitalist Who Wants to Have the World in the Back of His Cabs," *The Guardian*, 20 December, https://www.theguardian.com/theobserver/2014/dec /21/travis-kalanick-uber-cab-app-observer-proifile. Also see Mike Isaac, 2019, *Super Pumped: The Battle for Uber* (New York: W.W. Norton), 13. For discussion on corporate civil disobedience, see Thomas Wedell-Wedellsborg, 2014, "The Case for Corporate Civil Disobedience," *Harvard Business Review*, 2 June, https://hbr.org/2014/06/the -case-for-corporate-disobedience. Also see Ben Wear, 2016, "Wear: Of Uber, Lyft and How 'Corporate Civil Disobedience' Works in Austin," *Austin American-Statesman*, 24 September, https://www.statesman.com/story/news/2016/09/24/wear-of-uber-lyft -and-how-corporate-civil-disobedience-works-in-austin/10045601007.

18. Eric Eldon, 2011, "How Uber Is Launching Its Newest City, Washington, D.C.," *TechCrunch*, 15 December, https://techcrunch.com/2011/12/15/uberdc.

19. Mike DeBonis, 2012, "Uber Car Service Busted by D.C. Authorities," *Washington Post*, 13 January, https://www.washingtonpost.com/local/dc-politics/uber-car -service-busted-by-dcauthorities/2012/01/13/gIQAnL2DxP_story.html.

20. The D.C. Council is the legislative body for the city. It is composed of thirteen elected members.

21. Tusk, 2018, *The Fixer*, 114.

22. "Strike Down the Minimum Fare Language in the DC Uber Amendment," 2012, Uber, 9 July, https://www.uber.com/blog/washington-dc/strike-down-the -minimum-fare.

23. Andy Kessler, 2013, "Travis Kalanick: The Transportation Trustbuster," *Wall Street Journal*, 25 January, https://www.wsj.com/articles/SB10001424127887324235510 4578244231122376480. Operation Rolling Thunder was the name of a U.S. aerial

bombardment campaign that killed more than forty thousand North Vietnamese civilians from 1965 to 1968. See Stephen Emerson, 2018, *Air War over North Vietnam: Operation Rolling Thunder, 1965–1968* (Barnsley, UK: Pen and Sword Books).

24. See Emily Badger, 2014, "Free Market Advocates Say D.C. Is the Uber-Friendliest City in the Nation," *Washington Post*, 12 November, https://www.washington post.com/news/wonk/wp/2014/11/12/free-market-advocates-say-d-c-is-the-uber -friendliest-city-in-the-nation.

25. See Nick Gillespie, 2013, "Taxi Wars: How Govt Tries to Kill Innovative Ride Services Customers Want," *Reason*, 26 October, https://reason.com/2013/10/26/taxi -wars-how-govt-tries-to-kill-innovat.

26. Shervin Pishevar (@Shervin), Twitter, 10 July, https://twitter.com/shervin /status/222819101310062592.

27. Alexandrea Ravenelle, 2019, *Hustle and Gig: Struggling and Surviving in the Sharing Economy* (Berkeley: University of California Press), 6.

28. Alex Rosenblat, 2018, *Uberland: How Algorithms Are Rewriting the Rules of Work* (Berkeley: University of California Press); Sarah Kessler, 2018, *Gigged: The End of the Job and the Future of Work* (New York: St. Martin's Press); Juliet Schor, 2020, *After the Gig: How the Sharing Economy Got Hijacked and How to Win It Back* (Berkeley: University of California Press); Veena Dubal, 2017, "The Drive to Precarity: A Political History of Work, Regulation, & Labor Advocacy in San Francisco's Taxi & Uber Economies," *Berkeley Journal of Employment and Labor Law* 38 (1): 73–135; Trebor Scholz, 2017, *Uberworked and Underpaid: How Workers Are Disrupting the Digital Economy* (New York: Polity Press); Tom Slee, 2015, *What's Yours Is Mine: Against the Sharing Economy* (New York: OR Books).

29. Scholz, 2017, *Uberworked and Underpaid*, 5.

30. Ravenelle, 2019, *Hustle and Gig*, 5.

31. Ibid., 6.

32. Ibid., 209.

33. Ibid.

34. Slee, 2015, *What's Yours Is Mine*.

35. Shoshana Zuboff, 2019, *The Age of Surveillance Capitalism: The Fight for a Human Future at the New Frontier of Power* (New York: Public Affairs).

36. Sophia Rosenfield, 2011, *Common Sense: A Political History* (Cambridge, MA: Harvard University Press), 1.

37. See Daniel Greene, 2021, *The Promise of Access: Technology, Inequality, and the Political Economy of Hope* (Cambridge, MA: MIT Press).

38. Ibid., 23.

39. See Miriam Greenberg and Penny Lewis, 2017, *The City Is the Factory: New Solidarities and Spatial Strategies in an Urban Age* (Ithaca, NY: Cornell University Press); Josh Freeman, 2000, *Working-Class New York: Life and Labor since World War II* (New York: New Press); Gabriel Winant, 2021, *The Next Shift: The Fall of Industry and the Rise of Healthcare in Rust Belt America* (Cambridge, MA: Harvard University Press).

40. See Sharon Zukin, 2020, *The Innovation Complex: Cities, Tech, and the New Economy* (Oxford: Oxford University Press); Sarah Barns, 2019, *Platform Urbanism:*

Negotiating Platform Ecosystems in Connected Cities (London: Springer Nature); Ben Green, 2019, *The Smart Enough City: Putting Technology in its Place to Reclaim Our Urban Future* (Cambridge, MA: MIT Press); Jathan Sadowski, 2020, *Too Smart: How Digital Capitalism Is Extracting Data, Controlling Our Lives, and Taking Over the World* (Cambridge, MA: MIT Press); Donald McNeill, 2016, "Governing a City of Unicorns: Technology Capital and the Urban Politics of San Francisco," *Urban Geography* 37 (4): 494–513; Donald McNeill, 2021, "Urban Geography 1: 'Big tech' and the Reshaping of Urban Space," *Progress in Human Geography* 45 (5): 1311–1319.

41. Although the list of scholarship in this vein is extensive, the foundational texts often include John Mollenkopf, 1975, "The Post-war Politics of Urban Development," *Politics and Society* 5 (1): 247–295; Harvey Molotch, 1976, "The City as a Growth Machine: Toward a Political Economy of Place," *American Journal of Sociology* 82 (2): 309–332; Paul Peterson, 1981, *City Limits* (Chicago: University of Chicago Press); John Logan and Harvey Molotch, 2007, *Urban Fortunes: The Political Economy of Place* (Berkeley: University of California Press); Peter Eisinger, 1988, *The Rise of the Entrepreneurial State: State and Local Economic Development Policy in the United States* (Madison: University of Wisconsin Press); David Harvey, 1989, "From Managerialism to Entrepreneurialism: The Transformation in Urban Governance in Late Capitalism," *Geografiska Annaler* 71 (1): 3–17; Clarence Stone, 1989, *Regime Politics: Governing Atlanta 1945–1988* (Lawrence: University of Kansas Press). For commentary on the broad sweep of this scholarship, see Kevin Cox, 1993, "The Local and the Global in the New Urban Politics: A Critical View," *Environment and Planning D: Society and Space* 11(4): 433–448. In an article published in 1995, Cox goes as far as to argue that "the central object in the study of urban politics in the U.S. has become 'urban development' or what might more accurately be called the politics of local economic development." See Kevin Cox, 1995, "Globalisation, Competition and the Politics of Local Economic Development," *Urban Studies* 32 (2): 213–224.

42. Peterson, 1981, *City Limits*, 4.

43. Harvey, 1989, "From Managerialism to Entrepreneurialism," 12.

44. Jason Hackworth, 2007, *The Neoliberal City: Governance, Ideology, and Development in American Urbanism* (Ithaca, NY: Cornell University Press), 16.

45. Harvey, 1989, "From Managerialism to Entrepreneurialism," 5.

46. See Don Mitchell and Lynn Staeheli, 2006, "Clean and Safe? Property Redevelopment, Public Space, and Homelessness in Downtown San Diego," in *The Politics of Public Space*, ed. Setha Low and Neil Smith (New York: Routledge): 143–175.

47. Peterson, 1981, *City Limits*, 4.

48. See note 27.

49. Hackworth, 2007, *The Neoliberal City*, 16.

50. For recent discussion on urban governance, see forum in *Dialogues in Human Geography*, 2020, 10(3); John Lauermann, 2018, "Municipal Statecraft: Revisiting the Geographies of the Entrepreneurial City," *Progress in Human Geography* 42 (2): 205–224; Matthew Thompson, Vicky Nowak, and Alan Southern, 2020, "Re-grounding the City with Polanyi: From Urban Entrepreneurialism to Entrepreneurial Municipalism," *Environment and Planning A: Economy and Space* 52 (6): 1171–1194; Gordon MacLeod,

2011, "Urban Politics Reconsidered: Growth Machine to Post-democratic City?" *Urban Studies* 48 (2): 2629–2660; Erik Swyngedouw, 2009, "The Zero-Ground of Politics: Musings on the Post-political City," *New Geographies* 1 (1): 52–61; Mark Davidson and Kevin Ward, 2021, "Post–Great Recession Municipal Budgeting and Governance: A Mixed Methods Analysis of Budget Stress and Reform," *Environment and Planning A: Economy and Space* 54 (4): 0308518X211068051; Luis F. Alvarez León and Jovanna Rosen, 2020, "Technology as Ideology in Urban Governance," *Annals of the American Association of Geographers* 110 (2): 497–506; Don Mitchell, Kafui Attoh, and Lynn Staeheli, 2015, "Whose City? What Politics? Contentious and Non-contentious Spaces on Colorado's Front Range," *Urban Studies* 52 (14): 2633–2648.

51. Hilary Angelo and David Wachsmuth, 2014, "Urbanizing Urban Political Ecology: A Critique of Methodological Cityism," *International Journal of Urban and Regional Research*. 39 (1): 16–27; Neil Brenner and Christian Schmidt, 2014, "The 'Urban Age' in Question," *International Journal of Urban and Regional Research* 38 (3): 731–755: Neil Brenner, 2019, *New Urban Spaces: Urban Theory and the Scale Question* (Oxford: Oxford University Press).

52. Eric Swyngedouw, 2011, *Post-democratic Cities for Whom and for What?* Paper presented at the Regional Studies Association Annual Conference, Pecs, Hungary, 26 May.

53. "Uber and the American Worker: Remarks from David Plouffe" (transcribed by Natalia), 2015, Uber, 3 November, https://www.uber.com/newsroom/1776.

54. Ibid.

55. Ibid.

56. Ibid.

57. For a study on Uber's broadly negative impact on the lower end of the labor market, see Lawrence Mishel, 2018, *Report: Uber and the Labor Market* (Washington, DC: Economic Policy Institute), https://www.epi.org/publication/uber-and-the-labor-market-uber-drivers-compensation-wages-and-the-scale-of-uber-and-the-gig-economy. For a competing study that shows Uber's positive benefits on urban poverty rates, see Ziru Li, Yili Hong, and Zhongju Zang, 2021, "The Empowering and Competition Effects of the Platform-Based Sharing Economy on the Supply and Demand Sides of the Labor Market," *Journal of Management Information Systems* 38 (1): 140–165.

58. Swisher, 2014, "The $17 Billion Man."

59. Peterson, 1981, *City Limits*, 4.

60. Juliet B. Schor and Steven P. Vallas, 2021, "The Sharing Economy: Rhetoric and Reality," *Annual Review of Sociology* 47 (1): 369–389.

61. Doug Henwood, 2015, "What the Sharing Economy Takes," *The Nation*, 27 January, https://www.thenation.com/article/archive/what-sharing-economy-takes.

62. Ibid.

63. Ibid.

64. Ibid.

65. Ibid.

66. Borrowed from the article "Social Contagion: Microbiological Class War in China," 2020, *Chuang* (February), https://chuangcn.org/2020/02/social-contagion.

67. Nikil Saval, 2017, "Disrupt the Citizen," *n+1*, 27 June, https://www.nplusonemag .com/online-only/online-only/disrupt-the-citizen.

68. Ibid.

69. Ibid.

70. At one level, Uber's "Operation Rolling Thunder" may seem to run counter to our argument about democracy. From one perspective, by directing angry constituents to email the D.C. Council, Uber was acting to give voice to a long-frustrated public and to bolster democratic participation. We take a different view. Part of taking the idea of democracy seriously means acknowledging that the choices available to us are often shaped by powerful interests. We should be careful to equate Uber's consumer base with the public at large. Treating "Operation Rolling Thunder" as an expression of democratic decision-making not only ignores the hundreds of thousands of D.C. residents who did not participate in the operation but also refuses to see the nature of Uber's influence. That influence is reflected in Uber's ability to mobilize voters and to shift the ground of public debate in ways that support its bottom line and also narrow the scope of democratic decision-making.

71. Interview with Jim Fallows and Travis Kalanick at Washington Ideas Forum, Washington, D.C., 2013, CSPAN, video, 18:06, https://www.c-span.org/video/?316217 -3/travis-kalanick-washington-ideas-forum.

72. Tusk, 2018, *The Fixer*, 115. Also see Kathleen Thelen, 2018, "Regulating Uber: The Politics of the Platform Economy in Europe and the United States," *Perspectives on Politics* 16 (4): 938–953.

73. For discussion, see Wilfred Chan, 2020, "The Future of the Gig Economy Is on the Ballot," *The Nation*, 9 October, https://www.thenation.com/article/politics/prop -22-ab5-california; Veena Dubal and Juliet Schor, 2021, "Gig Workers Are Employees. Start Treating Them That Way," opinion, *New York Times*, 18 January, https:// www.nytimes.com/2021/01/18/opinion/proposition-22-california-biden.html; Levi Sumagaysay, 2021, "From Treatment of Gig Workers to Tip Transparency, the App-Based Economy Could See Key Changes in 2022," *MarketWatch*, 30 December, https:// www.marketwatch.com/story/from-treatment-of-gig-workers-to-tip-transparency -the-app-based-economy-could-see-key-changes-in-2022-11640900832. See also Matt Stout, 2022, "Lyft Makes Largest One-Time Political Donation in Massachusetts History, Fueling Gig Worker Ballot Fight," *Boston Globe*, 18 January, https://www .bostonglobe.com/2022/01/18/metro/lyft-makes-largest-one-time-political-donation -massachusetts-history-fueling-gig-worker-ballot-fight.

74. Max Smith, 2017, "Metro Track Fires on the Rise over Last Three Months," WTOP News, 23 October, https://wtop.com/tracking-metro-24-7/2017/10/metro -track-fires-rise-last-three-months.

75. Chris Myers Asch and George Derek Musgrove, 2017, *Chocolate City: A History of Race and Democracy in the Nation's Capital* (Chapel Hill: University of North Carolina Press), 355–390; Michael K. Fauntroy, 2003, *Home Rule or House Rule: Congress and the Erosion of Local Governance in the District of Columbia* (Lanham, MD: University Press of America), 11–16. Since 1973, the federal limits placed on D.C.'s authority to govern

itself (the imposition of an emergency control board in 1995, congressional control of its budget, and the fiscal constraints given a dearth of taxable property) have been notable. See Asch and Musgrove, 2017, *Chocolate City*, 129.

76. See Paul L. Knox, 1991, "The Restless Urban Landscape: Economic and Sociocultural Change and the Transformation of Metropolitan Washington, D.C.," *Annals of the Association of American Geographers* 81 (2): 181–209; Richard Florida, 2013, "Washington Is Nation's Most Post-industrial Metro Area," *Bloomberg CityLab*, 8 April, https://www.bloomberg.com/news/articles/2013-04-08/america-s-most-post-industrial-metros.

77. Katie J. Wells, "A Housing Crisis, a Failed Law, and a Property Conflict: The U.S. Urban Speculation Tax," *Antipode* 47 (4): 1043–1061; Howard Gillette Jr., 2011, *Between Justice and Beauty: Race, Planning, and the Failure of Urban Policy in Washington, D.C.* (Philadelphia: University of Pennsylvania Press); Stephen McGovern, 1998, *The Politics of Downtown Development: Dynamic Political Cultures in San Francisco and Washington* (Lexington: University Press of Kentucky).

78. Leonard Downie Jr. and Jim Hoagland, 1969, "Speculators Gained Control of Some S. & L.'s," *Washington Post*, 11 January, A1.

79. See Gabriella Modan and Katie J. Wells, 2015, "Gentrification in the Media," in *Capital Dilemma: Growth and Inequality in Washington*, ed. Derek Hyra and Sabiyha Prince (New York: Routledge), 315–331.

80. Brandi Summers, 2019, *Black in Place: The Spatial Aesthetics of Race in a Post-Chocolate City* (Chapel Hill: University of North Carolina Press), 4.

81. Readers may ask: "Why Uber? Why not any of the plethora of other platform companies that are busily transforming our cities?" First, Uber is a popular, well-known, and frequently used platform. In fact, it is so popular that it has quickly entered everyday language usage as a verb: to Uber. Second, its popularity reflects its place at the forefront of much of the gig economy's growth. It has been one of the gig economy's fastest-growing and most highly valued companies, one of Silicon Valley's "unicorns." Third, Uber has an important role as a political wrecking ball that has sought to destroy—or "disrupt," in industry parlance—industries and regulations that stand in the way of its business model. As an economic force, Uber is important. Yet we argue that, in the realm of politics, it has been equally innovative.

Chapter 1: On Not Being a Dinosaur

1. Interview with the authors, 28 July 2016.

2. Vasily Grossman, [1980] 2011, *Life and Fate* (New York: Random House).

3. Mike DeBonis, 2012, "Uber Car Impounded, Driver Ticketed in City Sting," *District of DeBonis* (blog), *Washington Post*, 13 January, https://www.washingtonpost.com/blogs/mike-debonis/post/uber-car-impounded-driver-ticketed-in-city-sting/2012/01/13/gIQA4Py3vP_blog.html.

4. Washington Field Office, Federal Bureau of Investigation, 2009, "Thirty-Nine Individuals Charged with Conspiring to Bribe Chair of D.C. Taxicab Commission," press

release, 2 October, https://archives.fbi.gov/archives/washingtondc/press-releases/2009/wfo100209.htm.

5. Del Quentin Wilber, 2012, "D.C. Taxi Official Turned FBI Informant Recalls Role in Corruption Probe," *Washington Post*, 2 April, https://www.washingtonpost.com/local/crime/dc-taxi-official-turned-fbi-informant-recalls-role-in-corruption-probe/2012/04/02/gIQAErYhrS_story.html; Pete Tucker, 2011, "Leon Swain, Chairman at Arms," *The Fight Back*, 23 March, http://thefightback.org/2011/03/leon-swain-chairman-at-arms; Alan Suderman, 2011, "Taxicab Confessions," *Washington City Paper*, 25 May, https://washingtoncitypaper.com/article/349588/taxicab-confessions-2; Alan Suderman, 2011, "Why Was Leon Swain Fired?" *Washington City Paper*, 28 April, https://washingtoncitypaper.com/article/349681/why-was-leon-swain-fired.

6. Tom Sherwood, 2011, "Journalists Handcuffed, Removed from Taxi Commission Meeting," NBC4 Washington, 22 June, https://www.nbcwashington.com/news/local/journalists-handcuffed-removed-from-taxi-commission-meeting/1895810.

7. Ron Linton, 2012, "The D.C. Taxi Commission's Problem with Uber," opinion, *Washington Post*, 27 January, https://www.washingtonpost.com/opinions/the-dc-taxi-commissions-problem-with-uber/2012/01/25/gIQAglzHWQ_story.html.

8. Grossman, 2011, *Life and Fate*.

9. This blog would come to rival the *Washington Post* as a source for local news, as well as become "one of the area's most influential advocates for thoughtful growth and better transportation options." See Andrew Beaujon, 2019, "Greater Greater Washington Lost a Big Chunk of Its Funding. Now What?," *Washingtonian*, 8 March, https://www.washingtonian.com/2019/03/08/greater-greater-washington-lost-a-big-chunk-of-its-funding-now-what.

10. David Alpert, 2012, "In Uber Fight, Silicon Valley and Washington Philosophies Clash," *Greater Greater Washington* (blog), 10 July, https://ggwash.org/view/28328/in-uber-fight-silicon-valley-washington-philosophies-clash.

11. David Alpert, 2012, "The Uber Cab Model Deserves a Chance to Succeed," opinion, *Washington Post*, 13 January, https://www.washingtonpost.com/opinions/the-uber-cab-model-deserves-a-chance-to-succeed/2012/01/12/gIQAksh2wP_story.html.

12. Of course, the history of metered taxis in D.C. is also a history of congressional oversight. In the 1930s, Congress banned the city from adopting metered pricing for its taxis. See Sam Smith, 2007, "The End of the Taxi Zone System," *Washington History* 19/20: 98–100.

13. Interview with the authors, 31 July 2019.

14. Interview with the authors, 17 July 2019.

15. Interview with the authors, 19 October 2016.

16. Interview with the authors, 16 July 2019.

17. Interview with the authors, 19 July 2019.

18. Interview with the authors, 19 July 2019.

19. Interview with the authors, 15 July 2016.

20. Interview with the authors, 27 September 2019.

21. Interview with the authors, 15 July 2019.

22. Interview with the authors, 27 September 2019.

23. David Weigel, 2012, "The Uber Battle," *Slate*, 10 July, https://slate.com/news-and-politics/2012/07/ubers-popular-and-pricey-sedan-service-is-posing-a-challenge-to-d-c-laws-and-regulations-governing-taxi-cabs.html.

24. Interview with the authors, 4 January 2017.

25. Interview with the authors, 1 November 2019.

26. Interview with the authors, 31 July 2019.

27. Weigel, 2012, "The Uber Battle."

28. Weigel, 2012, "The Uber Battle."

29. Elizabeth Chacko, 2016, "Ethiopian Taxicab Drivers: Forming an Occupational Niche in the US Capital," *African and Black Diaspora: An International Journal* 9 (2): 200–213

30. Dan McDermott, 2012, "'Oh God, My God'—Frustrated D.C. Council Chairman before Uber Vote," *Huffington Post*, 10 July, https://www.huffpost.com/entry/oh-god-my-god-frustrated-_b_1663531.

31. Liz Farmer, 2012, "Uber Founder Strikes Back at D.C. Proposed Rules for Car Service," *Washington Examiner*, 24 September, https://www.washingtonexaminer.com/uber-founder-strikes-back-at-dc-proposed-rules-for-car-service.

32. Patrick Madden and Martin DiCaro, 2012, "Uber Car Service Makes Its Case (Again) at D.C. Council," WAMU, 24 September, https://wamu.org/story/12/09/24/uber_car_service_makes_its_case_again_at_dc_council.

33. Bradley Tusk, 2018, *The Fixer: My Adventures Saving Startups from Death by Politics* (New York: Portfolio), 114.

34. Brad Stone, 2017, *The Upstarts: How Uber, Airbnb, and the Killer Companies of the New Silicon Valley Are Changing the World* (New York: Random House).

35. Benjamin Freed, 2012, "Cheh Shelves Amendment after Backlash from CEO and Customers," *DCist*, 10 July, https://dcist.com/story/12/07/10/cheh-shelves-uber-amendment-after-b.

36. Mike Debonis, 2012, "Uber Triumphant," *District of DeBonis* (blog), *Washington Post*, 3 December, https://www.washingtonpost.com/blogs/mike-debonis/wp/2012/12/03/uber-triumphant.

37. "Never Underestimate the Power of #UberDCLove," 2012, Uber, 10 July, https://newsroom.uber.com/us-dc/never-underestimate-the-power-of-uberdclove.

38. Shervin Pishevar (@shervin), 2012, Twitter, 10 July, https://twitter.com/shervin/status/222819101310062592.

39. Stone, 2017, *The Upstarts*, 194.

40. Interview with the authors, 31 July 2019.

41. Interview with the authors, 27 September 2019.

42. Office of Mary M. Cheh letter to D.C. Council members, 2012, "Subject B19-892, the Public Vehicle-for-Hire Innovation Amendment Act of 2012," 5 November, https://ggwash.org/files/2012-taxiinnovationmemo.pdf (emphasis added).

43. D.C. Act 19-631, Sedan Class Amendment Act of 2012, https://lims.dccouncil.us/Legislation/B19-0892.

44. Debonis, 2012, "Uber Triumphant."

45. Ibid.

46. Travis Kalanick (@travisk), 2012, Twitter, 5 December, https://twitter.com /travisk/status/276267461463126016.

47. Benjamin Freed, 2012, "After Bill Passes, Uber CEO Now Likes D.C. Council," *DCist*, 5 December, https://dcist.com/story/12/12/05/after-bill-passes-uber-ceo -now-like.

48. Steven Musil, 2012, "Uber on the Road to Reconciliation in D.C. with New Legislation," *CNET*, 4 December, https://www.cnet.com/tech/services-and-software /uber-on-the-road-to-reconciliation-in-d-c-with-new-legislation.

49. Rob Montz, 2013, "Uber Wars: How D.C. Tried to Kill a Great New Ride Technology," *Reason*, 22 October, https://reason.com/2013/10/22/uber-wars-how-dctried -to-kill-a-great-n.

50. See Will Sommer, 2013, "D.C. Taxi Regulations: The Movie," *Washington City Paper*, 22 October, https://washingtoncitypaper.com/article/345298/d-c-taxi -regulations-the-movie; Benjamin Freed, 2013, "2 Years of Uber Fighting D.C. Government in 11 Minutes," *Washingtonian*, 22 October, https://www.washingtonian.com /2013/10/22/two-years-of-uber-fighting-dc-government-in-11-minutes-video; Matt Cohen, 2013, "Uber vs. D.C. Taxi Commission: The Movie," *DCist*, 22 October, https:// dcist.com/story/13/10/22/uber-wars.

51. Montz, 2013, "Uber Wars."

52. Hubert Horan, 2017, "Can Uber Ever Deliver? Part Nine: The 1990s Koch Funded Propaganda Program That Is Uber's True Origin Story," *Naked Capitalism*, 15 March, https://www.nakedcapitalism.com/2017/03/can-uber-ever-deliver-part-nine -1990s-koch-funded-propaganda-program-ubers-true-origin-story.html.

53. Benjamin Freed, 2015, "Former D.C. Taxi Commissioner Ron Linton Dies at 86," *Washingtonian*, 29 June, https://www.washingtonian.com/2015/06/29/former -dc-taxi-commissioner-ron-linton-dies-at-86.

54. Tusk, 2018, *The Fixer*, 115.

55. See Elizabeth Pollman and Jordan M. Barry, 2016, "Regulatory Entrepreneurship," *Southern California Law Review* 90 (3), 383.

56. See Ryan Calo and Alex Rosenblat, 2017, "The Taking Economy: Uber, Information, and Power," *Columbia Law Review* 117 (March), 1623.

57. Interview with the authors, 19 October 2016.

58. See Government of the District of Columbia Board of Ethics and Government Accountability Lobbyist Activity Report for Uber Technologies July 2014; Government of the District of Columbia Board of Ethics and Government Accountability Lobbyist Activity Report for Uber Technologies January 2015; Supplemental Activity Report January 2015. Copies of reports available from authors.

59. Interview with the authors, 4 January 2017.

60. Interview with the authors, 3 August 2016.

61. Interview with the authors, 31 July 2019.

62. Maya Rhodan, 2014, "Taxi Drivers Protest Uber and Lyft, Stop D.C. Traffic," *Time*, 8 October, http://time.com/3482420/taxis-uber-lyft-washington-dc.

63. In addition, the taxi lobby suggested that Uber would submit for review any substantial changes it made to the platform's operating technology.

64. The effort to form the association was doomed, in part because of the strained relationship between the teamsters and the Amalgamated Transit Union, which represented D.C. bus drivers and Metro workers.

65. For decades, taxi driving in D.C. had offered "an unusual opportunity for lower income residents and immigrants" to achieve upward mobility. See Smith, 2007, "The End of the Taxi Zone System."

66. Chacko, 2016, "Ethiopian Taxicab Drivers."

67. Paulina Firozi, 2015, "Lawsuit Alleges That Four D.C. Cab Companies Ignored Blind Passengers," *Washington Post*, 17 March, https://www.washingtonpost.com/local /trafficandcommuting/lawsuit-alleges-that-four-dc-cab-companies-ignored-blind -passengers/2015/03/17/b61fb05e-cce0-11e4-a2a7-9517a3a70506_story.html.

68. District of Columbia Taxicab Commission Disability Advisory Committee, 2014, *Comprehensive Report and Recommendations on Accessible Taxicab Service*, 20 February, https://dfhv.dc.gov/sites/default/files/dc/sites/dc%20taxi/page_content/attachments /DC%20Taxicab%20Comission%20Disability%20Advisory%20Committee%20 Comprehensive%20Report%20022014%20FINAL%20w%20Addendum.pdf.

69. Ibid.

70. See ADA National Network, "The ADA & Accessible Ground Transportation," https://adata.org/factsheet/ADA-accessible-transportation; and Federal Regulations for the ADA, Sec. 37.29 "Private Entities Providing Taxi Service," https://www.transit .dot.gov/regulations-and-guidance/civil-rights-ada/part-37-transportation-services -individuals-disabilities#sec.37.29.

71. Benjamin Freed, 2013, "Sting Reveals D.C. Taxis Ignore Nearly Half of All Customers with Disabilities," *Dcist*, 14 May, https://dcist.com/story/13/05/14/sting -reveals-dc-taxis-ignore-nearl.

72. All names of interviewed stakeholders are pseudonyms.

73. Interview with the authors, 16 July 2019.

74. Interview with the authors, 16 July 2019.

75. D.C. Act A20-0489, "The Vehicle-for-Hire Innovation Amendment Act of 2014," https://lims.dccouncil.us/downloads/LIMS/31519/Signed_Act/B20-0753 -SignedAct.pdf, 4.

76. See Donald McNeill, 2015, "Global Firms and Smart Technologies: IBM and the Reduction of Cities," *Transactions of the Institute of British Geographers* 40 (4): 562–574; Donald McNeill, 2016, "Governing a City of Unicorns: Technology Capital and the Urban Politics of San Francisco," *Urban Geography* 37 (4): 494–513; Donald McNeill, 2021, "Urban Geography 1: 'Big Tech' and the Reshaping of Urban Space," *Progress in Human Geography* 45 (5): 1311–1319.

77. Eric Hal Schwartz, 2014, "How Uber Will Get More Wheelchair-Accessible Cars in D.C.," *Washington Business Journal*, 8 December, https://www.bizjournals .com/washington/inno/stories/news/2014/12/08/uber-wheelchair-accessible-car -program-dc.html.

78. "Wheelchair Accessible Taxis at the Tap of a Button," 2015, Uber, 11 December, https://www.uber.com/blog/washington-dc/wheelchair-accessible-taxis-at-the-tap -of-a-button.

79. Faiz Siddiqui, 2016, "Uber Aims to Put More Deaf Drivers on the Roads," *Washington Post*, 19 April, https://www.washingtonpost.com/local/trafficandcommuting/uber-aims-to-put-more-deaf-drivers-on-the-roads/2016/04/19/75a898fa-0638-11e6-b283-e79d81c63c1b_story.html.

80. Perry Stein, 2014, "Uber's Next Fight with the D.C. Council? A Wheelchair-Accessibility Bill," *Washington City Paper*, 20 November, https://washingtoncitypaper.com/article/447357/ubers-next-fight-with-the-d-c-council-a-wheelchair-accessibility-bill.

81. Bryan Casey, 2017, "Uber's Dilemma: How the ADA May End the On-Demand Economy," *UMass Law Review* 12 (1): 124.

82. Washington Lawyers' Committee for Civil Rights and Urban Affairs, 2021, "In Important Opinion for Disability Access and Inclusion, Federal Judge Rules That Uber Is Subject to Anti-discrimination Laws," 17 March, https://www.washlaw.org/in-important-opinion-for-disability-access-and-inclusion-federal-judge-rules-that-uber-is-subject-to-anti-discrimination-laws.

83. Ibid., 14.

84. Ibid., 15.

85. Uber's FOIA requests in D.C. are allegedly filed using third-party proxies, which makes it difficult for researchers and journalists to determine the frequency and scope of the company's FOIA use.

86. Interview with the authors, 19 October 2016.

87. Alex Rosenblat, 2018, *Uberland: How Algorithms Are Rewriting the Rules of Work* (Berkeley: University of California Press).

88. Interview with the authors, 27 September 2019.

89. Interview with the authors, 28 July 2016.

90. Interview with the authors, 28 July 2016.

91. Interview with the authors, 28 July 2016.

92. Martin DiCaro, 2015, "How the D.C. Region Became among the Most Uber-Friendly in the U.S.," WAMU, 20 April, https://wamu.org/story/15/04/20/how_the_dc_region_became_among_the_most_uber_friendly_regions_in_the_us.

93. For discussion, see Mike Isaac, 2017, "How Uber Deceives the Authorities Worldwide," *New York Times*, 3 March, https://www.nytimes.com/2017/03/03/technology/uber-greyball-program-evade-authorities.html.

94. For discussion on urban governance and technology, see Philip Ashton, Rachel Weber, and Matthew Zook, 2017, "The Cloud, the Crowd, and the City: How New Data Practices Reconfigure Urban Governance?," *Big Data & Society* 4 (1): 2053951717706718; Sarah Barns, 2016, "Mine Your Data: Open Data, Digital Strategies and Entrepreneurial Governance by Code," *Urban Geography* 37 (4): 554–571; Pauline McGuirk, Robyn Dowling, and Pratichi Chatterjee, 2021, "Municipal Statecraft for the Smart City: Retooling the Smart Entrepreneurial City?," *Environment and Planning A: Economy and Space* 53 (7): 1730–1748.

95. Interview with the authors, 26 October 2016.

96. Daniel Greene, 2021, *The Promise of Access: Technology, Inequality, and the Political Economy of Hope* (Cambridge, MA: MIT Press).

97. Interview with the authors, 17 July 2019.

98. For discussion about widespread trends, see Lee Vinsel and Andrew L. Russell, 2020, *The Innovation Delusion: How Our Obsession with the New Has Disrupted the Work That Matters Most* (New York: Currency).

99. Interview with the authors, 27 September 2019.

100. Martin DiCaro, 2016, "Metro Enters First Partnership with Uber in Bid to Boost Sagging Ridership," WAMU, 9 December, https://wamu.org/story/16/12/09/metro-enters-first-partnership-uber-bid-boost-sagging-ridership.

101. Nick Iannelli, 2021, "DC Schools Partner with Uber to Offer Free Rides to Meal Sites," WTOP, 16 July, https://wtop.com/dc/2021/07/dc-schools-partner-with-uber-to-offer-free-rides-to-meal-sites.

102. Rachel Dovey, 2017, "Uber Offers City Planners a Slice of Traffic Data," *Next City*, 9 January, https://nextcity.org/daily/entry/uber-movement-traffic-data.

103. Hamzat Sani, 2018, "Uber Partners with D.C. on the Future of Urban Mobility," *Afro News*, 13 April, https://afro.com/uber-partners-d-c-future-urban-mobility.

104. Executive Office of the Mayor, Government of the District of Columbia, 2018, "Mayor Bowser Joins Uber CEO to Discuss the Future of Mobility," 11 April, https://mayor.dc.gov/release/mayor-bowser-joins-uber-ceo-discuss-future-mobility.

105. D.C. Sustainable Transportation, undated letter to D.C. Council, circa 2018, https://ggwash.org/files/DCST,_industry,_and_experts_statement_on_ride-hailing_and_DCs_FY2019_budget.pdf.

106. Executive Office of the Mayor, Government of the District of Columbia, 2017, "Mayor Bowser Celebrates Uber Greenlight Hub in Ward 7," news release, 19 October, https://mayor.dc.gov/release/mayor-bowser-celebrates-uber-greenlight-hub-ward-7.

107. Interview with the authors, 19 October 2016; interview with the authors, 26 October 2016.

108. Interview with the authors, 19 October 2016.

109. This official also mentioned two caveats that reveal important (and popular) beliefs about the platform workplace: First, he cautioned that driving for Uber "is a supplemental job," not something that you can do to "make a living." Next, he argued that taxi driving was never "a good job" anyway. This second point is an important one. It points to the persistent idea in D.C. and elsewhere that taxi drivers' jobs are not worthy of protection.

110. Interview with the authors, 13 January 2016.

111. See Jamie Peck and Nik Theodore, 2012, "Politicizing Contingent Work: Countering Neoliberal Labor Market Regulation . . . from the Bottom Up?," *South Atlantic Quarterly* 111 (4): 741–761; Jovanna Rosen and Luis F. Alvarez León, 2022, "The Digital Growth Machine: Urban Change and the Ideology of Technology," *Annals of the American Association of Geographers*, advance online publication, https://doi.org/10.1080/24694452.2022.2052008; Jathan Sadowski, 2021, "Who Owns the Future City? Phases of Technological Urbanism and Shifts in Sovereignty," *Urban Studies* 58 (8): 1732–1744; Niels van Doorn, 2020, "A New Institution on the Block: On Platform Urbanism and Airbnb Citizenship," *New Media & Society* 22 (10): 1808–1826; Dillon Mahmoudi, Anthony M. Levenda, and John G. Stehlin, 2020, "Political Ecologies of

Platform Urbanism: Digital Labor and Data Infrastructures," in *Urban Platforms and the Future City: Transformations in Infrastructure, Governance, Knowledge and Everyday Life*, ed. Mike Hodson, Julia Kasmire, Andrew McMeekin, John G. Stehlin, and Kevin Ward (New York: Routledge), 40–52.

112. Loraine Kennedy and Ashima Sood, 2015, "Outsourced Urban Governance as a State Rescaling Strategy in Hyderabad, India," *Cities* 85 (February): 130–139.

113. Just as individual drivers pay for and maintain the vehicles through which Uber sells rides, so too do individual cities pay for and maintain the roads, traffic signals, and curbside drop-off zones on which Uber's services rely. For discussion on the nuances of platform partnerships, see Niels van Doorn, Eva Mos, and Jelke Bosma, 2021, "Actually Existing Platformization: Embedding Platforms in Urban Spaces through Partnerships," *South Atlantic Quarterly* 120 (4): 715–731.

114. These strategies are not unique to Uber, nor are their effects. For discussion of similar patterns, see John Stehlin, John, Michael Hodson, and Andrew McMeekin, 2020, "Platform Mobilities and the Production of Urban Space: Toward a Typology of Platformization Trajectories," *Environment and Planning A: Economy and Space* 52 (7): 1250–1268; Aaron Shapiro, 2022, "Platform Urbanism in a Pandemic: Dark Stores, Ghost Kitchens, and the Logistical-Urban Frontier," *Journal of Consumer Culture*, advance online publication, https://doi.org/10.1177/14695405211069983; Mark Graham, 2020, "Regulate, Replicate, and Resist—the Conjunctural Geographies of Platform Urbanism," *Urban Geography* 41 (3): 453–457; Jathan Sadowski, 2020, "The Internet of Landlords: Digital Platforms and New Mechanisms of Rentier Capitalism," *Antipode* 52 (2): 562–580; Desiree Fields, 2022, "Automated Landlord: Digital Technologies and Post-crisis Financial Accumulation," *Environment and Planning A: Economy and Space* 54 (1): 160–181; Alan Wiig and Michele Masucci, 2020, "Digital Infrastructures, Services, and Spaces: The Geography of Platform Urbanism," in *Urban Platforms and the Future City: Transformations in Infrastructure, Governance, Knowledge and Everyday Life*, ed. Mike Hodson, Julia Kasmire, Andrew McMeekin, John G. Stehlin, and Kevin Ward (New York: Routledge), 70–84.

115. See Amanda Huron, 2015, "Working with Strangers in Saturated Space: Reclaiming and Maintaining the Urban Commons," *Antipode* 47 (4): 963–979.

Chapter 2: UberKente

1. Levi Sumagaysay, 2020, "Protesters Call Uber's Antiracism Billboards 'Hypocritical and Offensive,'" *MarketWatch*, 9 September, https://www.marketwatch.com/story/protesters-call-ubers-antiracism-billboards-hypocritical-and-offensive-11599686425.

2. Oscar Wilde, 1893, *Lady Windermere's Fan* (London: E Mathews and J Lane), 95.

3. Cornell Belcher, 2015, "As a Black Man, It's Hard to Catch a Cab. And My Research Shows Even White People Know That," *Post Everything* (digital daily magazine), *Washington Post*, 23 July, https://www.washingtonpost.com/posteverything/wp/2015/07/23/as-a-black-man-its-hard-to-catch-a-cab-research-shows-even-white-people-know-that.

4. Ibid.

5. See Gene Demby, 2014, "Apps Make Googly Eyes at Riders Tired of Being Snubbed by Cabbies," *Code Switch*, National Public Radio, 2 October, https://www.npr .org/sections/codeswitch/2014/10/21/357645869/apps-makes-googly-eyes-at-riders -tired-of-being-snubbed-by-cabbies; Laura Washington, 2016, "Uber Upends Problem of 'Hailing While Black,'" *Chicago Sun-Times*, 24 June, https://chicago.suntimes .com/2016/6/24/18455960/laura-washington-uber-upends-problem-of-hailing-while -black; Anne Brown, 2018, "L.A.'s Taxi Industry Discriminates against Black Riders. If We Don't Force Them to Change, They Won't," op-ed, *Los Angeles Times*, August 12, https://www.latimes.com/opinion/livable-city/la-oe-brown-racism-taxi-uber-lyft -201812-story.html; Doug Glanville, 2015, "Why I Still Get Shunned by Taxis," *The Atlantic*, 24 October, https://www.theatlantic.com/politics/archive/2015/10/why-i -still-get-shunned-by-taxi-drivers/411583.

6. Clinton Yates, 2012, "Uber: When Cabs Whiz By, It's a Pick Me Up," *The Root DC* (blog), *Washington Post*, 28 September, https://www.washingtonpost.com/blogs /therootdc/post/uber-when-cabs-whiz-by-its-a-pick-me-up/2012/09/28/06a41f0c -082f-11e2-858a-5311df86ab04_blog.html.

7. Ibid.

8. Cornell Belcher and Dee Brown, 2015, *Hailing While Black: Navigating the Discriminatory Landscape of Transportation* (Chicago: Brilliant Corners), http://www .brilliant-corners.com/post/hailing-while-black.

9. Ibid., 3.

10. For coverage of the incident, see Ben Mathis-Lilley, 2014, "*Washington Post* Story about Taxi Racism Study Didn't Mention Study Was Funded by Uber," *Slate*, 23 July, https://slate.com/news-and-politics/2015/07/washington-post-taxi-racial -discrimination-study-uber-sponsored-it.html. See also Erik Wemple, 2015, "*Washington Post* Refuses to Comment on Compromised Cab Story," *Erik Wemple* (blog), *Washington Post*, 24 July, https://washingtonpost.com/blogs/erik-wemple/wp/2015 /07/24/washington-post-refuses-to-comment-on-compromised-cab-story.

11. See Sissi Cao, 2019, "7 Biggest Winners of Uber's Blockbuster IPO This Week," *Observer*, 9 May, https://observer.com/2019/05/uber-ipo-nyse-7-investor-winners . For more on Jeff Bezos and *Washington Post* and the potential conflict of interest, see Adam Johnson, 2015, "Bezos' Stake in Uber Goes Under the Radar at *Washington Post*," FAIR, 10 November, https://fair.org/home/bezos-stake-in-uber-goes-under-the -radar-at-washington-post.

12. For more on the legend of the Georgetown Metro, see Zach Schrag, 2006, *The Great Society Subway: A History of the Washington Metro* (Baltimore: Johns Hopkins University Press), 155. Also see Katya Schwenk, 2018, "Branching Out: Georgetown's Campaign against Public Transport," *Georgetown Voice*, 7 December, https://georgetownvoice.com/2018/12/07/branching-out-georgetowns-campaign -against-public-transport.

13. Between 2001 and 2011 alone, the city's White population grew by 31%. Over the same period, its Black population declined by 11%. See Sabrina Tavernise, 2011, "A Population Changes, Uneasily," *New York Times*, 18 July, A9. For the loss of D.C.'s majority Black status, see Mike DeBonis, 2015, "D.C., Where Blacks Are No Longer a

Majority, Has a New African-American Affairs Director," *Washington Post*, 4 February, https://www.washingtonpost.com/local/dc-politics/dc-where-blacks-are-no-longer-a -majority-has-a-new-african-american-affairs-director/2015/02/04/e8bd65a0-ac8e -11e4-ad71-7b9eba0f87d6_story.html.

14. Tavernise, 2011, "A Population Changes, uneasily." In 2016, the D.C. Fiscal Policy Institute found that while the bottom fifth of D.C. households held only 2% of total D.C. income, the top fifth held 56%. Minahil Naveed, 2017, "Income Inequality Highest in the Nation," *D.C. Fiscal Policy Institute* (blog), 15 December, https://www .dcfpi.org/all/income-inequality-dc-highest-country.

15. Harry Jaffe, 2014, "Will 2014 Be the Year D.C. Elects a White Mayor?," *Washingtonian*, 26 February, https://www.washingtonian.com/2014/02/26/will-2014-be -the-year-dc-elects-a-white-mayor.

16. Ibid.

17. Timothy Gibson, 2015, "The Rise and Fall of Adrian Fenty, Mayor-Triathlete: Cycling, Gentrification and Class Politics in Washington DC," *Leisure Studies* 34 (2): 230–249. Also see Brandi Summers, 2019, *Black in Place: The Spatial Aesthetics of Race in a Post-Chocolate City* (Chapel Hill: University of North Carolina Press).

18. Both Fenty's Creative Action Agenda and Gray's Creative Economy Strategy are available through the D.C. Office of Planning. For a critique of both, see Nathalie Delgadillo, 2018, "D.C. Is Being Sued for Gentrification, Here's What to Know about the Case," *DCist*, 15 June, https://dcist.com/story/18/06/15/dc-is-being-sued-for -gentrifying-he.

19. Gibson, 2015, "The Rise and Fall of Adrian Fenty, Mayor-Triathlete," 239.

20. Guy Debord, [1967] 2002, *The Society of the Spectacle* (Detroit: Black & Red Press), 34.

21. Paul Schwartzman, 2014, "As Term Ends, Gray Reflects on Success and Struggles," *Washington Post*, 21 December, https://www.washingtonpost.com/local/as-term -ends-gray-reflects-on-success-and-struggles/2014/12/21/528e3e00-84a8-11e4-b9b7 -b8632ae73d25_story.html.

22. All names of interviewed stakeholders are pseudonyms.

23. Interview with the authors, 28 July 2016.

24. Ibid. In many ways, Zack's comments here are a throwback to the cloying language of the sharing economy and the fallacious notion that Uber's purpose was not to generate wealth for shareholders but simply to bring people together across difference.

25. Ibid.

26. Jane Jacobs, 1961, *The Life and Death of the Great American City* (New York: Vintage Books). In her famous book, Jacobs touted the importance of diversity, both in land use and in terms of people, to the securing the vitality of urban life. Rather than separating people and breaking the city into distinct areas by land use type, Jacob's urged urban planners to create spaces in which people of different background might interact. William Julius Wilson, [1987] (2012), *The Truly Disadvantaged: The Inner City, the Underclass, and Public Policy* (Chicago: University of Chicago Press). Seeking to address the persistence of a "Black underclass" despite the legislative victories of the civil rights era, Wilson focused on the structural transformation of the U.S. economy.

Wilson rejected cultural explanations for Black poverty as well as explanations focused on racial prejudice. The issue was one of jobs, particularly the absence of entry-level industrial jobs capable of supporting a family on one income.

27. Interview with the authors, 28 July 2016.

28. Ibid.

29. For discussion of technological solutionism, see Evgeny Morozov, 2013, *To Save Everything, Click Here: The Folly of Technological Solutionism* (New York: PublicAffairs); Langdon Winner, 1980, "Do Artifacts Have Politics?" *Daedalus* 109 (1): 121–36, http://www.jstor.org/stable/20024652.

30. Interview with the authors, 19 October 2016.

31. Interview with the authors, 19 October 2016.

32. Interview with the authors, 4 January 2017.

33. See Yangbo Ge, Christopher Knittel, Don MacKenzie, and Stephen Zoepf, 2016, "Racial and Gender Discrimination in Transportation Network Companies," NBER Working Paper Series 22776, National Bureau of Economic Research, Cambridge, MA.

34. Interview with the authors, 30 July 2019.

35. Interview with the authors, 30 July 2019.

36. Interview with the authors, 28 July 2016.

37. The emails were published in three separate PDFs, totaling 2,688 pages. These PDFs were made available via DocumentCloud, at https://www.documentcloud.org/documents/406276-uber3.html.

38. Gibson, 2015, "The Rise and Fall of Adrian Fenty," 239.

39. See the Equal Rights Center, 2003, *Service Denied: Responding to Taxicab Discrimination in the District of Columbia*, October, https://equalrightscenter.org/wp-content/uploads/taxicab_report.pdf. See also Will Wrigley, 2013, "WUSA9 Investigation Finds D.C. Cab Drivers Discriminating against Black Customers," *Huffington Post*, 23 May, http://www.huffingtonpost.com/2013/05/23/wusa9-taxidiscrimination-video_n_3326228.html; Bill Miller, 2000, "D.C. Cab Company Accused of Racial Bias," *Washington Post*, 8 June, https://www.washingtonpost.com/archive/local/2000/06/08/dc-cab-company-accused-of-racial-bias/2c1eeb7e-d3fd-4951-8cc2-ce223beac6b1.

40. "Driving Impact in Wards 7 and 8," 2015, Uber, 4 November, https://www.uber.com/blog/washington-dc/uberx-driving-impact-dc-ward-7-ward-8.

41. Ge et al., 2016, "Racial and Gender Discrimination in Transportation Network Companies," 19.

42. Akshat Pandey and Aylin Caliskan, 2020, "Disparate Impact of Artificial Intelligence Bias in Ridehailing Economy's Price Discrimination Algorithms," arXiv preprint arXiv:2006.04599. See also Rachel G. McKane and David J. Hess, 2022, "Ridesourcing and Urban Inequality in Chicago: Connecting Mobility Disparities to Unequal Development, Gentrification, and Displacement," *Environment and Planning A: Economy and Space* 54 (3): 572–592.

43. Interview with the authors, 24 May 2016.

44. See Elizabeth Chacko, 2016, "Ethiopian Taxicab Drivers: Forming an Occupational Niche in the US Capital," *African and Black Diaspora: An International*

Journal 9 (2): 200–213, and Sam Smith, 2007, "The End of the Taxi Zone System," *Washington History* 19/20: 98–100.

45. In addition to the 53% who self-identified as African American or Black, in 2000 between 57% and 62% of D.C. drivers were foreign-born. Bruce Schaller, 2004, *The Changing Face of Taxi and Limousine Drivers* (New York: Schaller Consulting), http://www.schallerconsult.com/taxi/taxidriver.pdf.

46. For the 2016 fiscal year, 60% of Metro ridership (for both bus and rail services) was identified as a racial minority. 28% were low-income. The demographic differences between bus and rail services are quite notable. While 81% of all Metro bus riders are minority, they constitute only 45% of all Metro rail riders. See Jan Bryant, 2020, *2020 Title VI Program Update* (Washington, DC: Washington Metropolitan Area Transit Authority), 6, https://www.wmata.com/about/board/meetings/board-pdfs/upload /20200910-EXEC-3B-Title-VI-Update-2020.pdf. As early as the late 1970s, Black transit operators outnumbered White operators; see Craig G. Simpson, 2020, "George Davis and the Turbulent Times of D.C. Area Transit Union—1974–1980," *Washington Area Spark* (blog), 16 March, https://washingtonareaspark.com/2020/03/16/george -davis-and-the-turbulent-times-of-d-c-area-transit-union-1974-80. In 2012, in an article critical of D.C.'s Metro system, writer Luke Rosiak noted that 97% of bus and train operators working for the Washington Metropolitan Area Transit Authority were Black. See Luke Rosiak, 2012, "Metro Derailed by Culture of Complacence, Incompetence, Lack of Diversity," *Washington Times*, 26 March, https://www.washingtontimes.com/news /2012/mar/26/metro-derailed-by-culture-of-complacence-incompete.

47. William Whyte, 2009, *City: Rediscovering the Center* (Philadelphia: University of Pennsylvania Press), 110.

48. Errol Louis, 2015, "How Uber Saved Me from Cabs: Mayor de Blasio Is Leaving N.Y.ers Stranded—Like a Black Man Trying to Hail a Taxi Uptown," opinion, *New York Daily News*, 21 July, https://www.nydailynews.com/opinion/errol-louis-uber-saved -cabs-article-1.2298250.

49. See, e.g., Jen Chung, 2018, "8th NYC Taxi Driver Commits Suicide, Reportedly Due to Debt," *Gothamist*, 15 November, https://gothamist.com/news/8th-nyc-taxi -driver-commits-suicide-reportedly-due-to-debt.

50. Jeffrey Mays, 2018, "Uber Gains Civil Rights Allies against New York's Proposed Freeze," *New York Times*, 29 July, https://www.nytimes.com/2018/07/29/nyregion /uber-cap-civil-rights.html.

51. Cary Head, 2018, "Uber and Spike Lee Celebrate Brooklyn's Drivers," Uber, 11 July, https://www.uber.com/newsroom/uber-spike-lee-celebrate-brooklyns-drivers.

52. See Veena Dubal, 2022, "Economic Security and the Regulation of Gig Work in California: From AB5 to Proposition 22," *European Labour Law Journal* 13(1): 51–65.

53. John Bowden, 2020, "Uber Eats Waives Fees for Black-Owned Restaurants," *The Hill*, 10 June, https://thehill.com/policy/technology/502192-uber-eats-waives-fees -for-Black-owned-restaurants.

54. Ryan Lovelace, 2020, "Uber Encourages Riders to Join D.C. Protestors," *Washington Times*, August 28, https://www.washingtontimes.com/news/2020/aug/28/uber -encourages-riders-join-dc-protests.

55. See Laura Bliss, 2017, "Hailing an Uber Just Got Way More Political," Bloomberg, 29 January, https://www.bloomberg.com/news/articles/2017-01-30/-deleteuber-and-lyft-s-aclu-donation-follow-muslim-ban. See also Lucinda Shen, 2017, "200,000 Users Have Left Uber in the #DeleteUber Protest," *Fortune*, 3 February, https://fortune.com/2017/02/03/uber-lyft-delete-donald-trump-executive-order.

56. For a critical take on this ad campaign, see Erica Smiley, 2020, "The Racist Business Model behind Uber and Lyft," *The Guardian*, 29 October, https://www.theguardian.com/commentisfree/2020/oct/29/uber-lyft-racist-business-model-prop-22.

57. For a critical take on Proposition 22, see Veena Dubal, 2020, "The New Racial Wage Code," *Harvard Law & Policy Review* 15 (2): 511–549. Dubal argues that Proposition 22 is reminiscent of the New Deal carve-outs that excluded the largely African American agricultural and domestic workforce from labor standards. Despite Uber's appeals to racial justice, Proposition 22, she argues, will ensure that ride-hailing drivers share the same fate as domestic and agricultural workers did in the wake of the New Deal.

58. Kate Canales, 2020, "Prop 22 Has Courted the Endorsements of California's NAACP President," *Business Insider*, 21 October, https://www.businessinsider.com/uber-lyft-paid-naacp-alice-huffman-prop-22-2020-10. Indeed, a study in San Francisco found 78% of gig workers to be people of color. See Chris Benner (with Erin Johansson, Kung Feng, and Hays Witt), 2020, *On-Demand and On-the-Edge: Ride Hailing and Delivery Workers in San Francisco* (Los Angeles: UC Santa Cruz Institute for Social Transformation), https://transform.ucsc.edu/on-demand-and-on-the-edge.

59. For kente cloth reference, see Danielle Paquette, 2020, "Kente Cloth Is Beloved in Ghana. Why Did Democrats Wear It?," *Washington Post*, 9 June, https://www.washingtonpost.com/world/africa/democrats-kente-cloth-ghana/2020/06/08/dc33bcc4-a9b5-11ea-a43b-be9f6494a87d_story.html.

60. See full list of demands at "March on Washington for Jobs and Freedom," 1963, *Lincoln Memorial Program*, 28 August, https://www.crmvet.org/docs/mowprog.pdf, 3.

61. Bayard Rustin, 1965, "From Protest to Politics: The Future of the Civil Rights Movement," *Commentary Magazine* 39 (2): 1.

62. Ibid.

63. Asa Philip Randolph and Bayard Rustin, 1967, *Freedom Budget for All Americans: A Summary* (New York: A. Philip Randolph Institute), 9, https://www.prrac.org/pdf/FreedomBudget.pdf.

64. Ibid., 1.

65. Ronald Walters and Toni-Michelle C. Travis, eds., 2010, *Democratic Destiny and the District of Columbia: Federal Politics and Public Policy* (Lanham, MD: Lexington Books).

66. Chris Myers Asch and George Derek Musgrove, 2017, *Chocolate City: A History of Race and Democracy in the Nation's Capital* (Chapel Hill: University of North Carolina Press), 394.

67. Amanda Huron, 2018, *Carving Out the Commons: Tenant Organizing and Housing Cooperatives in Washington, D.C.* (Minneapolis: University of Minnesota Press).

68. Katie J. Wells, 2015, "A Housing Crisis, a Failed Law, and a Property Conflict: The U.S. Urban Speculation Tax," *Antipode* 47 (4): 1043–1061.

69. Michael Greenberger, Elizabeth Brown, and Anne Bowden, eds., 1993, *Cold, Harsh, and Unending Resistance: The District of Columbia Government's Hidden War against Its Poor and Its Homeless* (Washington, DC: The Washington Legal Clinic for the Homeless), https://www.legalclinic.org/wp-content/uploads/2014/01/Cold-Harsh -Unending-Resistance-Report.pdf.

70. Michael K. Fauntroy, 2003, *Home Rule or House Rule: Congress and the Erosion of Local Governance in the District of Columbia* (Lanham, MD: University Press of America).

71. Harry S. Jaffe and Tom Sherwood, 1994, *Dream City: Race, Power and the Decline of Washington, D.C.* (New York: Simon and Schuster).

72. Fauntroy, 2003, *Home Rule or House Rule.*

73. Zachary Schrag, 2006, *The Great Society Subway: A History of the Washington Metro* (Baltimore: Johns Hopkins University Press), 2.

74. For a history of Marion Barry's summer jobs program, see Martin Austermuhle, 2019, "40 Years Later, Marion Barry's Summer Jobs Program Still Employing Thousands of D.C. Youth," WAMU, 24 June, https://wamu.org/story/19/06/24/40-years -later-marion-barrys-summer-jobs-program-still-employing-thousands-of-d-c-youth.

Chapter 3: The Work of Data

1. Interview with the authors, 31 July 2019.

2. Interview with the authors, 19 May 2016.

3. Rick Perlstein, 2017, "Outsmarted: On the Liberal Cult of the Cognitive Elite," *The Baffler* 34 (April): 52–64, https://thebaffler.com/salvos/outsmarted-perlstein.

4. All names of interviewed drivers are pseudonyms.

5. Interview with the authors, 19 May 2016.

6. Interview with the authors, 19 May 2016.

7. Interview with the authors, 19 May 2016.

8. Jay Cassano, 2016, "How Uber Profits Even While Its Drivers Aren't Earning Any Money," *Vice*, 2 February, https://www.vice.com/en/article/wnxd84/how-uber -profits-even-while-its-drivers-arent-earning-money.

9. See Heather Somerville, 2019, "The Answer to Uber's Profit Challenge? It May Lie in Its Trove of Data," Reuters, 9 May, https://www.reuters.com/article/us-uber -ipo-profit/the-answer-to-ubers-profit-challenge-it-may-lie-in-its-trove-of-data -idUSKCN1SF0O5.

10. Interview with the authors, 19 May 2016.

11. See Jordan Gilbertson and Andrew Saltzberg, 2017, "Introducing Uber Movement," press release, 9 January, https://www.uber.com/newsroom/introducing-uber -movement-2.

12. Elizabeth Dwoskin and Faiz Siddiqui, 2017, "Uber Is Finally Releasing a Data Trove That Officials Say Will Make Driving Better for Everyone," *Washington Post*, 8 January, https://www.washingtonpost.com/news/the-switch/wp/2017/01/08

/uber; See also Alyssa Newcomb, 2017, "Why Uber Is Opening Up a Treasure Trove of Data," NBC News, 11 January, https://www.nbcnews.com/tech/tech-news/why -uber-opening-treasure-trove-data-n705461.

13. Mike Isaac, 2017, "Uber, Trying to Hook Municipal Planners, Puts Out a Lure: Its Data," *New York Times*, 9 January, 3B.

14. Ibid.

15. Jason Shueh, 2017, "Uber Launches Open Data Platform Revealing City Traffic Flows," *StateScoop*, 9 January, https://statescoop.com/uber-launches-open-data -platform-revealing-city-traffic-flows.

16. Sharon Zukin, 2020, *The Innovation Complex: Cities, Tech, and the New Economy* (Oxford: Oxford University Press).

17. Interview with the authors, 27 September 2019.

18. Daniel Greene, 2021, *The Promise of Access: Technology, Inequality, and the Political Economy of Hope* (Cambridge, MA: MIT Press).

19. Interview with the authors, 27 September 2019.

20. Ibid.

21. Tajha Chappellet-Lanier, 2016, "DC Is Cisco's First US 'Lighthouse City,'" *TechnicallyDC*, 21 October, https://technical.ly/dc/2016/10/21/dc-smart-cities-cisco.

22. Interview with the authors, 5 February 2016.

23. David Alpert, 2014, "The Next Step for Regulating Uber," opinion, *Washington Post*, 19 September, https://www.washingtonpost.com/opinions/the-next-step-for -regulating-uber/2014/09/19/0e730c8e-3514-11e4-8f02-03c644b2d7d0_story.html.

24. According to one person familiar with the debates around the legislation, at least two factors played a role in the exclusion of data-sharing provisions from the 2014 law. The first was that "lobbyists wrote the bill," and the second was that the council— still chastened from Uber's aggressive campaign against a price floor in 2012—remained "nervous about crossing these companies," given the companies' proven popularity. Interview with the authors, 11 November 2019. See also Bradley Tusk, 2018, *The Fixer: My Adventures Saving Startups from Death by Politics* (New York: Portfolio).

25. For general discussion of the Budget Support Act of 2018, see Martin Austermuhle, 2018, "Taxes on Booze and Uber Set to Go Up in D.C. to Help Pay for Metro," WAMU, 15 May, https://wamu.org/story/18/05/15/taxes-booze-uber-set-go-d-c-help -pay-metro. For text of the act (DC Act 22-442) and its data-sharing provision, see https://lims.dccouncil.us/downloads/LIMS/39944/Signed_Act/B22-0753-SignedAct .pdf.

26. Elena Cresci, 2017, "#DeleteUber: How Social Media Turned on Uber," *The Guardian*, 30 January, https://www.theguardian.com/technology/2017/jan/30 /deleteuber-how-social-media-turned-on-uber.

27. For more on #DeleteUber, see Mike Isaac, 2017, "What You Need to Know about #DeleteUber," *New York Times*, 31 January, https://www.nytimes.com/2017/01 /31/business/delete-uber.html.

28. See Regina Clewlow and Gouri Shankar Mishra, 2017, *Disruptive Transportation: The Adoption, Utilization, and Impacts of Ride-Hailing in the United States* (Davis, CA: UC Davis Institute of Transportation Studies), https://usa.streetsblog.org/wp

-content/uploads/sites/5/2017/10/2017_UCD-ITS-RR-17-07.pdf. See also Michael Graehler, Richard Mucci, and Gregory Erhardt, 2019, *Understanding the Recent Transit Ridership Decline in Major U.S. Cities: Service Cuts or Emerging Modes?* (Washington, DC: Transportation Research Board).

29. Interview with the authors, 18 July 2019.

30. Interview with the authors, 18 July 2019.

31. Interview with the authors, 18 July 2021.

32. Interview with the authors, 17 July 2019.

33. Interview with the authors, 17 July 2019.

34. Interview with the authors, 19 July 2019.

35. Ibid.

36. Ibid.

37. For discussion of DDOT's adoption of MDS, see David Alpert, 2020, "Why a Battle between Tech Visionaries, Privacy Advocates, Uber, and Transportation Officials Is about Much More Than Scooter Data," *Greater Greater Washington* (blog), 20 May, https://ggwash.org/view/77285/mobility-data-standard-scooters-bikes -autonomous-vehicles-uber-lyft-ddot-los-angeles. For more discussion of MDS, also see David Zipper, 2019, "Cities Can See Where You Are Taking That Scooter," *Slate*, 2 April, https://slate.com/business/2019/04/scooter-data-cities-mds-uber-lyft-los -angeles.html.

38. Full text of letter at https://ggwash.org/files/Coalition_Letter_to_DDOT_re _Dockless_Mobility_Data_3.26.20_--_FINAL_.pdf.

39. See Laura Bliss, 2020, "This City Was Sick of Tech Disruptors. So It Decided to Become One," *Bloomberg City Lab*, 21 February, https://www.bloomberg.com/news /articles/2020-02-21/as-l-a-plays-tech-disruptor-uber-fights-back.

40. See full legal complaint at https://www.aclusocal.org/sites/default/files /sanchez_v_ladot_-_complaint.pdf.

41. Jamie Williams, 2020, "Unchecked Smart Cities Are Surveillance Cities. What We Need Are Smart Enough Cities," *Electronic Frontier Foundation*, 18 March, https:// www.eff.org/deeplinks/2020/03/unchecked-smart-cities-are-surveillance-cities-what -we-need-are-smart-enough.

42. Alpert, 2020, "Why a Battle between Tech Visionaries, Privacy Advocates, Uber, and Transportation Officials Is about Much More Than Scooter Data."

43. Interview with the authors, 30 July 2019.

44. Ibid.

45. Interview with the authors, 19 May 2016.

46. Interview with the authors, 19 May 2016.

47. Cassano, 2016, "How Uber Profits Even While Its Drivers Aren't Earning Any Money."

48. Interview with the authors, 26 August 2016.

49. Interview with the authors, 28 June 2016.

50. Ibid.

51. Interview with the authors, 28 June 2016.

52. Ben Zipperer, Celine McNicholas, Margaret Poydock, Daniel Schneider, and Kristen Harknett, 2022, *National Survey of Gig Workers Paints a Picture of Poor Working*

Conditions, Low Pay (Washington, DC: Economic Policy Institute), https://shift
.hks.harvard.edu/wp-content/uploads/2022/06/gig_brief.pdf. Studies in California and
Colorado similarly found that ride-hailing drivers' net earnings are below $7 an hour.
See Elizabeth McCullough, Brian Dolber, Justin Scoggins, Edward-Michael Muna,
and Sarah Treuhaft, 2022, "Prop22 Depresses Wages and Deepens Inequities for California Workers," National Equity Atlas, 21 September, https://nationalequityatlas
.org/prop22-paystudy; Kari Paul, 2022, "Colorado Drivers Make an Average of Just
$5.48 an Hour, Study Finds," *The Guardian*, 9 November, https://www.theguardian
.com/us-news/2022/nov/09/gig-drivers-colorado-wages-less-than-minimum
-study.

53. Ibid., 5.

54. For discussion of how the gig economy obfuscates meaningful wage calculations and can be similar to underpaid piecework arrangements, see Veena Dubal,
2020, "The Time Politics of Home-Based Digital Piecework," *C4E Journal: Perspectives on Ethics, Symposium Issue (The Future of Work in the Age of Automation and
AI)*, https://c4ejournal.net/2020/07/04/v-b-dubal-the-time-politics-of-home-based
-digital-piecework-2020-c4ej-xxx.

55. Katie J. Wells, Kafui Attoh, and Declan Cullen, 2019, *The Uber Workplace in
D.C.* (Washington, DC: Georgetown University Kalmanovitz Initiative for Labor and
the Working Poor), March, https://lwp.georgetown.edu/wp-content/uploads/sites
/319/uploads/Uber-Workplace.pdf.

56. David Harvey, 2009, *Social Justice and the City*, rev. ed. (Athens: University
of Georgia Press), 145.

57. Interview with the authors, 19 July 2019.

58. Interview with the authors, 27 September 2019.

59. Isaac, 2017, "Uber, Trying to Hook Municipal Planners, Puts Out a Lure."

60. Jathan Sadowski, Salome Viljoen, and Meredith Whitaker, 2021, "Everyone
Should Decide How Their Digital Data Are Used—Not Just Tech Companies," *Nature*
595 (July): 169–171, https://www.nature.com/articles/d41586-021-01812-3.

61. Perlstein, 2017, "Outsmarted."

Chapter 4: Flying Cars and Other Urban Legends

1. David Graeber, 2016, *The Utopia of Rules: On Technology, Stupidity, and the Secret
Joys of Bureaucracy* (London: Melville House), 113.

2. Peter Norton, 2021, *Autonorama: The Illusory Promise of High-Tech Driving*
(Washington, DC: Island Press), 21.

3. The U.S. National Highway Traffic Safety Administration uses a six-level classification system to evaluate the level of automation in a vehicle. See National Highway Traffic Safety Administration, U.S. Department of Transportation, "The Road
to Full Automation," https://www.nhtsa.gov/technology-innovation/automated
-vehicles-safety#the-topic-road-to-full-automation. Most discussions of "autonomous" vehicles are actually referring to highly automated vehicles. See Peter Norton,
2021, *Autonorama: The Illusory Promise of High-Tech Driving* (Washington, DC: Island
Press), 4.

4. Amir Efrati, 2012, "Google's Driverless Car Draws Political Power," *Wall Street Journal*, 12 October, https://www.wsj.com/articles/SB1000087239639044349330457 8034822744854696.

5. Tim Craig, 2012, "Google's Self-driving Car Makes D.C. Council Members Giddy," *D.C. Wire* (blog), *Washington Post*, 17 May, https://www.washingtonpost .com/blogs/dc-wire/post/googles-self-driving-car-makes-dc-council-members-giddy /2012/05/17/gIQAIOAQWU_blog.html.

6. Duncan Madden, 2018, "The Future Is Almost Here and It's Full of Flying Cars," *Forbes*, 30 April, https://www.forbes.com/sites/duncanmadden/2018/04/30/the -future-is-almost-here-and-its-full-of-flying-cars; Jack Stewart, 2017, "Can't Decide What Flying Car to Get? Try These 10," *Wired*, 22 June, https://www.wired.com/2017 /06/flying-car-concepts-prototypes; "Flying Cars Are Almost Here but They Don't Look Like Cars," *The Economist*, 30 May, https://www.economist.com/technology -quarterly/2019/05/30/flying-cars-are-almost-here-but-they-dont-look-like-cars.

7. See Doris Elin Urrutia, 2019, "NASA and Uber Are Getting Serious about Flying Cars," Space.com, 11 May, https://www.space.com/40553-nasa-uber-flying-car -simulation-plan.html; Jeremy Bogaisky, 2018, "Your Flying Car May Be Almost Here," *Forbes*, May 24, https://www.forbes.com/sites/jeremybogaisky/2018/05/24/your -flying-car-is-almost-here/#473eb37e5724. On the historical dream of flying cars and their relationship to technology and capitalism, see David Graeber, 2012, "Of Flying Cars and the Declining Rate of Profit," *The Baffler* 19 (March): 66–84.

8. Norton, 2021, *Autonorama*, introduction.

9. Aaron Benanav, 2020, *Automation and the Future of Work* (New York: Verso), chapter 1; Malene Freudendal-Pedersen, Sven Kesselring, and Eriketti Servou, 2019, "What Is Smart for the Future City? Mobilities and Automation," *Sustainability* 11 (1): 2–21.

10. Aaron Benanav, 2019, "Automation and the Future of Work—I," *New Left Review* 119 (Sept/Oct): 5–38, https://newleftreview.org/issues/ii119/articles/aaron -benanav-automation-and-the-future-of-work-1.

11. Rupert Neate, 2020, "Uber Sells Loss-Making Flying Taxi Division to Joby Aviation," *The Guardian*, 9 December, https://www.theguardian.com/technology /2020/dec/09/uber-sells-loss-making-flying-taxi-division-to-joby-aviation. Lyft has also drastically shrunk its projections for AV deployment. In 2016 it predicted that the majority of Lyft rides would be automated by 2021. In 2021 it projected that 5% of rides would be automated in the near future. See Ali Griswold, 2022, "Lyft Resets Its Driverless Ambitions," *Oversharing*, 14 June, https://oversharing.substack.com/p/lyft -resets-its-driverless-ambitions.

12. Graeber, 2012, "Of Flying Cars and the Declining Rate of Profit."

13. Uber, 2016, *Uber Elevate: Fast-Forwarding to a Future of On-Demand Urban Air Transportation*, white paper, 27 October, https://evtol.news/__media/PDFs/Uber ElevateWhitePaperOct2016.pdf.

14. Alex Davies, 2016, "Inside Uber's Plan to Take Over the Skies with Flying Cars," *Wired*, 27 October, https://www.wired.com/2016/10/uber-flying-cars-elevate -plan.

15. "On-demand aviation, has the potential to radically improve urban mobility, giving people back time lost in their daily commutes. Uber is close to the commute pain that citizens in cities around the world feel. We view helping to solve this problem as core to our mission and our commitment to our rider base. Just as skyscrapers allowed cities to use limited land more efficiently, urban air transportation will use three-dimensional airspace to alleviate transportation congestion on the ground" (*Uber Elevate*, 2).

16. Elaine L. Chao, 2019, "Remarks Prepared for Delivery by U.S. Secretary of Transportation Elaine L. Chao, Uber Elevate Symposium, Arlington, VA," U.S. Department of Transportation, 11 June, https://www7.transportation.gov/briefing-room/uber-elevate-symposium.

17. "Uber Elevate Summit 2019: News, Photos, and Videos," 2019, *Electric VTOL News*, 12 June, https://evtol.news/news/uber-elevate-summit-2019-news-photos-videos.

18. For histories of the environmental promise of futuristic automobiles, see Norton, 2021, *Autonorama*; Paris Marx, 2022, *Road to Nowhere: What Silicon Valley Gets Wrong about the Future of Transportation* (New York: Verso); Levi Tillemann, 2016, *The Great Race: The Global Quest for the Car of the Future* (New York: Simon and Schuster); Alex Davies, 2021, *Driven: The Race to Create the Autonomous Car* (New York: Simon & Schuster).

19. Davies, 2016, "Inside Uber's Plan to Take Over the Skies with Flying Cars."

20. Hannah Murphy, 2019, "The Investor Who Turned Down Uber at a $5m Valuation," *Financial Times*, 11 May, https://www.ft.com/content/de38388e-73a0-11e9-bbfb-5c68069fbd15.

21. Michael J. de la Merced and Kate Conger, 2019, "Uber I.P.O. Values Ride-Hailing Giant at $82.4 Billion," *New York Times*, 9 May, https://www.nytimes.com/2019/05/09/technology/uber-ipo-stock-price.html.

22. Hubert Horan, 2016, "Can Uber Ever Deliver? Part Three: Understanding False Claims about Uber's Innovation and Competitive Advantages," *Naked Capitalism* (blog), 2 December, https://www.nakedcapitalism.com/2016/12/can-uber-ever-deliver-part-three-understanding-false-claims-about-ubers-innovation-and-competitive-advantages.html.

23. Interview with the authors, 19 July 2019.

24. Interview with the authors, 19 July 2019.

25. Derek Thompson, 2022, "The End of the Millennial Lifestyle Subsidy," *The Atlantic*, 13 June, https://www.theatlantic.com/newsletters/archive/2022/06/uber-ride-share-prices-high-inflation/661250.

26. Luis F. Alvarez León and Jovanna Rosen, 2020, "Technology as Ideology in Urban Governance," *Annals of the American Association of Geographers* 110 (2): 497–506.

27. Langdon Winner, [1987] 2010, *The Whale and the Reactor: A Search for Limits in an Age of High Technology* (Chicago: University of Chicago Press).

28. "Uberworld," 2016, *The Economist*, 3 September, https://www.economist.com/leaders/2016/09/03/uberworld.

29. For recent examples, see Aaron Benanav, 2020, *Automation and the Future of Work* (New York: Verso); Phil Jones, 2021, *Work without the Worker: Labour in the Age of Platform Capitalism* (New York: Verso). For earlier discussions, see Stanley Aronowitz and William DiFazio, 2010, *The Jobless Future* (Minneapolis: University of Minnesota Press); Jeremy Rifkin, 1995, *The End of Work* (New York: G.P. Putnam); Ulrich Beck, 2000, *The Brave New World of Work*, trans. P. Camiller (Cambridge, UK: Polity).

30. Benanav, 2019, "Automation and the Future of Work—I," 12.

31. Eric Brynjolfsson and Andrew McAfee, 2014, *The Second Machine Age: Work, Progress, and Prosperity in a Time of Brilliant Technologies* (New York: W.W. Norton); Martin Ford, 2015, *Rise of the Robots: Technology and the Threat of a Jobless Future* (New York: Basic Books); Andy Stern and Lee Kravitz, 2016, *Raising the Floor: How a Universal Basic Income Can Renew Our Economy and Rebuild the American Dream* (New York: Public Affairs); Carl Benedikt Frey and Michael Osborne, 2017, "The Future of Employment: How Susceptible Are Jobs to Computerisation?" *Technological Forecasting and Social Change* 114 (January): 254–280; Klaus Schwab, 2017, *The Fourth Industrial Revolution* (New York: Crown); Carl Benedikt Frey, 2019, *The Technology Trap* (Princeton, NJ: Princeton University Press); Daniel Susskind, 2020, *A World without Work: Technology, Automation and How We Should Respond* (London: Penguin UK).

32. Biz Carson, 2017, "Uber Isn't Sure if It Can 'Remain a Viable Business' without Building Self-driving Cars," *Business Insider*, 8 April, https://www.businessinsider.com /uber-questions-future-of-being-a-viable-business-without-self-driving-cars-2017-4.

33. Ibid.

34. Julia Carrie Wong, 2016, "'We're Just Rentals': Uber Drivers Ask Where They Fit in a Self-driving Future," *The Guardian*, August 19, https://www.theguardian.com /technology/2016/aug/19/uber-self-driving-pittsburgh-what-drivers-think.

35. All names of interviewed drivers are pseudonyms.

36. Interview with the authors, 12 May 2016.

37. Interview with the authors, 28 June 2016.

38. "Self driving Lyft Ride," 2018, UberPeople.net (forum), 5 September, https:// www.uberpeople.net/threads/self-driving-lyft-ride.282669/#post-4286633.

39. Interview with the authors, 26 August 2016.

40. Interview with the authors, 18 July 2016.

41. Interview with the authors, 27 June 2016.

42. On the role of retraining as a solution to technological change in the economy, see Daniel Greene, 2021, *The Promise of Access: Technology, Inequality, and the Political Economy of Hope* (Cambridge, MA: MIT Press).

43. Michael Samers, 2021, "Futurological Fodder: On Communicating the Relationship between Artificial Intelligence, Robotics, and Employment," *Space and Polity* 25 (2): 237–256.

44. Felicity Lawrence, 2022, "'They Were Taking Us for a Ride': How Uber Used Investor Cash to Seduce Drivers," *The Guardian*, 12 July, https://www.theguardian.com /news/2022/jul/12/they-were-taking-us-for-a-ride-how-uber-used-investor-cash-to -seduce-drivers; Noam Scheiber, 2017, "How Uber Uses Psychological Tricks to Push

Its Drivers' Buttons," *New York Times*, 2 April, https://www.nytimes.com/interactive /2017/04/02/technology/uber-drivers-psychological-tricks.html.

45. Interview with the authors, 26 August 2016.

46. Ibid.

47. Interview with the authors, 24 August 2016.

48. Norton, 2021, *Autonorama*, 73.

49. Johana Bhuiyan and Pamela Duncan, 2022, "From Eureka Moment to Global Domination: A Timeline of Uber's Aggressive Expansion," *The Guardian*, 10 July, https://www.theguardian.com/news/2022/jul/10/uber-files-timeline-parisian-eureka -moment-global-domination.

50. Interview with the authors, 28 July 2016.

51. Alberto Vanolo, 2014, "Smartmentality: The Smart City as Disciplinary Strategy," *Urban Studies* 51 (5): 883–898; Alan Wiig and Elvin Wyly, 2016, "Introduction: Thinking through the Politics of the Smart City," *Urban Geography* 37 (4): 485–493; Jathan Sadowski and Roy Bendor, 2019, "Selling Smartness: Corporate Narratives and the Smart City as a Sociotechnical Imaginary," *Science, Technology, & Human Values* 44 (3): 540–563; Igor Calzada and Cristobal Cobo, 2015, "Unplugging: Deconstructing the Smart City," *Journal of Urban Technology* 22 (1): 23–43; Alvarez León and Rosen, 2020, "Technology as Ideology in Urban Governance."; Paolo Cardullo, Cesare Di Feliciantonio, and Rob Kitchin, eds., 2019, *The Right to the Smart City* (Bingley, UK: Emerald Group Publishing).

52. Martin Austermuhle, 2012, "Google's Self-Driving Car Gives Hope That D.C. Can Eventually Be Saved from Maryland Motorists," *DCist*, 17 May, https://dcist.com /story/12/05/17/google-self-driving-car-gives-hope/#photo-1.

53. *Autonomous Vehicle Act of 2012*, D.C. Law 19-278, 60 DCR 2119 (2013), https:// code.dccouncil.gov/us/dc/council/laws/19-278.

54. Marc Scribner, 2012, "Driverless Cars Are on the Way. Here's How Not to Regulate Them," opinion, *Washington Post*, 12 November, https://www.washingtonpost .com/opinions/driverless-cars-are-on-the-way-heres-how-not-to-regulate-them/2012 /11/02/a5337880-21f1-11e2-ac85-e669876c6a24_story.html.

55. *Autonomous Vehicle Act of 2012*, D.C. Law 19-278, 60 DCR 2119 (2013).

56. Sarah Anne Hughes, 2014, "D.C. Prepares for Terrifying Future of Self-driving Cars," *DCist*, 7 April, https://dcist.com/story/14/04/07/dc-preparing-for-terrifying -future.

57. Interview with the authors, 17 July 2019.

58. Ryan Ferguson, 2017, "D.C. Will Take Global Lead on Self-driving Cars," *DC Inno*, 11 January, https://www.bizjournals.com/washington/inno/stories/news/2017 /01/11/d-c-will-take-global-lead-on-self-driving-cars.html.

59. Skip Descant, 2018, "Washington, D.C., Dips Its Toe into Self-driving Cars," *Government Technology*, 20 February, https://www.govtech.com/fs/washington-dc -dips-its-toe-into-self-driving-cars.html.

60. Alvarez León and Rosen, 2020, "Technology as Ideology in Urban Governance." Luis F. Alvarez León, 2019, "Eyes on the Road: Surveillance Logics in the Autonomous Vehicle Economy," *Surveillance & Society* 17 (1/2): 198–204.

61. Tillemann, 2015, *The Great Race*; Yuko Aoyama and Luis F. Alvarez Léon, 2021, "Urban Governance and Autonomous Vehicles," *Cities* 119 (December): 103410.

62. "Five More Cities Join Bloomberg Philanthropies and The Aspen Institute's Global Initiative on Autonomous Vehicles," 2017, Bloomberg Philanthropies, news release, 9 January, https://www.prnewswire.com/news-releases/five-more-cities-join -bloomberg-philanthropies-and-the-aspen-institutes-global-initiative-on-autonomous -vehicles-300387730.html.

63. D.C. has also partnered with U.S. Ignite as part of its Global Cities Team Challenge. See Office of the Deputy Mayor for Planning and Economic Development, Government of the District of Columbia, "D.C. Smart City Initiative," http://open .dc.gov/smart-city. The city has also been named a Cisco "lighthouse city," a program which sought to bring smart street lighting and public high-speed Wi-Fi to Pennsylvania Avenue. See Jake Williams, 2016, "D.C. Joins International Cisco-Supported Smart Cities Effort, Unveils Next Phase of PA 2040," *StateScoop*, 20 October, https:// statescoop.com/d-c-joins-international-cisco-supported-smart-cities-effort-unveils -next-phase-of-pa-2040.

64. Taylor Shelton, Matthew Zook, and Alan Wiig, 2015, "The 'Actually Existing Smart City,'" *Cambridge Journal of Regions, Economy and Society* 8 (1): 13–25, 17.

65. Andrew Giambrone, 2018, "To Attract HQ2, D.C. Pitched Amazon a Taxpayer-Funded 'Ambassador,' One-Day Permit Approvals," *Curbed*, 20 November, https://dc.curbed.com/2018/11/20/18102681/dc-amazon-hq2-incentives-bezos -bowser-arlington; Martin Austermuhle, 2018, "Building Permits in a Flash, an Amazon 'Ambassador': Here's All of What D.C. Offered Amazon for HQ2," WAMU, 11 November, https://wamu.org/story/18/11/19/one-day-building-permits-an-amazon -ambassador-heres-all-of-what-d-c-offered-amazon-for-hq2.

66. Muriel Bowser, 2017, "Uber Greenlight Hub Center Opening," 19 October, https://www.flickr.com/photos/teammuriel/37215638214/in/album-721576875 28273211.

67. Office of the Deputy Mayor for Planning and Economic Development, Government of the District of Columbia, 2018, "DMPED's March Madness," 5 March, https://content.govdelivery.com/accounts/DCWASH/bulletins/1db21b3.

68. Ibid.

69. Office of the Deputy Mayor for Planning and Economic Development, Government of the District of Columbia, 2018, "Mayor Bowser Establishes Autonomous Vehicle Working Group," 12 February, https://dmped.dc.gov/release/mayor-bowser -establishes-autonomous-vehicle-working-group.

70. District of Columbia Interagency Working Group on Autonomous Vehicles, 2018, "Autonomous Vehicles Principles Statement," Office of the Deputy Mayor for Operations and Infrastructure, Government of the District of Columbia, 19 October, https://dmoi.dc.gov/sites/default/files/dc/sites/dmped/publication/attachments /Autonomous%20Vehicles%20Principles%20Statement_0.pdf.

71. Luz Lazo, 2018, "D.C. Mayor Muriel E. Bowser Lays Out the Welcome Mat for Self-driving Cars," *Washington Post*, 13 February, https://www.washingtonpost.com

/news/dr-gridlock/wp/2018/02/13/d-c-mayor-muriel-bowers-lays-out-the-welcome-mat-for-self-driving-cars.

72. Office of the Deputy Mayor for Planning and Economic Development, 2018, "Mayor Bowser Establishes Autonomous Vehicle Working Group."

73. See Government of the District of Columbia Board of Ethics and Government Accountability Lobbyist Activity Report for Uber Technologies July 2014; Government of the District of Columbia Board of Ethics and Government Accountability Lobbyist Activity Report for Uber Technologies January 2018, July 2018, Q1 2019, Q2 2019, Q3, 2019, Q4 2019, Q1 2020, Q2 2020, https://efiler.bega.dc.gov/LRRSearch.

74. Andrew Giambrone, 2019, "Self-driving Cars Are Coming. D.C. Lawmakers Want to Regulate Them," *Curbed, Washington DC*, 3 April, https://dc.curbed.com/2019/4/3/18294167/autonomous-vehicles-dc-self-driving-cars-regulations.

75. Committee on Transportation and the Environment, Council of the District of Columbia, 2019, *Public Roundtable: "The Integration of Autonomous Vehicles in the District,"* 31 January, video, 2:48:00. Full transcript and video recording at http://dc.granicus.com/ViewPublisher.php?view_id=29.

76. Ibid., at 36:30.

77. Ibid., at 36:35.

78. Ibid., at 38:40.

79. Michael Laris, 2020, "Uber Is Bringing Its Testing of Self-driving Vehicles to D.C. Streets," *Washington Post*, 23 January, https://www.washingtonpost.com/local/trafficandcommuting/uber-is-bringing-its-self-driving-vehicle-testing-to-dc-streets/2020/01/23/bb97b226-3e04-11ea-b90d-5652806c3b3a_story.html.

80. Self-Driving Coalition for Safer Streets, 2018, *Model Legislation for Autonomous Vehicles*, https://www.uniformlaws.org/HigherLogic/System/DownloadDocumentFile.ashx?DocumentFileKey=f6e813fe-0845-e5c3-f8ae-81b40fd2bc4a. The group has since rebranded itself as the Autonomous Vehicle Industry Association.

81. Committee on Transportation and the Environment, 2019, *Public Roundtable*, at 2:18:10.

82. Ibid., at 2:18:30.

83. Ibid., at 26:30.

84. Ibid., at 26:07.

85. Ibid., at 1:42:26.

86. Ibid., at 1:37:40.

87. Ibid.

88. Ibid., at 34:00.

89. Ibid.

90. District Department of Transportation, AECOM, and DC Sustainable Transportation, 2020, *DC AV Study: Final Report* (Washington, DC: Government of the District of Columbia), https://lims.dccouncil.us/downloads/LIMS/44545/Introduction/RC23-0172-Introduction.pdf.

91. Here we note that DCST has deep ties to David Alpert, the blogger and founder of *Greater Greater Washington*, whose advocacy around Uber's initial entry to the

city and data-sharing agreements is discussed, respectively, in chapters 1 and 3. DCST includes Uber as a member of its working group. Both DCST and Alpert's blog-turned-advocacy organization received varying amounts of funding from Uber between 2016 and 2021. Interview with the authors, 1 November 2019.

92. In the same month the AV working group published its report, researchers at the University of Maryland's National Center for Smart Growth Research and Education published a range of model scenarios. Smart City advocates in the region reported that "the future of [the] D.C.-Baltimore region depends on AV adoption." (Chris Teale, 2018, "Report: Future of DC-Baltimore Region Depends on AV Adoption," *Smart-Cities Dive*, 20 April, https://www.smartcitiesdive.com/news/dc-baltimore-region-av-adoption-growth/521770). The report itself, however, showed that only one of the four models, named Blue Planet, would have positive effects. Prospects for Regional Sustainability Tomorrow (PRESTO), 2020, *Smarter Roads, Smarter Cars, Smarter Growth? Baltimore-Washington 2040* (Baltimore: University of Maryland), https://www.umdsmartgrowth.org/wp-content/uploads/2020/07/DRAFT_PRESTOvol2_11012020_2.pdf.

93. District Department of Transportation, AECOM, and DC Sustainable Transportation, 2020, *DC AV Study*, 158.

94. Ibid., 16.

95. Liz Ellis Mayes, 2017, "DC Will Be the First US City to Pilot Food Delivery Bots," *Technical.ly*, 6 January, https://technical.ly/startups/food-delivery-bots-starship.

96. Julia Airey, 2017, "D.C. Delivery Robot Program Gets Extension," *Washington Times*, 12 December, https://www.washingtontimes.com/news/2017/dec/12/dc-delivery-robot-program-gets-extension.

97. Washington, D.C., 2016, § 50-1552, Establishment of a personal delivery device pilot program, https://code.dccouncil.gov/us/dc/council/code/titles/50/chapters/15C.

98. Michael Laris, 2016, "Driverless Delivery Robots Could Be Hitting D.C. Sidewalks Soon," *Washington Post*, 23 March, https://www.washingtonpost.com/news/dr-gridlock/wp/2016/03/23/driverless-delivery-robots-could-be-hitting-d-c-sidewalks-soon.

99. Ibid.

100. Sara Gilgore, 2016, "What the Skype Founders' Delivery Robots Will Look Like in Washington—and When You'll See Them Rolling Around," *Washington Business Journal*, 12 October, https://www.bizjournals.com/washington/news/2016/10/12/what-the-skype-founders-delivery-robots-will-look.html.

101. Scholars and food justice advocates have pushed back against the term "food deserts," arguing that 'taking racialized metaphors like "food desert" at face value privileges the persistence of "lack" that is nearly synonymous with Blackness in much social science research with little regard for how that lack gets transformed by the communities in question.' Ashanté M. Reese, 2018, "'We will not perish; we're going to keep flourishing': Race, Food Access, and Geographies of Self-Reliance," *Antipode* 50 (2): 415.

102. Liz Ellis Mayes, 2016, "Could Robots Eliminate D.C.'s Food Deserts?" *Technical.ly*, 24 March, https://technical.ly/dc/2017/03/24/delivery-bots-food-deserts.

103. Shira Ovide, 2022, "The Good News about Food Delivery," *New York Times*, 11 May, https://www.nytimes.com/2022/05/11/technology/food-delivery-apps-access .html; Caroline George and Adie Tomer, 2022, "The Potential—and Pitfalls—of the Digitalization of America's Food System," Brookings Institution, 11 May, https://www .brookings.edu/essay/the-potential-and-pitfalls-of-the-digitalization-of-americas -food-system; Nena Perry-Brown, 2018, "Delivery Robots, Farmshares: DC Looks for Solutions to Serve Food Deserts," *DC Urban Turf*, 9 February, https://dc.urbanturf .com/articles/blog/solutions-to-serve-dcs-food-deserts/13554.

104. Ibid.

105. Jessica Sidman, 2018, "More Delivery Robots Are Coming to DC," *Washingtonian*, 11 May, https://www.washingtonian.com/2018/05/11/more-delivery-robots -are-coming-to-dc; "D.C. Law 22-137. Personal Delivery Device Act of 2018," Council of the District of Columbia, https://code.dccouncil.gov/us/dc/council/laws/22-137.

106. Ibid.

107. Norton, 2021, *Autonorama*, 21.

108. Phil Allmendinger and Graham Haughton, 2012, "Post-political Spatial Planning in England: A Crisis of Consensus?" *Transactions of the Institute of British Geographers* 37 (1): 89–103.

109. Winner, 2010, *The Whale and the Reactor*, 10.

110. Aoyama and Alvarez Léon, 2021, "Urban Governance and Autonomous Vehicles."

111. Robert Macrorie, Simon Marvin, and Aidan While, 2021, "Robotics and Automation in the City: A Research Agenda," *Urban Geography* 42 (2): 197–217.

112. A growing body of literature shows how smart urbanism interacts with and shapes different cities globally. Ayona Datta, 2015, "A 100 Smart Cities, a 100 Utopias," *Dialogues in Human Geography* 5, (10): 49–53; Andrea Pollio, 2016, "Technologies of Austerity Urbanism: The "Smart City" Agenda in Italy (2011–2013)," *Urban Geography* 37 (4): 514–534; Dietmar Offenhuber, 2019, "The Platform and the Bricoleur— Improvisation and Smart City Initiatives in Indonesia," *Environment and Planning B: Urban Analytics and City Science* 46 (8): 1565–1580; Clara Irazábal and Paola Jirón, 2021, "Latin American Smart Cities: Between Worlding Infatuation and Crawling Provincializing," *Urban Studies* 58 (3): 507–534; Margarita Angelidou, 2014, "Smart City Policies: A Spatial Approach," *Cities* 41: S3–S11; Vanessa Watson, "The Allure of 'Smart City' Rhetoric: India and Africa," *Dialogues in Human Geography* 5 (1): 36–39.

113. Macrorie, Marvin, and While, 2021, "Robotics and Automation in the City," 208.

114. Arielle Levin and Derek Hyra, 2020, *The Wharf: A Monumental Waterfront Urban Regeneration Development in Washington, D.C.* (Washington, DC: The Metropolitan Policy Center, American University).

115. Office of the Deputy Mayor for Planning and Economic Development, 2018, "Mayor Bowser Establishes Autonomous Vehicle Working Group."

116. Ibid.

117. Government of the District of Columbia, DMPED, Cityfi, and SWBID, 2020, "DC Mobility Innovation District—Call for Projects | On-Demand Mobility Service and Supporting Technology," https://www.swbid.org/mobilitymid.

118. "Mobility," Southwest Business Improvement District, https://www.swbid.org/mobility (accessed 20 December 2021).

119. Casey Dawkins and Rolf Moeckel, 2016, "Transit-Induced Gentrification: Who Will Stay, and Who Will Go?" *Housing Policy Debate* 26 (4–5): 801–818.

120. Mimi Montgomery, 2021, "As Interest in Luxury D.C. Apartments Soars, Developers Are Competing to Offer the Most Extravagant Amenities Possible," *Washingtonian*, 27 July, https://www.washingtonian.com/2021/07/27/as-interest-in-luxury-dc-apartments-soars-developers-are-competing-to-offer-the-most-extravagant-amenities-possible.

121. Patrick Sisson, 2019, "In the Apartment Amenity Arms Race, Service and Technology Win Out," *Curbed*, 26 March, https://archive.curbed.com/2019/3/26/18281713/rent-apartment-amenity-residential-real-estate.

122. Perry Stein, 2016, "This New Apartment Building Has an 'Uber Room' to Wait for Your Ride," *Washington Post*, August 17, https://www.washingtonpost.com/news/local/wp/2016/08/17/this-new-apartment-building-has-an-uber-room-to-wait-for-your-ride. Amazon Fresh's flagship automated store in D.C. is also part of a significant real estate development and is located within a mixed-use apartment building, The Liz, on 14th Street NW. This mixed-use development, built with former director of the D.C. office of planning, Ron Altman, has been hailed as a successful example of development without gentrification. A glowing *New York Times* article hailed the company's championing of "A gentler way to gentrify." See Brenda Richardson, 2019, "Former D.C. City Planner Is Revolutionizing Non-profit Sustainability with Mixed-Use Development," *Forbes*, 21 July, https://www.forbes.com/sites/brendarichardson/2019/07/21/former-dc-city-planner-is-revolutionizing-non-profit-sustainability-with-mixed-use-development; Stefanos Chen, 2019, "A Gentler Way to Gentrify?," *New York Times*, 16 August, https://www.nytimes.com/2019/08/16/realestate/developers-try-gentler-gentrification.html.

123. Daniella Byck, 2021, "Self-driving Cars Are Now Cruising through the Yards," *Washingtonian*, 19 February, https://www.washingtonian.com/2021/02/19/self-driving-cars-are-now-cruising-through-the-yards.

124. The company also suffered the same fate as Uber's AV division, raising an important question of what happens to public transit that is operated by private companies when the company is shut down or bought. Pranshu Verna, 2022, "Boston Self-driving Car Company Optimus Ride Closes Its Doors," *Boston Globe*, 11 January, https://www.bostonglobe.com/2022/01/11/business/boston-self-driving-car-company-optimus-ride-is-acquired.

125. Sharon Zukin, 1991, *Landscapes of Power: From Detroit to Disney World* (Berkeley: University of California Press); Michael Sorkin, ed., 1992, *Variations on a Theme Park: The New American City and the End of Public Space* (New York: Hill and Wang).

126. Brett Williams, 1988, *Upscaling Downtown: Stalled Gentrification in Washington, D.C.* (Ithaca, NY: Cornell University Press); Jonathan Jackson, 2015, "The Consequences of Gentrification for Racial Change in Washington, DC," *Housing Policy* 25 (2): 353–373; Amanda Huron, 2018, *Carving Out the Commons: Tenant Organizing and Housing Cooperatives in Washington* (Minneapolis: University of Minnesota Press).

127. Fredric Jameson, 2005, *Archaeologies of the Future: The Desire Called Utopia and Other Science Fictions* (New York: Verso).

128. Thomas More [1516], 2003, *Utopia* (London: Penguin).

129. Anthony M. Townsend, 2013, *Smart Cities: Big Data, Civic Hackers, and the Quest for a New Utopia* (New York: W.W. Norton).

130. David Bissell, 2018, "Automation Interrupted: How Autonomous Vehicle Accidents Transform the Material Politics of Automation," *Political Geography* 65 (July): 57.

131. Federico Cugurullo, 2018, "The Origin of the Smart City Imaginary: From the Dawn of Modernity to the Eclipse of Reason," in *The Routledge Companion to Urban Imaginaries*, ed. Christoph Lindner and Miriam Meissner (New York: Routledge), 113–124; Giuseppe Grossi and Daniela Pianezzi, 2017, "Smart Cities: Utopia or Neoliberal Ideology?," *Cities* 69: 79–85; Olivia Bina, Andy Inch, and Lavinia Pereira, 2020, "Beyond Techno-Utopia and Its Discontents: On the Role of Utopianism and Speculative Fiction in Shaping Alternatives to the Smart City Imaginary," *Futures* 115 (January): 102475.

132. Jathan Sadowski and Sophia Maalsen, 2020, "Modes of Making Smart Cities: Or, Practices of Variegated Smart Urbanism," *Telematics and Informatics* 55 (December): 101449.

133. Jathan Sadowski, 2021, "Who Owns the Future City? Phases of Technological Urbanism and Shifts in Sovereignty," *Urban Studies* 58 (8): 1732–1744.

Chapter 5: The Uber Workplace: "It Just Is What It Is"

1. Amanda Huron, 2015, "Working with Strangers in Saturated Space: Reclaiming and Maintaining the Urban Commons," *Antipode* 47 (4): 963–979.

2. Interview with the authors, 11 May 2016.

3. All names of interviewed drivers are pseudonyms.

4. Interview with the authors, 5 August 2016.

5. Ibid.

6. Three other drivers in this study participated in Uber's in-house leasing program. For one of them, Beatrice, the debt she took on to drive for Uber did not seem so different from that to which she was accustomed. She had worked for the previous seven years as a contractor, without benefits, in the asbestos-removal industry. Before that, she had had jobs in daycares, at restaurants, and as a cross-country truck driver. In the week before we met, Beatrice drove for Uber for 14 hours. After Uber took out its 25% commission and booking fees, she earned about $300 for that time spent driving. Given her weekly expenses of $170 for the lease and $63 for the insuring of the vehicle, Beatrice had netted less than $5 per hour. Moreover, these rates meant that if Beatrice continued to drive for Uber, she would have $12,040 worth of annual expenses in addition to the costs of gas and vehicle maintenance, which could be significant, as she had put three thousand miles on her car in the last month alone. (Interview with the authors, 1 August 2016.)

7. According to the Federal Trade Commission, Uber regularly deceived drivers about these costs. See Associated Press, 2017, "Uber Pays $20 Million to Settle Claims It Deceived Drivers about Pay," *Los Angeles Times*, 20 January, https://www.latimes.com

/business/la-fi-tn-uber-ftc-20170120-story.html. In addition, the Massachusetts attorney general found that Uber's former lender charged higher-than-allowed interest rates to drivers in low-income communities. See Deirdre Fernandes, 2015, "Santander Auto-Loan Unit to Pay Back $5.4m," *Boston Globe*, 5 November, https://www.bostonglobe.com/business/2015/11/05/santander-agrees-million-settlement-over-high-auto-loan-rates/NclpZuFeh8WR18RpnLJjuI/story.html. At the end of 2017, Uber phased out its in-house leasing program. But the company still advertises third-party leases at similar rates to drivers, and, in 2022, it celebrated a claim that fifteen thousand Uber drivers had rented Teslas through a partnership with Hertz. See Umar Shakir, 2022, "Uber Drivers Are Liking the Teslas," *The Verge*, 28 June, https://www.theverge.com/2022/6/28/23185468/uber-drivers-tesla-car-rentals-through-hertz-growth.

8. Phil LeBeau, 2015, "Record Highs of Americans Leasing Autos," CNBC, 1 June, https://www.cnbc.com/2015/06/01/record-highs-of-americans-leasing-vehicles.html.

9. Interview with the authors, 5 August 2016.

10. Interview with the authors, 18 July 2019.

11. Interview with the authors, 18 July 2019.

12. Interview with the authors, 24 June 2020.

13. See appendix B for a detailed breakdown of these participants.

14. Interview with the authors, 25 August 2016.

15. Interview with the authors, 13 May 2016.

16. Interview with the authors, 16 July 2016.

17. Interview with the authors, 1 August 2016.

18. Veena Dubal, 2017, "The Drive to Precarity: A Political History of Work, Regulation, & Labor Advocacy in San Francisco's Taxi & Uber Economies," *Berkeley Journal of Employment and Labor Law* 38 (1): 73–135; Niels van Doorn, 2017, "Platform Labor: On the Gendered and Racialized Exploitation of Low-Income Service Work in the 'On-demand' Economy," *Information, Communication & Society* 20 (6): 898–914. See also Alexandrea Ravenelle, 2019, *Hustle and Gig: Struggling and Surviving in the Sharing Economy* (Berkeley: University of California Press); Juli Ticona, 2022, *Left to Our Own Devices: Coping with Insecure Work in a Digital Age* (Oxford, UK: Oxford University Press); Trebor Scholz, 2017, *Uberworked and Underpaid: How Workers Are Disrupting the Digital Economy*; Tom Slee, 2015, *What's Yours Is Mine: Against the Sharing Economy* (New York: OR Books); Steven Hill, 2015, *Raw Deal: How the "Uber Economy" and Runaway Capitalism Are Screwing American Workers* (New York: St. Martin's Press); Sarah Kessler, 2018, *Gigged: The End of the Job and the Future of Work* (New York: St. Martin's Press).

19. See Andrew Herod, 2001, *Labor Geographies: Workers and the Landscapes of Capitalism* (New York: Guilford Press).

20. Interview with the authors, 20 August 2016.

21. See also Brenton J. Malin and Curry Chandler, 2017, "Free to Work Anxiously: Splintering Precarity among Drivers for Uber and Lyft," *Communication, Culture & Critique* 10 (2): 382–400.

22. Interview with the authors, 24 May 2016.

23. Interview with the authors, 19 May 2016.

24. Interview with the authors, 11 May 2016.

25. Interview with the authors, 9 July 2019.

26. Interview with the authors, 11 May 2016.

27. When these drivers began work on the platform, 45% said they did not know any other current or former Uber drivers. Another 43% reported knowing only one other current or former driver.

28. For discussion, see Alex Rosenblat, 2018, *Uberland: How Algorithms Are Rewriting the Rules of Work* (Berkeley: University of California Press).

29. Interview with the authors, 12 May 2016.

30. Ibid.

31. Interview with the authors, 11 May 2016.

32. Kafui Attoh, Katie J. Wells, and Declan Cullen, 2019, "'We're Building Their Data': Labor, Alienation, and Idiocy in the Smart City," *Environment and Planning D: Society and Space* 37 (6): 1007–1024.

33. Interview with the authors, 10 July 2019.

34. Interview with the authors, 24 Aug 2016.

35. Harry Campbell, 2017, "How to Calculate Per Mile Earnings Instead of Per Hour," *The Rideshare Guy* (blog), https://therideshareguy.com/how-to-calculate-per -mile-earnings-instead-of-per-hour.

36. For discussion, see Hannah Johnston, 2020, "Labour Geographies of the Platform Economy: Understanding Collective Organizing Strategies in the Context of Digitally Mediated Work," *International Labour Review* 159 (1): 25–45; Andrea Pollio, 2019, "Forefronts of the Sharing Economy: Uber in Cape Town," *International Journal of Urban and Regional Research* 43 (4): 760–775.

37. Interview with the authors, 15 July 2019.

38. Interview with the authors, 15 July 2019.

39. Interview with the authors, 10 August 2016.

40. Airport regulations were amended after four public hearings at which thirty-nine individuals, only five of whom were supportive of Uber, gave comments.

41. The National Airport Taxi Drivers Association, which won these victories, has not built an alliance with Uber drivers in the lot.

42. Dynamic pricing is a business strategy in which the price for a ride is not firmly set. Instead, the price changes based on increased demand at certain times. Digital technologies and their rapid exchange of geo-spatial data have helped integrate this model, which historically has been used in airline and hotel industries, into ride-hailing services.

43. See Jamie Woodcock and Mark R. Johnson, 2018, "Gamification: What It Is, and How to Fight It," *Sociological Review* 66 (3): 542–558; see also Sarah Mason, 2018, "High Score, Low Pay: Why the Gig Economy Loves Gamification," *The Guardian*, 20 November, https://www.theguardian.com/business/2018/nov/20/high-score-low -pay-gamification-lyft-uber-drivers-ride-hailing-gig-economy.

44. One way to understand the Uber workplace is through the idea of "just-in-place" labor. This concept draws from the ideas of "just-in-time" manufacturing (often associated with the automotive industry) and "just-in-time" staffing (often associated

with the retail sector). (See Andrew Herod, 2000, "Implications of Just-in-Time Production for Union Strategy: Lessons from the 1998 General Motors–United Auto Workers Dispute," *Annals of the Association of American Geographers* 90 (3): 521–547.) In both cases, "just-in-time" is a management technique aimed at decreasing response times between customers and suppliers, as well as reducing production times and inventory levels. In response to a change in the level of demand from customers, companies can quickly scale up or down in order to avoid losses associated with having too much inventory (in the case of the automotive industry) or too much paid staff (in the case of retail). Some scholars have argued that on-demand services are producing just-in-time workers with "hectic tempos." (See Julie Yujie Chen and Ping Sun, 2020, "Temporal Arbitrage, Fragmented Rush, and Opportunistic Behaviors: The Labor Politics of Time in the Platform Economy," *New Media & Society* 22 (9): 1561–1579. See also Valerio De Stefano, 2015, "The Rise of the 'Just-in-Time Workforce': On-Demand Work, Crowdwork, and Labour Protection in the 'Gig-Economy'," *Comparative Labor Law & Policy Journal* 37 (Fall): 471–504.) We argue that the assertion needs to be pushed further. The rise of the "just-in-place" worker associated with Uber is no different, except that it allows Uber to address not only temporal but also *spatial* spikes in demand. One of the big innovations of the Uber workplace arises not just from technological infrastructure but also from the everyday management of drivers that isolates them and, thus, limits the possibilities for solidarity. The Uber platform, which relies on algorithms not to schedule its drivers as much as to *place* them where it wants them across a city, strongly inhibits drivers from building relationships. See also Katie J. Wells, Kafui Attoh, and Declan Cullen, 2021, "'Just-in-Place' Labor: Driver Organizing in the Uber Workplace," *Environment and Planning A: Economy and Space* 53 (2): 315–331.

45. One way to think about this strategy is as "urban hackers capable of tinkering with the proprietary platform and its data flows." See Karen Gregory and Miguel Paredes Maldonado, 2020, "Delivering Edinburgh: Uncovering the Digital Geography of Platform Labour in the City," *Information, Communication & Society* 23 (8): 1187–1202.

46. Other gig workers have used "fake-GPS apps" to make it seem they are closer to a delivery zone in order to facilitate more matches or, in other cases, farther from the zone in order to hide from orders. See Heiner Heiland, 2021, "Controlling Space, Controlling Labour? Contested Space in Food Delivery Gig Work," *New Technology Work and Employment* 36 (1): 1–16.

47. It was not clear to drivers, and is not clear to the authors of this book, how this form of surge pricing was paid to the driver. Uber has designed its platform in such a way that riders and drivers do not have transparency while they're together over who is paying what and how their fees are being paid. Did passengers pay a $30 higher fare? Or did the company draw a decreased amount from the ride?

48. Interview with the authors, 26 August 2016.

49. Interview with the authors, 11 July 2019.

50. "Washington, D.C." forum thread, 2018, UberPeople.net (forum), 26 March, https://uberpeople.net/forums/WashingtonDC; "Washington, D.C." forum threads, 2019, UberPeople.net (forum), 9 January, 21 February, https://uberpeople.net/forums/WashingtonDC.

51. U.S. presidential candidates Bernie Sanders and Elizabeth Warren announced their support for striking drivers.

52. Interview with the authors, 16 July 2019.

53. For discussion of gig-worker strikes and strategies, see Jamie Woodcock and Callum Cant, 2022, "Platform Worker Organising at Deliveroo in the UK: From Wildcat Strikes to Building Power," *Journal of Labor and Society* 25 (2): 220–236.

54. For discussion of similar and other instances of agency in the gig economy, see Zizheng Yu, Emiliano Treré, and Tiziano Bonini, 2022, "The Emergence of Algorithmic Solidarity: Unveiling Mutual Aid Practices and Resistance among Chinese Delivery Workers," *Media International Australia* 183 (1): 107–123; Mohammad Amir Anwar and Mark Graham, 2020, "Hidden Transcripts of the Gig Economy: Labour Agency and the New Art of Resistance among African Gig Workers," *Environment and Planning A: Economy and Space* 52 (7): 1269–1291; Fabian Ferrari and Mark Graham, 2021, "Fissures in Algorithmic Power: Platforms, Code, and Contestation," *Cultural Studies* 35 (4–5): 814–832; Arianna Tassinari and Vincenzo Maccarrone, 2020, "Riders on the Storm: Workplace Solidarity among Gig Economy Couriers in Italy and the UK," *Work, Employment and Society* 34 (1): 35–54.

55. Interview with the authors, 10 July 2019.

56. Friedrich Engels famously asked a question about the meaning of similar limited actions by workers: "It will be asked, 'Why, then, do the workers strike in such cases, when the uselessness of such measures is so evident?' Simply because they must protest against every reduction, even if dictated by necessity; because they feel bound to proclaim that they, as human beings, shall not be made to bow to social circumstances, but social conditions ought to yield to them as human beings; because silence on their part would be a recognition of these social conditions, an admission of the right of the bourgeoisie to exploit the workers in good times and let them starve in bad ones." See Friedrich Engels, [1845] 1987, *The Condition of the Working Class in England* (Harmondsworth, UK: Penguin Books).

57. Brian Dolber, 2019, *From Independent Contractors to an Independent Union: Building Solidarity through Rideshare Drivers United's Digital Organizing Strategy* (Philadelphia: Media, Inequality and Change Center), https://www.asc.upenn.edu/sites/default/files/2020-11/Dolber_finall.pdf; Johnston, 2020, "Labour Geographies of the Platform Economy."

58. See Miriam Greenberg and Penny Lewis, eds., 2017, *The City Is the Factory: New Solidarities and Spatial Strategies in an Urban Age* (Ithaca, NY: Cornell University Press).

59. Between 2015 and 2019, the Metropolitan Washington Airport Authority spent $1 million to manage waiting areas for ride-hailing drivers.

60. Interview with the authors, 10 July 2019.

61. Sam Sweeney, 2019, "Uber, Lyft Drivers Manipulate Fares at Reagan National Causing Artificial Price Surges," WJLA7 News, 16 May, https://wjla.com/news/local/uber-and-lyft-drivers-fares-at-reagan-national.

62. Miriam Greenberg and Penny Lewis write that cities must be seen as the new factory. Workers are more likely to demonstrate in urban space, be it on sidewalks or

plazas, than at the gates of their workplace. In this light, the airport police are Uber's new foremen. See Greenberg and Lewis, 2017, *The City Is the Factory*, 7.

63. Edna Bonacich finds that central nodes such as ports—or, in our case, airports—are fundamental strengths *and* weaknesses for capital. See Edna Bonacich, 2003, "Pulling the Plug: Labor and the Global Supply Chain," *New Labor Forum* 12 (2): 41–48.

64. See Rosenblat, 2018, *Uberland*; Jonathan Woodside, Tara Vinodrai, and Markus Moos, 2021, "Bottom-Up Strategies, Platform Worker Power and Local Action: Learning from Ridehailing Drivers," *Local Economy: The Journal of the Local Economy Policy Unit* 36 (4): 325–343.

65. See Dolber, 2019, *From Independent Contractors to an Independent Union*.

66. Though driver organizing was fledgling at the start of the pandemic, enough groundwork had been covered that local leaders launched a series of Zoom sessions in 2020 about working conditions and unemployment insurance—specifically, how to get it. By the end of the year, the contact lists developed by local organizers were no longer useful, as many former drivers moved from ride-hailing platforms to instant delivery, construction, or other jobs. The pandemic seemed to have expedited turnover in an industry already rife with short tenure, a pattern that ensures significant barriers to workers' collective agency. In early 2021, D.C.'s first, and so far only, platform labor organization decided to sunset itself.

67. See Declan Cullen, Kafui Attoh, and Katie J. Wells, 2018, "Taking Back the Wheel," *Dissent*, 31 August, https://www.dissentmagazine.org/online_articles/uber-flying-car-silicon-valley-labor-technology-future-politics.

68. For a critique of this phrase and an argument for avoiding it, see Walter Johnson, 2003, "On Agency," *Journal of Social History* 37 (1): 113–124.

69. Sarah L. Holloway, Louise Holt, and Sarah Mills, 2019, "Questions of Agency," *Progress in Human Geography* 43 (3): 458–477.

70. Cindi Katz, 2004, *Growing Up Global: Economic Restructuring and Children's Everyday Lives* (Minneapolis: University of Minnesota Press), 256, emphasis added.

71. Amanda Huron, 2015, "Working with Strangers in Saturated Space: Reclaiming and Maintaining the Urban Commons," *Antipode* 47 (4): 963–979.

72. Heather McLean, 2020, "Spaces for Feminist Commoning? Creative Social Enterprise's Enclosures and Possibilities," *Antipode* 53 (1): 242–259.

73. For discussion of networks that have generated solidarity among gig workers in Jakarta, see Samuel Nowak, 2021, "The Social Lives of Network Effects: Speculation and Risk in Jakarta's Platform Economy," *Environment and Planning A: Economy and Space*, advance online publication, https://doi.org/10.1177/0308518X211056953; Rida Qadri, 2021, "What's in a Network? Infrastructures of Mutual Aid for Digital Platform Workers during COVID-19," *Proceedings of the ACM [Association for Computer Machinery] on Human-Computer Interaction* 5 (CSCW2): 1–20.

74. Katz, 2004, *Growing Up Global*, 242.

75. See Lizzie Richardson and David Bissell, 2019, "Geographies of Digital Skill," *Geoforum* 99 (February): 278–286; Emily Reid-Musson, 2014, "Historicizing Precarity: A Labour Geography of 'Transient' Migrant Workers in Ontario Tobacco," *Geoforum* 56 (September): 161–171.

Conclusion: A New Common Sense

1. "Expectations, n.1b." *OED Online*, Oxford University Press.

2. Charles Dickens, 1890 [1861], *Great Expectations* (New York: Collier).

3. For discussion of Uber's track record, see Harry Davies, Simon Goodley, Felicity Lawrence, Paul Lewis, and Lisa O'Carroll, 2022, "Uber Broke Laws, Duped Police and Secretly Lobbied Governments, Leak Reveals," *The Guardian*, 11 July, https://www.theguardian.com/news/2022/jul/10/uber-files-leak-reveals-global-lobbying-campaign; Mike Isaac, 2019, *Super Pumped: The Battle for Uber* (New York: W.W. Norton).

4. We are echoing geographer Don Mitchell's style of questioning. See Don Mitchell, 2006, "Property Rights, the First Amendment, and Judicial Anti-Urbanism: The Strange Case of *Virginia v Hicks*," *Urban Geography* 26 (7): 565–586.

5. Iris Marion Young, 1990, *Justice and the Politics of Difference* (Princeton, NJ: Princeton University Press), 256.

6. Ruth Wilson Gilmore, 2002, "Fatal Couplings of Power and Difference: Notes on Racism and Geography," *Professional Geographer* 54 (1): 16.

7. All names of interviewed drivers are pseudonyms.

8. Interview with the authors, 11 May 2016.

9. A related unpublished poem by Kafui Attoh: "The law locks up the man or woman / who dodges the fare and steals Metro service from the public / but lets the greater culprit go / who steals the public from the Metro."

10. See Martin DiCaro, 2016, "Episode 11: Track Fires vs. Garbage Fires," in *Metropocalypse*, produced by Brendan Sweeney, Joe Warminsky, et al., podcast, 22:28, WAMU, 8 August, https://wamu.org/story/16/08/08/episode_11_track_fires_vs_garbage_fires.

11. Interview with the authors, 11 May 2016.

12. Interview with the authors, 15 July 2019.

13. Ibid.

14. Interview with the authors, 3 March 2022.

15. Ibid.

16. For a discussion of "structure of feeling," see Raymond Williams, 1983 [1976], *Keywords: A Vocabulary of Culture and Society* (New York: Oxford University Press).

17. Amanda Michelle Gomez, 2022, "Ward 4 Councilmember Introduces D.C. 'Green New Deal' Bills for Housing and Lead Pipe Removal," *DCist*, 26 April, https://dcist.com/story/22/04/26/dc-ward-4-councilmember-introduces-green-new-deal.

18. Margaret Barthel, 2022, "MetroAccess Workers Reach Tentative Union Agreement with Private Contractor, End Strike," *DCist*, 11 August, https://dcist.com/story/22/08/11/metroaccess-strike-union-contract.

19. For a discussion of the rarity of this strike, see Michael Haack, 2022, "The Strike That Shut Down Metro for Nearly a Week in 1978," *Washington Post*, 4 May, https://www.washingtonpost.com/history/2022/05/04/metro-wildcat-strike-1978.

20. "Press Release: Councilmember Christina Henderson to Pilot Universal Metrobus Access," 2022, *DC Line*, 27 October, https://thedcline.org/2022/10/27/press-release-councilmember-christina-henderson-introduces-legislation-to-pilot

-universal-metrobus-access; Martin Austermuhle, 2022, "Bill to Give D.C. Residents $100 a Month for Metro Clears Council Committee," *DCist*, 26 September, https://dcist .com/story/22/09/26/dc-advances-100-dollar-resident-metro-subsidy.

21. Ambar Castillo, 2022, "Bill Would Give D.C. Domestic Workers Legal Rights and Protections," *Washington City Paper*, 16 March, https://washingtoncitypaper.com /article/551347/bill-would-give-d-c-domestic-workers-legal-rights-and-protections.

22. Cuneyt Dil, 2022, "D.C. Ballot Will Again Ask Voters if Tipped Wage Should Rise," *Axios*, 6 April, https://www.axios.com/local/washington-dc/2022/04/06/dc -ballot-tipped-wage-raise.

23. Julie Zauzmer Weil, 2022, "Candidate Robert White Pitches Guaranteed Job for Every D.C. Resident," *Washington Post*, 21 April, https://www.washingtonpost.com /dc-md-va/2022/04/21/robert-white-dc-mayor-jobs-guarantee.

24. On four Saturdays in a row in 2021, the *New York Times* ran front-page Business Section articles about low-wage workers for ride-hailing and grocery-delivery services.

25. These workers' movements are not limited to the United States. In the United Kingdom, for instance, see the Worker Info Exchange (https://www .workerinfoexchange.org).

26. Ted van Green, 2022, "Majorities of Adults See Decline of Union Membership as Bad for the US and Working People," Pew Research Center, 18 February, https:// www.pewresearch.org/fact-tank/2022/02/18/majorities-of-adults-see-decline-of -union-membership-as-bad-for-the-u-s-and-working-people.

27. Justin McCarthy, 2022, "U.S. Approval of Labor Unions at Highest Point since 1965," Gallup, 30 August, https://news.gallup.com/poll/398303/approval-labor -unions-highest-point-1965.aspx.

28. Derek Thompson, 2021, "The Great Resignation Is Accelerating," *The Atlantic*, 15 October, https://www.theatlantic.com/ideas/archive/2021/10/great-resignation -accelerating/620382.

Appendix A: A Methodological Note

1. Donald Anderson, 2014, "Not Just a Taxi"? For-Profit Ridesharing, Driver Strategies, and VMT," *Transportation* 41 (5): 1099–1117; Alex Rosenblat, 2018, *Uberland: How Algorithms Are Rewriting the Rules of Work* (Berkeley: University of California Press); UCLA Labor Center Report, 2018, *More Than a Gig: A Survey of Ride-Hailing Drivers in Los Angeles*, https://www.labor.ucla.edu/wp-content/uploads/2018/06/Final-Report .-UCLA-More-than-a-Gig.pdf.

2. See also Noopur Raval and Paul Dourish, 2016, "Standing Out from the Crowd: Emotional Labor, Body Labor, and Temporal Labor in Ridesharing," *Proceedings of the 19th ACM [Association for Computing Machinery] Conference on Computer-Supported Cooperative Work & Social Computing* (27 February–2 March): 97–107.

3. Interview with the authors, 6 April 2016.

4. Funda Ustek Spilda, Kelle Howson, Hannah E. Johnston, Alessio Bertolini, Patrick Feuerstein, Louise Bezuidenhout, Oğuz Alyanak, and Mark Graham, 2022, "Is Anonymity Dead?: Doing Critical Research on Digital Labour Platforms through Platform Interfaces," *Work Organisation, Labour & Globalisation* 16 (1): 72–87.

5. Gift cards were used to compensate drivers for lost work time.

6. Eric Grenier, 2020, "Cooped Up by the Pandemic, More People Are Taking Part in Polls," CBC News, 31 May, https://www.cbc.ca/news/politics/covid19-poll-response-rates-1.5590429.

7. See Jonathan Hall and Alan Krueger, 2018, "An Analysis of the Labor Market for Uber's Driver-Partners in the United States," *International Labor Relations Review* 71 (3): 705–732.

INDEX

Page numbers in italics refer to figures and tables.